# Becoming
# Vulnerable to Grace

Bart Marshall

# Becoming Vulnerable to Grace

*Strategies for Self-Realization*

## Bart Marshall

REALFACE PRESS

Published by Realface Press
info@realface.com

ISBN: 978-0-9992583-3-0

Also published by Realface Press:

*Christ Sutras: The Complete Sayings of Jesus
from All Sources Arranged into Sermons,*
compiled and composed by Bart Marshall

*The Perennial Way: Expanded Edition,*
translations by Bart Marshall

*Bhagavad Gita: The Definitive Translation,*
translated by Bart Marshall

*The Triune Self: Confessions of a Ruthless Seer,* by Mike Snider

*Letters of Transmission: The Enlightenment Method of
Zen Master Alfred Pulyan,* edited by Bart Marshall

*After the Absolute,* by David Gold with Bart Marshall

*Magic, White and Black,* by Franz Hartmann, M.D.,
edited by Bart Marshall

*Verses Regarding True Nature,* by Bart Marshall

*Ashtavakra Gita,* translated by Bart Marshall

*The Torah: The Five Books of Moses,
King James Reader's Version,* translated by Bart Marshall

*Poetry and Wisdom of the Old Testament,
King James Reader's Version,* translated by Bart Marshall

*The Conquest of Illusion,* by J.J. van der Leeuw,
90th Anniversary Edition, edited by Bart Marshall

*Pearl of the Orient,* a screenplay by Bart Marshall

*Book of Psalms: A Psalter for Seekers in Extraordinary Times,*
translated by Bart Marshall

*The Emerald Tablets of Thoth the Atlantean,*
edited by Bart Marshall

*The Four Gospels and the Gospel of Thomas,
King James Reader's Version,* translated by Bart Marshall

"There is a black leopard on the stairs. You meet him! What will you do? You can't pretend he isn't there. You can run away, you can fight furiously, you can say 'nice pussy,' you can try tricks to divert him, you can call for help—you can try many things. But he must eat you."

— Alfred Pulyan

"Amazing Grace,
How sweet the sound
That saved a wretch like me.
I once was lost, but now am found.
Was blind, but now I see."

— John Newton (traditional hymn)

"The spiritual path is a process of wearing down your resistance to a gift that is on constant offer. It is a process of becoming vulnerable to Grace."

— Bart Marshall

# Table of Contents

# Preface

This is a book about spiritual enlightenment—what it is, how it happened for me, and how you might live in such a way that it could happen for you. I've been avoiding writing it for sixteen years. Those sixteen years have given me a lot more to write about, however, so perhaps my avoidance and procrastination have put me right on schedule.

Few undertakings are more pretentious than writing about Absolute Truth and the "path" to it. For starters, positioning oneself as an authority on the subject is obscenely audacious, and takes a lot of *chutzpah*. Second, words cannot touch it, so no matter how well you might be able to choose and order yours, the end result will fall so far short of the mark it may as well be an outright lie.

And yet, to have something informed to say about Truth and not speak it is almost impossible. To have True Nature reveal Itself to Itself in "your" presence is the greatest gift anyone could ever receive, and leaves you wishing that gift be given to everyone.

During those sixteen years of avoidance I did a lot of other writing, mostly translations/versions of ancient spiritual texts that speak of these things in a beautiful, timeless fashion that leaves one feeling nothing more can be said. I've also edited and published some public domain books I felt should be tidied up and offered to contemporary seekers.

Over the years, though, people kept asking, "Why don't you write your own stuff?" I'd usually laugh it off and say, "Sounds a lot like *work*," but I knew they were right, and that eventually I'd have to do it. Because no one but me can tell my story, or speak about spiritual matters from my perspective, and the longer I avoided it, the more I felt compelled to take a stab at it before giving up the ghost.

One reason I've avoided doing my own book is that I'm not drawn to the spotlight or being center stage, and if you're telling your own story it's pretty difficult to avoid it. Also, I don't like to toot my own horn or be too confessional, and it seems that when writing about oneself you're always leaning one way or the other. Some things in my life I'm proud of, others not so much, others could go either way. Regardless, I own it all, and I'm immensely grateful for every bit of it. In this book I've tried to just tell things straight out, without pride or shame.

In the narrative portion, I've tried to focus on stories and life passages I feel in some way may have contributed to my Realization, or to my perspective now, sixteen years later. Of course I have no way of knowing what if anything set me up for the *coup de grace*. I agree with Richard Rose's response to a question about what aspects of his life and path caused his Realization. "All of it and none of it," he said, "and a million things besides."

The later chapters are pretty much straight up "teachings" aimed at helping seekers on their own paths to Realization, and are the *raison d'etre* for this book at all. The memoir portion mainly serves as a way to get to know who you're listening to if you make it to the latter part, but hopefully it also provides an entertaining read.

Writing this book has been an educational experience. Memoir writing requires a good deal of self-inquiry and leaves you with a more detailed and objective perspective on your character and story than you would have otherwise. The Yaqui and Toltec shamanic traditions recommend a spiritual practice called *recapitulation*, which involves remembering and reliving events from one's past in great detail as a method of *self-healing*. The process of memoir writing is much like that.

Organizing my thoughts on spiritual practice has also been good for me. Mostly when talking about these matters I don't know what I'm going to say until I hear myself say it, and I hear myself telling different people different things depending on where they are in their thinking. Certainly there are themes and specifics that have recurred over the years, things I might say to anyone, regardless of where they are on the path, but it's all been sort of scattered and mostly driven by questions. I never tried to pull it all together.

Writing this book has forced me to create a more generic, comprehensive teaching, and I learned a lot about how and what I think by doing it. In my daily life I do not think much about spiritual matters. I just do what comes to be done, and it's pretty much a "chop wood, carry water" way of being. When I'm asked questions about it, though, it immediately comes front and center, then recedes again when the questions stop. So in many ways writing this book was a process of asking myself questions, or recalling questions I've been asked, and writing my response.

I've been surprised by some of what I see appearing on the screen as I type, but it's more of an "uncovering" of what's already there, rather than an emergence of new thoughts. Joan Didion said, "I write to find out what I'm thinking," and I know what she means.

The things I say about spiritual matters are not intended to inform your mind and bring understanding. They are Trojan horses aimed at destroying all that. I'm not interested in saying things satisfying to the intellect. I'm interested in saying things that might weaken your fascination with a false reality, that might put your mind on shaky ground, that might make you vulnerable to Grace.

You'll probably find some passages in here that are worded well enough to make it sound like I know what I'm talking about. Do not be mislead by this. "I" know nothing. Bart is a conduit for what flows through. He just tries not to get in the way. If you find anything here that's of value to you, great. If not, that's great too — one less rock you need to look under to find what you seek.

It's not possible for me or anyone else to speak the "truth." Every word of every language is a lie. How can they be strung together into truth? So I end up saying the same thing in lots of different ways, none of them "true," because you never know what might weaken an arrogant intellect or resonate with an attentive witness.

My actual purpose is to arrange my words in such a way as to cause your mind to collapse in on itself, and there are numerous phrases and passages within this book capable of doing that. Other books of this category are similarly filled with phrases that could stop a ripe mind and trigger Self-Realization.

The problem is not a lack of catalysts. Your life is filled with myriad invitations to "Know Thyself." When you are ready — when you have the capacity to *receive* — the thought that stops the mind will happen and *transmission* will occur. This is my deepest wish for you, but only if you wish it for yourself.


Bart Marshall
February 2021

X

# First of All

In 2004 my 37-year search for Truth, my pursuit of "enlightenment," came suddenly to an end, 30,000 feet above the north Atlantic. In a talk I was asked to give eight months later, I encapsulated the occurrence like this:

> "Something happened on the plane that corrected a basic mistake in perception I'd lived with all my life. Prior to this occurrence I thought I was an individual consciousness experiencing an infinitely vast, infinitely old external universe of solid separate objects, one of which was Me. What I discovered, however, is that the consciousness I mistakenly believed belonged to a separate entity (Me), is in actuality God Consciousness, the One Consciousness, and that Me, the Universe, and everything in it are vague, ephemeral thought forms appearing in and out of Emptiness in a timeless, spaceless Now."

Despite all my readings, despite all the teachers I'd listened to, this was not what I expected or hoped to find. Who would? The discovery that the universe and everything in it does not actually exist as a substantial reality is one few in their right mind want to be presented with. We want enlightenment to shower the cherished "I" we've come to know and love with beautiful spiritual experiences, profound insights, secret wisdom and special powers.

Buddha addressed this issue by giving the back-of-the-book answer to seekers up front. His advice to followers was this: "First of all," he said, "*First of all*, understand that the universe, everything in it, and you yourself have no substance whatever. Then let the mind fight it out with the mind."

To find yourself in a condition where you pick up books like this one is a mixed bag. On the one hand it indicates at least a preliminary interest in discovering the truth about yourself and reality, which, being the highest work of man and all, is generally a noble enterprise. On the other, it means you're dissatisfied enough with your current state that you'd consider the possibility that you don't exist a potential improvement.

It is in the nature of Man to want to understand himself and his environment, but most people are satisfied with very rudimentary, superficial understandings, almost all of which they've been told by others. They accept external authorities as the final word and never look into anything themselves. They form deeply-held beliefs based on speculative theoretical "knowledge" and third-hand teachings, and go to their graves without ever having had an original thought or question about matters of fundamental importance.

In every generation, however, there are a smattering of rebels who have a curiosity that cannot be satisfied with pre-packaged dogma and inexplicable explanations. If you're in the habit of reading books like this one, you may be one of these few.

Congratulations and condolences. You are in the company of Buddha, Jesus, and all the great ones who discovered their true nature as the infinite clear emptiness of God.

But you are also in the company of countless numbers who sought Self-Realization but could not sustain the necessary effort or endure the forces of adversity that haunt and hound earnest seekers of Truth. There's a quote from Mencius that's relevant in this regard, and even more so, a variation of that quote attributed to Moshi:

> *When Heaven is about to confer great office upon a man, it first exercises his mind with suffering, and his bones and sinews with toil. It exposes him to poverty and confounds all his undertakings. In this way, it is seen if he is ready.*

Needless to say, this path is not for everyone. Most of the people who are still reading this should probably put the book down and back slowly away. As it says in the *Ashtavakra Gita*:

> *Knowledge of Truth*
> *turns an eloquent, wise and active man*
> *mute, empty, and inert.*
> *Lovers of the world therefore shun it.*

The vast majority of those who profess to be interested in spiritual matters are looking for personal growth, emotional comfort, material success, better relationships, spiritual community, and a solid belief system to lean on in times of need. The opposite is offered here.

The pursuit of Truth can quite literally ruin your life if you're not destined for it, and none of us can possibly know if we're destined for it or not. It's a suicide mission. As one Zen master put it, "Better not to start. But if you start, better to finish."

There's no good word for what this mission is aimed at. It's called many things — awakening, self-realization, nirvana, salvation, liberation, satori, enlightenment, samadhi... All have slightly different connotations, and all hit false notes. But what they try to point at is a state in which the illusion of individual personhood is seen through and God alone exists. Jesus used the phrase *kingdom of heaven* to denote this state, which has been misinterpreted over the millennia to mean something quite different. I tend to use the words *Self-Realization* and *enlightenment*.

Most religions hint at this state of being, and some have an inner teaching that addresses it directly — the most explicit and potentially helpful teachings being found in the traditions of Zen Buddhism and Advaita Vedanta. Even to call it a "state of being" is misleading, though, because it is not a state.

But enough with the caveats about words. I promise to choose mine carefully and define how I use them, if you agree not to mistake what is said for truth. The best we can hope for is that some of the things said badly here, will collide and combine with things you've heard said badly elsewhere, and by some mysterious alchemical magic cause a wordless perception to take place.

My own spiritual search began in Vietnam on February 20, 1968 when a hand grenade or mortar round (the situation made it difficult to determine which) landed next to me and blew me into an infinite clear blackness that felt like "Home." That search ended in an airplane over the north Atlantic on August 31, 2004, when in a quiet explosion of a different sort all questions vanished and "I" was revealed as the infinite clear emptiness of God.

The intervening 37 years, 6 months, 11 days were filled with innumerable life experiences and events, both dramatic and banal, that may or may not have been contributing factors to the occurrence on the plane. Some of those experiences, as well as some prior to the explosion and after the flight, are related in this book to provide a narrative background and framework for the more overtly "spiritual" offerings of the later chapters.

But all of that is merely story. Events and experiences are isolated incidents. Story is the somewhat arbitrary linking of events together in a way that suggests cause and effect, passage of time, progress and defeat, problem and resolution—and most tantalizing of all, *meaning*. As humans, we are addicted to story. We live for story. Without story we feel bereft. Without our story, our sense of being an individual entity separate from all else quite literally disappears.

To "disappear" in this way is the whole point of an earnest spiritual search. This is not what anyone wants to hear, of course. Why would we? To embark on an enterprise aimed at the full-Monty exposure of the protagonist as an imaginary thought-form is sheer folly to the ego-mind. It constantly wants to know, "What's in it for me? Will I be a better person? Will my pain go away? Will life get easier. Will people like and respect me more?" The answer to these and all similar questions is again and again, "No." Why? Because you are not a person. You are the infinite clear emptiness of God.

The apparent person we are so concerned about—the identity, the ego, the character, whatever you want to call it—is an ephemeral, non-locatable matrix of thoughts and so-called memories. Everyone is worried about what the life of their imaginary entity will be like after it is discovered that the entity does not exist as a separate "being," and that the awareness they have always thought belonged to their entity is in fact the singular Awareness of God—the One.

On the other side of the discovery, of course, this ludicrously laughable conundrum will no longer be a concern. But as a seeker, obsessive worry about the fate of an imaginary self is perhaps the primary obstacle to Self-Realization, and if stubbornly clung to, probably insures it will never happen. Grace is kind. Unless you are fearlessly all-in, it keeps its distance and bides its time.

The discovery of Truth carries with it such powerful self-evidence you don't even realize you're Awake. There is no *experience* of being "enlightened." It feels like this is the way it's always been, the only way it can be, and the way it will forever persist—all of which is absolutely true.

In the aftermath of the occurrence on the plane I thought, "Is this it? Is this the experience I've been chasing all these years? Is this enlightenment?" It seemed too simple. It seemed as if I'd always known. Even though there was joy and weeping and profundity and all that, it still seemed too simple, too self-evident. Surely enlightenment must be something less obvious. It's such a subtle shift, and yet everything is new. Everything is ever-new. I had the thought, "We'll just have to wait and see how this plays out."

The intense, life-changing "experience" of Self-Realization happens only once. Like every experience, it is not sustainable. It cannot be held onto or perpetuated, nor is there any need for it to be. The gift of it is that from that point on you can stop seeking it.

It also provides a homing beacon, so that no matter how the world pulls at you, True Nature is just a thought (or no-thought) away. This does not mean you have a realization experience each time you engage Truth. It's just a quiet certainty that nothing is as it appears, and that all is perfect. The emptiness that you are shines through the veil and winks at you.

Self-Realization leaves you in a state of true Faith, wherein no matter what befalls you, you know that all is well and just as it must be. This does not mean the character doesn't sometimes cavil, plead and lash out — maybe even curse the power that seemingly inflicts or fails to alleviate pain. But even as it does, Faith remains and the outburst soon fades. The baseline emotion is deep gratitude, and the separation between the character and that which it thanks or curses, while temporarily expedient, is clearly seen to be imaginary.

When a so-called enlightened person engages in the affairs of the world he is acting as the false identity, and is subject to all the slings and arrows of the dream paradigm. The difference is that he knows for sure that freedom is a small step away, because that step has already been taken.

It is the false identity only that feels the sting of criticism and rejection, the fear of financial discomfort or ill-health, the torture and uncertainty of hope. Take one step away from it and you are free. But don't expect to be able to step back into the false identity and carry that freedom with you. Freedom is a thing apart. Ego can never be free. It holds itself prisoner in a cell of it's own design, decorated to taste.

After "great office" is conferred, life goes on pretty much as before. It does not make you wise, at not least in the sense of knowing things. Nor do you become immune to the vagaries of inhabiting a human body. None of your emotional wiring is cut, and most of your preferences and opinions remain unchanged.

You find, simply, that you see the world in two ways now instead of one. You see it as a solid, substantial world of separate objects evolving and aging over time, as before, and simultaneously as an imaginary dream transpiring in the frozen moment of Absolute Now with no one watching.

Are there greater realizations than this? For me, there is only one thing to realize and it's too simple to be superseded. There may be degrees of intensity with which it is felt, and the accompanying story of the moment of realization will certainly vary in drama and tumult from person to person. There may be a variance of depth to which it penetrates the body — for some skin deep, for others straight through — and there are probably different levels of deepening that can occur as one's life proceeds. I don't know. All I can say is that this occurrence silenced my incessant questioning, my pleading for certainty. What was given was far greater than anything I could have imagined. To ask more would be ungracious. If more awaits unbidden, however, I say bring it on.

Is it possible to become re-seduced into the dream world after Self-Realization? Yes, to a degree. The old life is full of hooks, and in fact it seems sometimes that after Realization the dream world re-doubles it's efforts to elicit fear and desire, to "pull you back in." This is why there is such a temptation for some, myself included, to just wander off and be alone afterwards.

But there's nothing wrong in exploring and enjoying the dream world. It's an incredibly beautiful, multi-sensory holographic extravaganza of continual amazements. Why throw it away? Seeing that it does not arise in the way one formerly believed does not sully its mysterious thrall. If anything, witnessing it spontaneously arising ever-new in timeless emptiness is even more amazing than imagining it to be an infinitely vast, infinitely old universe of solid separate objects.

If you habitually read books like this, and are still reading this one after I've tried to scare you off, chances are you're in too deep to get out now. You are unlikely to be deterred by warnings of travail or absence of personal reward. Perhaps you feel as Francis Thompson did that you are being pursued by *The Hound of Heaven*. Perhaps you understand what Alfred Pulyan meant in the quote used as an epigraph for this book. Perhaps you have been chosen. As Jesus said, speaking as God the Father, "You do not choose me. I choose you. One out of a thousand, two out of ten thousand. And you shall be as a single One."

Perhaps you have already entered the tractor beam of the Beloved. Perhaps even as we speak It is drawing you inexorably into

*What Is.* How long it takes to reel you in depends on how much of a fight you put up.

If you want to slow the process down, stay interested in the story you constantly play in your head telling you who you are, what you like and don't like, what happened to you in the past, what problems you're dealing with in the present. Take offense at every opportunity. Feel victimized by the people and events around you. Be distracted by as many trivialities as possible. Seek wealth and fame, and worship those who have it. Worry about your future and whine about your life as often as possible. If you want to go faster, cut the shit.

On the one hand, Self-Realization is as egalitarian as it gets— available to anyone at any time. On the other, it is incredibly elitist and self-selective. Immense obstacles and distractions are in place to keep a person from becoming even the least bit interested, or capable of hearing even it's most non-belief-threatening premises.

Those who do cross the first barrier into the realm of curiosity about spiritual matters, invariably then look for their place of maximum comfort in the marketplace of religious belief and New Age cul-de-sacs. Almost everyone who gets this far stops here.

A few, however, intrigued to the point of obsession by the concept of Final Realization, determine to summit—with or without oxygen. Of these, some make it, some do not. But none who have come far enough to wait in the ante-room of the Absolute regrets having chosen to be there, whether or not the door ever opens. Regret is for those who never tried. As it says in the *Dhammapada*:

> One who does what is wrong
> and fails to do what is right,
> who pursues sense pleasures
> and ignores the path of truth,
> will one day meet a man who pursues Truth
> and be filled with envy.

Enlightenment
is a sudden
catastrophic
seeing
of the
blatantly
obvious.

Bart Marshall

# The Brochure

I did not go into Special Forces because I was a badass. I went in because I felt deficient in badass and was looking to ramp it up. It was a tribal coming-of-age, rite of passage, transition to manhood thing every bit as much as those found in myth and primitive cultures. I sent myself into the jungle with a spear and a knife, on a quest to return with the hide of a tiger.

I remember well the first time I became aware of SF. I had recently flunked out of college after one semester and was enduring a palpable I-told-you-so attitude from my father.

A CIA officer and "Greatest Generation" WWII veteran, he was a man of few words. But in a rare heart-to-heart talk after high school he told me I wasn't ready for college and should join the Army, grow up some first. He had good reason for his opinion. I had graduated high school by the skin of my teeth, and my name was not even printed in the graduation program because it was such a long shot I'd pass.

In those days you had to have two years of a foreign language to graduate, and late in my senior year I was failing second-year Latin so badly there was only one way I might eek out a D for the year, and that was to get a near-perfect A on the final. Hence leaving my name off the graduation program.

On the last day of school, however, during the 6th period announcements over the PA system, the principal called me to his office. I went down and he told me I'd passed Latin and would be allowed to graduate.

How did I pull that off, one might ask. Well, it's not a story I'd put on my application for sainthood, but it is what it is. I had a key to my high school that had been passed down to me from an older friend when he graduated. He got it by giving a janitor $20 to lend him his long enough to make a copy.

So one night I broke into the school and stole the Latin final exam from a cabinet I knew the teacher kept his tests in. Sadly, I was so out of it with schoolwork even having the test didn't do me much good. So I enlisted the help of Betsy, a straight-A cheerleader who probably had never before done a dishonest thing in her life.

I missed only one question on the test—the same one Betsy missed. With a little foresight we might have anticipated something like that and taken measures, but no. The teacher was so angry at me that when he was handing back the papers he threw mine in my general direction from two rows away. Betsy just got a reproving look and a disappointed shake of the head. It didn't seem to phase her. She looked over and gave me a wink, perhaps beginning to embrace her bad girl side.

As I think back, having Betsy involved may have been the only thing that saved me. Without her complicity, the teacher probably would have brought me up on charges. But Betsy was captain of the cheerleaders and popular with everyone, students and teachers alike, and he would not have wanted to drag her through the mud with me. Thank you, Betsy.

So anyway, I told my father I wanted to try college, and if it didn't work out, then maybe the Army. We lived in Silver Spring, Maryland, and at that time the University of Maryland had to accept all state residents regardless of high school grades. He said he would not pay for it, but if I paid my own tuition ($300) he'd reimburse me if I passed the first semester, then pick up the tab from then on.

He never had to. In high school when you cut class you get in trouble. In college, no one cares if you go to class, and so, more often than not, I didn't. It was a strange, even bizarre, semester. Going into it I resolved to mend my ways and truly excel at this college thing. The "new me" even ran for freshman class president—though I quickly soured on the idea and did little to try to win.

I went to all my classes for awhile, but gradually slipped into my old slacker ways. I got hooked on playing bridge in the student union, and fell in with some guys who liked to go the track and bet the ponies. The further I fell behind in my classes, the less I wanted to go back, and at the end of the semester I failed all of them except one, gym, in which I strangely got a "A," even though I had stopped attending that one, too.

It was a swimming class, and in those days men's swimming classes at Maryland were done naked. (Yes, girls did peek through the windows and door cracks.) The reason I probably got an "A" despite all my absences, is that I turned out to be a very fast freestyle sprinter. I had no technique—I just kicked like hell and windmilled my arms—but the instructor even asked me to try out for the Maryland team. I didn't. I wasn't big on swimming as a sport, and besides, I had bridge hands to play and ponies to bet on.

All of which brings me to the night I was drinking with my racetrack buddies at a seedy bar in Shepherd Park, just over the D.C. line, where the legal age was 18 and they didn't check IDs anyway. I had just screwed the pooch with college and had no clue where to go from here, or what I wanted to do with my life. Plus, I was now in a precarious position. The draft was in effect then and not being in school made me prime meat.

The other guys at the table were in pretty much the same boat, and one had already been to an Army recruiter. The deal then was that if you were drafted it was for two years, but you had no say in what they did with you. Whereas if you enlisted, it was for three years, but you could pick something you wanted and they would honor it. It could be a place you wanted to be assigned, or a specific job training, or whatever.

Anyway, he had a bunch of brochures he'd picked up at the recruiting office and laid them on the table. Each was advertising a certain job or specialty you could enlist for—tanks, electronics, engineering... They all left me cold. Then I got to the last one.

The featured picture was twelve badass motherfuckers built like linebackers, standing shoulder-to-shoulder in tiger fatigues, with green berets cocked over their foreheads at various fuck-you angles. The description had phrases like "elite warriors," "special operations," "clandestine missions," "guerilla warfare..."

Tumblers in my mind I didn't know existed slid into place and locked. I wanted in. I wanted in bad.

At the recruiter's office I found out you can't volunteer for Special Forces until after you're already in the Army. You have to take a battery of physical and intelligence tests to qualify, then go through months of training with a ridiculously low graduation rate. Undeterred, I signed up and picked Jump School as my request because it was a prerequisite for SF.

# Basic

In the Army you meet all types, especially in those days when the draft was in effect. Growing up in a relatively safe, homogenous suburban environment, most everyone I knew had more or less the same background, and shared more or less the same kinds of experiences. Not so in the Army. Young men from every conceivable walk of life, and with every conceivable psychological makeup were thrown together and trained to not just get along, but to work together for common goals.

To this end, heads are shaved, uniforms are issued, and all expressions of individuality are drummed out — except those deemed of benefit to the Army. Recruits are put through long periods of exhausting training and shared misery that both instills programming to obey orders no matter what, and creates bonding among the troops. It's a formula that has worked for centuries.

I was 19 when I started Basic Training, which was followed by Advanced Infantry Training (AIT), during which I found out you had to be 20 to enter Special Forces — a detail my recruiter had somehow failed to mention. I passed all my SF physical and intelligence tests while in AIT, but I would not turn 20 in time to avoid being assigned to a non-SF Airborne unit after Jump School, and I'd be headed for Jump School soon. Shit. I didn't know what to do. I had no interest in being a grunt in an ordinary Airborne unit. For me, it was SF or nothing.

Enter the hand of the Divine. In Basic Training my platoon sergeant — the "ole Sarge" as he referred to himself — would sometimes extort money from us, saying things like whichever squad gave the ole Sarge the most money would get a pass off base next Saturday. I never thought much about it. What did I know? This was just how the Army was, I figured. But somebody ratted him out, and he got busted. Apparently he'd been doing it for years.

So just as I was about to graduate AIT and head to Jump School, I was notified I was a potential witness at his court martial, and was sent to a holding company after AIT. A lot of the other guys in this holding company were awaiting their own court martials for various offenses, and my time there was an adventure in itself. Fights frequently broke out, and a couple of the friends I made there went AWOL in an attempt to avoid the stockade. One of them woke me up in the middle of the night he left, wanting to trade me his dirty civilian shirt for one of my clean ones before he headed out. Two days later he was brought back in handcuffs by MPs, still wearing my shirt. He'd gone home. They always go home. Easy pickings.

My days in the holding company were spent on various manual labor details around the base, and a few times I drew the fireman night shift, which meant you had to stay up all night stoking the coal furnaces that heated the company buildings. Everyone hated fireman night duty, but I enjoyed it. In the wee hours everything was quiet, and I had time to daydream in relative peace.

Sometimes I'd sit in front of a furnace for awhile on my rounds and just stare into the fiery coals without thinking. It would be a gross overstatement to say I was beginning to become contemplative, but those times of "no-mind" at night in the midst of unpredictable days made an impression on me, and I can still remember how they felt, and how I looked forward to them.

When the time for the court martial arrived, I donned my dress uniform and was driven to the courtroom with the other guys from my basic training unit who were being held over. When we got there the waiting room was filled with potential witnesses from other basic training units the ole Sarge had extorted. Eventually, witnesses were called one by one and went into the courtroom. I waited nervously for my name to be called.

My plan was to claim ignorance on the stand, saying I never heard the sergeant ask for money and never gave any. I hated rats, and was determined not to be one. In basic training I was ratted out for leaving base with two buddies — both of whom were in the Army because a judge gave them the option as an alternative to jail — for a relatively innocent afternoon excursion one Saturday.

Technically we were AWOL since we did not have permission to be off base, and while at the lake we ran into our trainee "company commander," Sterling Stahler, who did have permission. Stahler was an unlikeable sort who enjoyed throwing his weight around. We became immediately concerned he'd turn us in, but we included him in our activities and hoped for the best.

The next day, as the company stood in formation waiting to go into the mess hall for dinner, my two cohorts and I were called into the CO's office. I knew what that meant. We'd been ratted out. Sterling Stahler stood in front of the formation with his armband of authority, a cigarette dangling from his mouth. I made a point to walk in front of him on my way to the office, thinking only to give him the evil eye as I passed. But he smiled at me, and I reflexively

14

smacked the cigarette out of his mouth. We got into it and ended up on the ground before being separated by First Sergeant Pirtle.

In the CO's office we told our stories. Pirtle also hated rats apparently. He suggested to the CO that Stahler and I be given boxing gloves and be allowed to work it out. The CO seemed to consider it, but instead gave all four of us an Article 15—including Stahler! And so I had a couple weeks extra duty and a minor black mark on my record. A small price to pay for wiping Stahler's smile off his face.

As an aside, I learned later that Stahler got busted for falsifying records to get into the Army. He had previously been in the Marines and been dishonorably discharged. Sterling was his younger brother's name, which he used to enlist in the Army. He got found out and was sentenced to five years in Leavenworth. *Schadenfreude*? You bet.

I was never called as a witness at the court martial. After hearing some number of witnesses testify against him, the ole Sarge changed his plea to guilty and was sentenced to seven years. A week later I got orders for Jump School at Fort Benning, Georgia, where I arrived on my 20th birthday. Three weeks later I graduated and was assigned to Special Forces Training Group at Fort Bragg, North Carolina.

# Mrs. A.

Special Forces training takes a long time, and my three-year enlistment was half up before I finished. In addition to the physical training and instruction in SF strategy and tactics, we were trained in one of the SF Military Operational Specialties (MOS). The basic SF unit is the 12-man A-team, which consists of two officers, and two sergeants for each of five MOSs: Intelligence, Weapons, Engineering, Communications, and Medic. The Intelligence and Weapons slots were usually filled by older SF lifers, so new trainees could choose between the other three, based on the needs of Special Forces.

My first choice was Medic, but it was the longest training — over a year for that alone — and I was concerned it would not leave me enough time to go to Vietnam, which I very much wanted to do. I also heard from old hands that Communications was the most mission critical, in that few operations or patrols went out without a commo man. So I chose Communications, which included becoming an expert in Morse code.

Virtually all of my Training Group instructors had at least one Vietnam tour, and much of the classroom and field instruction was specific to Vietnam, including six weeks of language training in Vietnamese. All of which fueled my desire to experience the war.

After graduation I was assigned to the 3rd SF Group at Fort Bragg, where I asked my company commander to put me in for orders to the 5th SF Group in Vietnam, which he did. But orders didn't come. And didn't come. It became a concern because Vietnam tours lasted exactly one year, and they would not send you if you had less than a year left on your enlistment. If I didn't get orders soon I'd either have to re-up or miss out on experiencing war. I decided to take matters into my own hands.

Now, every set of orders for every Special Forces soldier, be it a minor stateside transfer or orders for Vietnam or any other part of the world, were signed "Mrs. Alexander." Mrs. A., as she was known, had a certain mythic quality among SF soldiers, and was regarded as royalty by SF old hands, some of whom told me they had contacted her directly to request orders from time to time.

So one weekend I asked for leave, borrowed a car and drove to the Pentagon. I got a later start Friday than I'd planned and it was mid-afternoon by the time I pulled into the parking lot, leaving me two or three hours max to find Mrs. A.

I lucked into a close parking spot and stepped out of the car to quickly change from civvies to my dress uniform before going in. A car pulled up in front of me and stopped. An Air Force general rolled down his window. I held up my pants and saluted.

"At ease. You coming or going?"

"Just got here, sir."

"Five bucks for your spot."

"Sorry, sir, I'm in kind of a hurry."

"Very well. Carry on."

In those days you could just walk into the Pentagon with little or no security checks, especially if you were in uniform. Inside I was overwhelmed by the massive size of the place and the labyrinthine network of floors and halls and back halls. My heart sank at the shrinking possibility of finding the Mrs. A. needle in this haystack. But I just started walking around, asking people if they knew where Mrs. Alexander's office was, or where Special Forces orders were created, or whatever.

Nobody knew, until finally somebody did. And lo and behold, I eventually found myself in a cramped cubbyhole of an office with the legendary Mrs. A. Her office was full of Special Forces memorabilia, and it was obvious this was more than just a job to her. We schmoozed a bit, then I told her my situation and requested she put me on the next manifest for Vietnam.

She looked at me without speaking for a few moments.

"Are you sure?"

"Yes, Ma'am."

"You're just a baby."

"I'll be fine."

She didn't say anything.

"I'll be fine."

"Okay, you'll get your orders. But don't let me see your name on a casualty list. Promise?"

"Yes, Ma'am. I promise."

As I walked back to the car, I felt a certain elation, and a "mission accomplished" pride in myself. I got in, started the engine, then just sat there with it running as an uncomfortable feeling flooded my body. I shut the engine off and stared blankly through the windshield.

What the fuck did I just do?

Mrs. Billyea Alexander

MIKE FORCE

# Mike Force

I took off in nine airplanes before I landed in one. It took me to Oakland, California, where I boarded a commercial Continental Airlines flight to Saigon full of replacement troops. I sat next to a Special Forces lifer going back for his third tour. We were the only SF on the plane. We drank whiskey and smoked—him cigars, me Winstons. We flirted with stewardesses and talked about his Nam experiences. He told me to get assigned to the Central Highlands if I could, work with the Montagnards—advice I ended up taking.

As we approached the city lights of Saigon at night I remember thinking, "For the next year I could die at any moment." Almost immediately an unfamiliar voice in my head rejoined, "It's the same for every other time in life." That voice has been with me ever since, and I have come to think of it as the voice of my death. It is this voice that will tell me, "It's time."

From Saigon I went to Nha Trang, 5th Special Forces Group Headquarters, then to the II Corps C-Team in Pleiku, then the B-Team in Qui Nhon, then to my assignment on an A-Team in the boonies.

I spent a couple months there and got a feel for the country and for SF operations, but the area surrounding that A-camp was not particularly hot at the time, and our patrols often ended without any enemy contact or firefights. In the beginning I was grateful for this. It gave me time to learn the ropes without being thrown off the deep end. But after awhile I began to feel I was missing out somehow. I was in Vietnam, but I wasn't in the *war*.

As I'd passed through the Pleiku C-Team I'd spent a couple nights drinking with some guys from a special SF unit called Mike Force (Mobile Strike Force), a unit you had to volunteer for and be accepted into—after you had some combat experience. The basic mission of Mike Force was to reinforce A-camps that were under attack, and generally to go where the fighting was most intense.

They also went on month-long "Blackjack" operations into all parts of the Central Highlands, and sometimes across borders (illegally) into Laos and Cambodia. On cross-border operations they wore "sterile" fatigues made in France and wore no dog tags, so that if a body had to be left behind it was not identifiable as American.

I'd had an immediate pull towards Mike Force as I talked with those guys, in much the same way I'd had towards SF when first seeing the brochure, and the more I thought about it, the more I realized Mike Force was where I wanted to be. So I volunteered and was accepted.

I can't really explain why I was so attracted to the most dangerous assignments, to being where I was most likely to be killed, except to say that my feeling was that this was my one chance to experience war, and I wanted to be in the belly of the beast, not do my time in some relatively safe cul-de-sac.

Well, I got what I wished for. Intense firefights became the norm in my life, so much so I couldn't tell you which firefights went with which operation. The individual memories I have are isolated, self-contained, dreamlike — a vague look and feel of a certain piece of jungle, imprints of myself doing certain things, bullets cracking overhead like popping corn, shredded foliage raining down...

My most lasting impression about firefights is that while bullets are flying, time stops. There is only the micro-moment of *What Is*. These experiences became a touchstone and a metaphor for me as I later encountered similar descriptions of "no-thought" and "no-time" in enlightenment literature, and began to occasionally experience it again in less life-threatening situations.

I have no continuity of memory about specific operations, or the order of the operations, or the order of events on each operation. It has all blurred together into a montage of long walks, tense nights, and firefights with no relation to each other.

Only two battles stand out in stark relief to this vagueness, and these I remember with remarkable clarity: Hill 875 and Tet. One reason for this is their extended duration. In the case of Hill 875, the battle lasted many days. In the case of Tet, weeks.

# White Holes

I was in Vietnam over 50 years ago. War was a lot different then. Fighting in Vietnam was not much different than fighting in World War II. Just some guys with rifles running around shooting at each other. It was a low-tech, old school war.

The standard rifle in Nam, the M-16, was arguably better than the standard M-1 in WWII, although it had a tendency to jam if not kept clean, and keeping it clean was sometimes difficult in the jungle. Many WWII infantry weapons were still in visible use in Vietnam, and even some M-1s were still around and being used by indigenous forces. Even the casualty rates were comparable. The percentage of Americans serving in combat in Vietnam who were killed or wounded was about the same as in WWII theaters of operation.

For air support we often used jets, but when we had a choice we called in A-1E Skyraiders, a single-prop close air support aircraft from the WWII era. They could carry a lot of weaponry and stay on station longer than jets could. Plus, the Mike Force  compound was located not far from the Pleiku airfield where the A-1Es were stationed, and there was a close relationship between the A-1E pilots and Mike Force. Sometimes when you were directing airstrikes with A-1Es you'd be on the radio with a pilot you'd had drinks with a few weeks earlier.

Another fact that may bring it home about how far back in history Nam was, is that when we were on long-range operations, my method of communicating nightly situation reports to the C-team was encrypted Morse code, tapped out on a telegraph key on my knee. It was the only way we could communicate over any distance.

The Central Highlands of Vietnam is a vast expanse of triple-canopy jungle mountains. At the time, they were mainly populated by primitive Montagnard (Hmong) tribes that hunted with crossbows and practiced slash-and-burn agriculture.

Each year they would cut down and burn a small section of jungle and plant crops there, benefitting both from the sunlight that could get in and the ashes that provided fertilizer. The next year, they would do the same to a new patch of forest, and the previous year's patch would begin reverting back to jungle. They also marked time in this way, naming these croplands, and referring to the past as, for instance, "The year we ate the forest of the stone spirit Goo."

The Hmong are the original indigenous inhabitants of Vietnam—the Vietnamese being descended from Chinese and Japanese invaders centuries ago. The French called the Hmong *Montagnards*, meaning mountain people. That term continued with the Americans, and was often shorted to "Yards."

Special Forces trained and used Montagnards as soldiers in the Central Highlands, and a close relationship developed between them. The Hmong men adapted amazingly well, and were excellent fighters, transitioning from primitive crossbow hunters in loincloths, to parachuting out of airplanes in training, and attacking enemy positions under fire with relative ease. We paid them well, from cardboard boxes of cash delivered by a CIA operative on paydays. A Hmong private in Mike Force made more than a master sergeant in the South Vietnamese Army.

I loved the look of those mountains, steep and abrupt and shrouded in mist. On operation, sometimes a vista would open up, revealing a landscape reminiscent of Chinese paintings. Humping up and down them, however, or hacking through dense foliage and bamboo thickets, was not so picturesque.

On operation we used compasses and topographic maps to navigate. Because it was such an isolated, unexplored region, some of these maps had large blank areas that had not yet been surveyed. I called these "white holes." It was more difficult to navigate inside a white hole because you had no terrain markings to check against or shoot azimuths from. Intellectually I knew nothing was different inside a white hole, but I was always a bit more alert, as if the laws of the universe might not apply here.

It was while operating in a white hole we got orders to change plans and check out Hill 875, a marked hill just outside the white hole. Hills got their names from their elevation indicated on the map.

When we got to the base of it we knew something was up. There were signs indicating a large number of troops in the area, and there was little effort put into disguising or camouflaging it. The map showed us we were on the side on the hill with the steepest slope. Another part of the hill had a much more gradual slope that was more inviting, but also more likely to be well-defended. We decided to go up the steep slope.

This may be a good place to explain who I mean by *we*. Mike Force operations were generally company size, a company consisting of four platoons of Montagnard strikers, each having about 20 soldiers — a small enough unit to move through the jungle with relative stealth, but large enough to engage in sustained combat when contact was made.

Each platoon was led by an SF sergeant, and sometimes there was a lieutenant or captain nominally in command of the company. I say "nominally" because relatively few officers were career SF. It was a dead-end if they had ambitions for higher rank. The smart path if you wanted to move up as an officer was to stick with conventional units. So SF officers tended to be on their first tour, and would often defer tactical decisions to the highest ranking sergeant on the operation, and rightly so. Many of these old SF hands had been coming to Nam since the late '50s and had three or four tours under their belts.

The Montagnard leader of my platoon was named Khong. He knew some basic English and was able to relay orders to the others when we had time. Often though, when we were being stealthy, or when we only had visual contact, we'd all communicate through a system of hand signals.

I had a radioman, Reeby, who carried the PRC-25 short-range radio used for voice communication between the SF on the operation, and with air support overhead. I also had a bodyguard, Baap Canh, whose job was to watch my back during firefights to make sure one of my own troops didn't shoot me. He also made me coffee. He was older than most strikers, and had been a village shaman before joining Mike Force. Baap Cahn and Reeby were my constant companions on operation. At night they slept on either side of me.

Montagnards were fiercely loyal to Special Forces, and the danger of being shot by one of your own men was very low in the Central Highlands, but there were a few Montagnard Viet Cong, so a good bodyguard was a definite asset. In areas of the country where SF used Vietnamese for strikers, the danger of being shot by your own men during a firefight was higher.

As we started moving up the steep slope it became increasingly clear this was no temporary NVA (North Vietnamese

Army) position. There were steps cut into the mountain, and bamboo handrails lashed to trees. We moved away from the steps and slowly clawed our way up. I could feel the eyes of the enemy.

Suddenly, the world erupted in gunfire, so much and so close you could hardly hear spaces between rounds—it was just a steady roar. It came not just from further up the hill, but from all around and behind us. We had unknowingly walked past spider holes and were now surrounded by enemy fire.

There was nothing to do but run downhill as fast as we could to at least get everything in front of us. We returned fire and dragged wounded downhill as fast as possible. Incredibly, nobody was left behind.

We moved to the base of the hill, called in A1-E airstrikes, and Dustoff choppers to evacuate casualties. A1-Es pounded the hill for a an hour or two, then we tried going back up. Same thing. If anything the fire was more intense. More casualties evacuated, more airstrikes. Then we tried going up again. Same thing only more so. We got the living shit kicked out of us, and our medic, Goldie, was among those who had to be medevac'd.

Word of all this got the attention of the U.S. high command. Obviously this was not a job for a rag-tag bunch of Montagnards, they probably figured. What was needed was a major American unit. We were informed that the commander of the 173rd Airborne Brigade would be choppering in to be briefed.

We told him that as bad as it was going up the steep slope, going up the gradual slope would almost certainly be worse. We recommended multiple attacks going up multiple slopes of the hill, to see which was least defended, and to not allow the NVA to concentrate their firepower. He rejected the idea, saying he didn't want to divide his forces. He said he'd send his full brigade up the gradual slope so fast and so hard "they won't know what hit 'em."

We were relegated to a blocking position to possibly pick off stray NVA deserting their positions when the Americans attacked. In preparation, jets bombed the hill relentlessly. The next day, the 173rd made their assault. And the next day. And the next day. We listened on our PRC-25s as the futility of their attacks unfolded. At one point, every 173rd soldier was required to carry a body bag because he'd likely have to be put in it before the day was done. Between their attacks, jets pounded and pounded the hill.

The 173rd commander finally cried uncle and requested reinforcements. The 4th Infantry Division was called in. We were ordered to clear an LZ for them on a nearby knoll. Chopper after chopper they came. In the background, jets constantly pounded 875. There were no trees left standing.

Then orders came for all of us to go up the hill at once — 26th Company Mike Force, 173rd Airborne Brigade, and 4th Infantry Division. So we did — on multiple fronts. And we all made it to the top without a shot being fired.

The NVA had been deeply dug in, and the remains of their bunkers, tunnels and trenches were still in evidence despite the intense bombing. We found some bodies in the mounds of dirt, but not many. Most had fled with their dead and wounded.

None of us knew what to do once we were up there. Did we win? What did we win? I wandered the surreal landscape of bombed and re-bombed earth, mounds and mounds of it, like a giant's sandbox, overwhelmed by the realization there is no victory in war, no glory in dying for a pile of dirt. Hundreds of mothers on both sides were about to get the worst news of their lives, and for what?

Hill 875, Dak To, Kon Tum province, November 1967

Hmong striker

# Eve of the First Morning of the First Day

In Vietnam everyone has the same birthday, which is also the beginning of the Vietnamese New Year. Understandably, the celebration of this occurrence is a very big deal. The occasion is called Tet, which is short for *Tết Nguyên Đán*, which translates as "Feast of the First Morning of the First Day."

Tet is not a fixed date, but is keyed to the Vietnamese spring calendar and the phases of the moon. The first day of Tet usually occurs from late January to mid-February and the celebration continues for some days after. In 1968, the first day of Tet was January 30.

It was the height of the war. Over 500,000 Americans were in country, and there was intense fighting in every province, from the DMZ to the Delta. My Mike Force company was humping the hills as usual in late January when we got word to clear an LZ. We were being extracted early. There had been a truce called for Tet and all combat operations were temporarily suspended.

Back at the Mike Force team house it was a major party. Everybody was in camp at once, which never happened. The jukebox played non-stop and beautiful women fast-danced with each other, showing off.

II Corps Mike Force was a very loose place. A number of women lived there with us, and others would often show up at the gate in groups of five or six, wanting to get in. A Montagnard gate guard would ring up the team house and say, "Girls, girls," and someone would go down to check them out and say okay.

To say I enjoyed this paradigm would be a major understatement. I took full advantage. But I also gradually came to realize I was more comfortable on operations than I was drinking and womanizing on standowns—which were usually about a week or ten days in length. Sometimes I had a nervous stomach between operations, and drank a lot of canned chocolate milk to calm it down. I looked forward to getting back out in the field, and once there my body relaxed and I was "comfortable."

My theory about this is that while on standown, enjoying the perks of life, is when the fear set in. My thoughts ranged to the future, to ambitions and anticipations of further enjoyments that could suddenly be snuffed out by a bullet. But when on operation, that was the only thing going on. I was focused, and time was compressed. My world was very small, and psychologically more manageable, even though being on operation was the situation where the bullet the snuffed out my future was most likely to come.

On the night before Tet '68 the gate guards were constantly calling up, saying, "Girls, girls." Literally dozens of women showed up and were let in to join the party. You could hardly move around the team house without brushing up against a tight ass, but nobody questioned it or thought much about it. Until 3:00 the next morning.

I awoke to the sound of explosions and gunfire in the distance, coming from the direction of town. I threw on clothes and burst into the team room. Others were gathering and listening to a radio that was picking up combat conversations. Pleiku was under attack by a large enemy force.

Then other conversations came in from other towns, and it soon became apparent that the same thing was happening all over the country. The Viet Cong and NVA had used the Tet truce as a ruse to attack every city and town in Vietnam.

Two companies quickly reinforced the camp perimeter defenses, and hasty plans were hatched to send a couple more companies into Pleiku to get into the fray. Mine was one of them. I went back to my room to get ready. The women in my bed were unfazed, sleepy. I told them what was happening. They barely reacted.

Then it hit me. They knew! They'd come to Mike Force as a safe haven from what they knew was coming but didn't warn us.

"You knew about this," I said. They nodded. "Why didn't you tell us?"

One shrugged. "What would you have done?"

I realized then this was no big deal to them. Constant war was all they'd ever known, all their parents had ever known, all their grandparents had ever known. To them, this was just how life was.

# Phan Tiet

City fighting's a lot different than jungle fighting. Snipers can clearly see you and take a bead. Every room you enter might have a rifle aimed at the doorway. Every corner you turn might be a trap.

We spent the next week commuting to and from the battle. By day we'd kick down doors and help American units clear the town house-by-house. Evenings, we'd catch a truck back to Mike Force to get drunk and sleep in our beds. Most of the other companies were fighting in other cities, so there weren't as many SF around. But all the women were still there, waiting for the town to be cleared.

One night I was drinking with the Mike Force Sergeant Major, SGM Kemmet, who had for some reason taken a liking to me, and we had developed a sort of mentor-student relationship. He was a highly-decorated veteran of WWII and Korea—including a Distinguished Service Cross—with multiple tours in Nam, plus a long list of minor skirmishes around the world no one was supposed to know about. He liked telling stories about all that and I liked listening.

He was built solid, with a square head and jaw, and an arm full of Montagnard bracelets that reached halfway to his elbow. A young lieutenant walked up while we were talking and said, "Sergeant Major, we need to kick out all the women as punishment for not telling us about the attack."

Kemmet barely glanced at him. "That ain't gonna happen." Then he continued our conversation like he wasn't there. The lieutenant fidgeted a few moments then slinked off. Kemmet cut his eyes slightly in his direction. "Fucking Christians." I laughed and said he should be in charge of the whole goddamn war.

"I could've been if I'd kept my nose clean. Shit, if I had all my promotions and none of my busts I'd be on my third term as President."

At some point when things calmed down in Pleiku, my company was pulled and sent to the town of Phan Tiet, where there was still heavy resistance. By now I'd learned more about fighting in cities and was getting more comfortable with it. The ranking NCO of our company, SFC Davis, even started sending me on "side jobs."

One day he informed me the 101st Airborne had to leave one of their wounded behind when they pulled out, and told me to go find him. The location he'd been given was pretty vague, but the soldier was in a "light green house." So I took half a dozen Yards and headed out.

I'd not been to that part of town and didn't know if it was supposedly cleared or not so we were cautious, keeping to backyards and alleys, avoiding streets. At one point we came to a large black sewage pond full of garbage and dead rats that blocked our way. It almost came to the edge of a building we had to pass, but there was enough room to go single file, hugging the wall, and not slip in.

We found him about an hour later, in a light green house as they said, lying on his back on the concrete floor. He'd been badly gut shot and also taken one through the face. He looked dead, but he was breathing.

I said, "Don't worry, I've got you." His eyes popped open so fast and wide it startled me.

"I got you," I said again softly. "I got you." His eyes closed. I hit him with a morphine syrette and told the Yards to find something to carry him on. He was a big man, over 200 pounds, and a fireman's carry was not an option, especially with gut wounds.

The Yards came back with a ladder and we carefully moved him onto it. I put four Yards on the corners of the ladder and we headed back the way we came. When we got to the sewage pond I stopped and told them to put him down. Those carrying the ladder would not be able to hug the wall. They'd have to wade through the pond, which was of unknown depth, and with a man that heavy weighing them down who knows what might happen.

I told them to wait, and went to check out the street. If it looked okay, we might have to risk it. I stuck my head around the corner and didn't see anything. Then I walked up the street in the direction we'd be taking. Suddenly I came under automatic weapons fire and scrambled to get back. I fired behind me at random as I ran, and heard shouts in Vietnamese. I thought they might be in pursuit, I didn't know.

As I ran towards my Yards I shouted for them to pick up the ladder. We had no choice now about our route and we had to hurry. I sent the ladder through the pond first. The two Yards closest to the wall had decent footing, but those on the deep side started slipping and sinking, and one of the Yards at the back of the ladder nearly went under, almost letting go of the ladder. I jumped in and grabbed the back of the ladder just before the wounded soldier slipped into the sewage, and we managed to get him safely to the other side. By the time I climbed out I'd been in up to my armpits.

34

We made our way back to where the rest of our company was and Davis radioed for an ambulance truck. Pat, our team medic, treated the 101st soldier and said he would probably make it, but not by much. I felt good about that. Real good. But God did I stink.

That night we camped in an old French colonial compound near a bridge by the river. It had been used before by other American units and the wrought-iron fence facing the neighboring buildings had been fortified with a high wall of sandbags, with scaffolding for firing positions. That was the wall my platoon was assigned.

It was a pitch-black moonless night and we had a Puff the Magic Dragon AC-47 gunship overhead dropping flares so we could see anyone sneaking up on us. Puff carried a big rapid-fire Gatling-type gun that fired so fast and furious it was said a one-second burst would put a bullet every square foot on a football field. They used only tracer rounds and a burst looked like a tongue of fire, hence the name. So we had that going for us, which was nice.

After I'd positioned the Yards, I sat on the ground with my back against the sandbags and started cleaning my bullets, which had sewage pond shit all in the magazines. It had just turned February 20 and we were scheduled to be replaced by another Mike Force company in the morning. My tour would be up in a week, so this was probably the last night of my last operation. I cleaned my bullets and thought about my future.

I had nothing back in the States pulling at me, no girlfriend, no job prospects, no desire to go back to college. Here I had found a place I felt I belonged. I liked what I was doing and was good at my job—hell, I just saved a man's life, for chrissake! I admired the SF old hands like SGM Kemmet and the adventures they'd had, and I had the respect of men I respected. A man could do worse than to spend his life like that. I thought about re-upping when I got back to Mike Force, and extending my Vietnam tour. I didn't want to leave.

Not much later Puff was called away to support an American unit that was under attack outside of town. We were left in the dark. I went around to my Yards manning the wall and told everybody to be alert, and to fire a burst into the neighborhood every so often— recon by fire. Then I sat back where I'd been.

Baap Canh and Khong sat down beside me. It occurred to me strongly then, how I had the option whether or not to stay in a war-torn country, they did not. I told Khong what I was considering. He said he hoped I would stay, as I knew he would. "Maybe you marry my sister," he said, and we laughed.

Several months before we were at a "feast" in the Mike Force dependent village where some of the striker's families lived, a few miles from the Mike Force compound. I sat flanked by Khong and Baap Canh, as I was now, drinking rice wine from tall earthen jars and eating Montagnard "delicacies." A pretty young woman came over a few times and fed me choice bits of food with a modestly flirtatious smile. Khong elbowed me.

"My sister," he said. I did not know whether he meant biologically, or metaphorically in a tribal sense. I smiled and politely said, "Very beautiful."

"Maybe you get married, stay Vietnam," he said. Montagnards are not much for subtlety.

In a flash an entire scenario ran through my imagination, one in which I lived in an isolated Hmong village in the jungle with a Hmong wife and a passel of half-Hmong kids. It was not an unpleasant vision. I laughed. "Maybe," I said.

Now, reclining against sandbags in the dark, I asked Khong to tell Baap Canh what I was thinking about and to ask the ex-shaman his advice. Baap Canh listened, and stayed silent for several minutes. Then in a low voice he intoned a chant in Rhade. Khong translated.

My memory of what they said has been enhanced by later finding records of Montagnard shamanic chants, where I ran across one that struck the same chord:

> Fear nothing. Do not flee.
> Eat the pig within.
> Eat the monkey within.
> Drink the rice wine within.
>
> Do not seek the soup of another.
> Do not seek the rice of another.
> Do not seek the house of another.

It did not make "sense" to me then, but it seemed to advise one to do what is right for oneself, not what others are doing. What I didn't know was whether he was advising me to stay or leave. Turns out, that decision was not mine anyway.

About that time a few Yards did their recon by fire and Khong left to check it out. Baap Canh stood up and put his hand on top of my head for a few seconds, then disappeared into the night. I just sat there against the sandbags, feeling very still and quiet inside. I thought about what I would do with the $9,600 re-up bonus I would get for signing away the next six years of my life. Enter the hand of the Divine.

Suddenly there was a bright explosion inside the compound off to my left, then immediately another, and another, then one to my right almost on top of me. I was lifted off the ground, and while in mid-air, time stopped. I felt pieces of shrapnel slowly enter my body, so slowly I had complete thoughts between each piece. After each one I prayed, "Not head, not head, please not my head…" Then another would slowly pierce my flesh. "Not head, not head…"

Then nothing. Blackness. At some point I "woke up" inside that blackness and was seemingly aware of everything about it. It was achingly familiar and I felt like I was "Home."

It was not a cloistered, claustrophobic blackness. It was the opposite—an infinite clear blackness filled with light. But there was nothing in that infinite clearness to reflect the light, and so it was blackness. I would gladly have stayed forever. Then a pinpoint of light appeared in the upper left of my view, and slowly blinked off and on. It gradually grew bigger and brighter, and a faint sound was heard. The sound got louder, and the light pulsated in rhythm with the sound. Then the sound became recognizable as a voice, a voice saying a name. I knew the name was meant for me so I took it on again. But I also knew it was not the name of the one who knows blackness. I opened my eyes to the earthly darkness of night.

At first light an ambulance truck came for me. I was the only one wounded. The medics slid me in the back on a stretcher and took off. They drove fast, worried about snipers. Suddenly they hit something and spun out until the truck came to a stop. Then backed up. The back doors flew open and the medics tossed an old Vietnamese man in with me. I could see his mangled cyclo on the street behind us. He was bleeding badly from the back of his head, and blood trickled from his mouth. The truck took off again and the old man's head bounced against the metal floor. I slid my arm under it for a pillow and we looked  into each other's eyes for a few minutes. Then he died.

Washington, D.C., 1968

# Stateside

From the aid station I was flown to a field hospital where they operated on my knee and cut out some of the other shrapnel. I was sort of awake during the whole thing. They numbed me from the waist down and gave me something that made me not give a shit about anything. The doctor talked to me the whole time.

"Some of the shrapnel in your knee is too deep in the bone to go after. The bone will grow around it, so it won't be a permanent problem."

"I'm not going to do any fine stitching on your knee. You'll want a good scar to show off and remember this by."

"I'm not touching the smaller flesh wounds. The shrapnel will dissolve over time and be like a mineral supplement."

While recovering in the crowded ward, I developed hepatitis. My piss looked like coffee, my shit like vanilla ice cream. It was the least problematic kind of hepatitis, thankfully, but they would not send anyone back to the States while they had it.

There are any number of reasons I could have gotten it, but it probably came from shrapnel carrying pieces of my sewage-soaked fatigues into my body. They kept me in-country for six weeks after my tour was up before sending me to a hospital in the States.

As it turned out, this hepatitis delay ended up shortening my time in the Army by almost two months, because when I had healed enough to be released from the stateside hospital I did not have enough time left on my enlistment to be reassigned, so they discharged me. Had I been reassigned, I might have had time to reconsider staying in the Army, so hepatitis saved me from that.

When they send you home wounded they send you to the military hospital closest to your hometown, so I was sent to Walter Reed in Washington, D.C., the hospital where I was born. My injuries were relatively minor, but for some reason I was placed on a ward with the most serious cases imaginable—triple amputees, head wounds, severed spines. From a "hand of the Divine" perspective, this may have been another way to dissuade me from any lingering ideas I might have had about re-upping and going back to Nam: "Take a good look, kid, this is what you'd be risking."

In the bed next to me was a guy with a piece of his skull missing, and likely a piece of his brain. He talked incessantly, but there was no way to understand what he was saying. I nodded and pretended to listen. I think he was either consciously or unconsciously trying to re-wire his brain and learn how to talk again.

I played poker with wheelchair amputees who were amazingly upbeat and cheerful in the protective, supportive hospital setting, but you could sense what awaited them when they were thrust back out into the world.

One guy I remember especially had lost both legs and his right arm. He hated being in bed and spent all day wheeling around the ward. We became good friends in that environment, but now I can't remember his name. No wait—it just came to me. Tommy. His name was Tommy…

I got out of the hospital and was discharged from the Army the same day. Then there I was, back in the old neighborhood, drinking with guys I knew in high school. They were doing things like clerking in a plumbing supply store or selling appliances at Sears. Some had a wife and kids.

I felt lost, like I no longer belonged there, or anywhere, in fact, except maybe Vietnam. I found new friends who had been to Nam and preferred their company. At least we had something in common to talk about. I had no idea what I wanted to do with my life, but I knew I didn't want any part of the banality I'd returned to.

My idea to re-up and stay in Mike Force had been taken from me, and once I was out of the war and the hospital I realized I didn't really want to be career Army anyway. I did want to somehow get back into the action, though. My experience of the "brilliant blackness" had changed things, and it called me in a way I didn't understand. At the time, I associated it with the danger and adventure of war, and the milieu of the Orient. I felt pulled to get back into that paradigm.

A couple of Nam vet Marines I was hanging out with talked about signing on with various mercenary outfits operating in Africa and South America, but that sort of thing had little appeal to me. It had the danger and adventure I was looking for, but those areas of the world did not have the "mystique" of the Orient, that subconsciously, at least, was a part of what beckoned me.

Another possibility that was floated by a vet friend was to open a bar in Bangkok, which had a certain allure, but still was not right. It was in Southeast Asia, but lacked the danger and adventure aspects I associated with my experience of brilliant blackness. I imagined myself becoming an aging, pot-bellied bar owner pimping out a stable of girls to soldiers and tourists, wondering where the hell my life had gone.

By far the most tantalizing possibility at the time was to go to work for Air America, the CIA airline. Even back then the CIA was in the drug business, and among other missions, Air America was how they transported opium from the Golden Triangle area of Southeast Asia. Working for them was a well-known option for ex-SF, and I'd actually discussed it with a few old hands while in Nam. If necessary I could ask my father to pull some strings, but that was a last resort.

It paid $20,000 a year to start, which was damn good money then, and I liked the romantic "Terry and the Pirates" aspect of the whole scene—at least as I imagined it. I made a couple calls to get the ball rolling.

Enter the hand of the Divine.

# Lucy in the Sky with Diamonds

Vandelia had been briefly married to a friend of mine but I didn't know her very well. One evening at a party she asked me if I wanted to try LSD sometime. I said, "Sure." I had no idea what LSD was, but a pretty woman was inviting me to do something with her. No-brainer.

So a day or two later she picks me up and takes me to her friend Ria's apartment, where the three of us dropped a tab and a half of robin's egg acid each, then drove to their friend Kathy's house.

Kathy's parents were rich and away on vacation. We had the place to ourselves. We laid out by the pool and tripped our asses off. I could not imagine any way back to "normal" consciousness from where I now was, but I didn't care. I fucking loved it, and if that was to be my reality from then on, I was more than fine with that.

Ria sat naked in meditation, and gestured me to come over. Her hair was in long raven-black braids and she looked like a Sioux princess. She guided my head onto her lap and read the *Tao Te Ching* to me with the voice of an angel—the first time I'd ever heard it. The words penetrated deep, and simultaneously reflected and created my experience…

*Supreme virtue is to abide in Tao alone.*

*Tao is elusive and empty—*
*Oh yes, utterly empty and elusive—*
*yet within it dreamlike images arise.*

*Oh yes, it is indistinct and nebulous,*
*but within it shadows take form.*

*Oh yes, it is mysterious and dark,*
*but within it appearances originate.*

*The origin of Creation is the Real.*
*Its manifestations are unceasing.*
*This can be witnessed.*

*How do I witness the origin of Creation?*
*By looking!*

Later, inside the house, Jimi Hendrix playing, Van and I made love for what seemed like hours as phantasmagoric fractal extravaganzas created our world… Air America dropped from my list of life options at free-fall speed.

Van and I continued to trip together often, and for a time it seemed we might be in love. Meanwhile, I was a man on a mission to turn on everyone I knew to acid, and became known as "Captain O.D." because of my "if a little's good, a lot's better" attitude.

Acid presented me with an alternate and radically different experience of "reality" that was every bit as convincing as what I'd previously never questioned as the *only* reality. I was compelled to explore this new reality as deeply as possible, while also wondering how many more alternate realities there might be.

Eventually, Van and I drifted apart, partly because of my wandering eye, partly because she started using heroin, which I had no interest in. I still think about her, and wonder how life unfolded for her. If I could see her now I'd thank her profoundly for introducing me to psychedelics in such a beautiful and intensely memorable way, and for the gift of her love, which I treated so carelessly. If she should find this book and read this passage, I want to say to her from the depths of my heart, "Thank you," and "I'm sorry."

All this occurred in the late Sixties, and along with the psychedelics had come the first wave of readily available spiritual books and teachers. I dived in. There was a relationship between the brilliant blackness of my experience in Phan Tiet and my LSD experiences that I could not comprehend but intuited existed, and the spiritual traditions and philosophies of the east seemed to spring from the same well.

I read everything I could get my hands on. When Indian gurus gave talks, I sat in rapt attention. When Buddhist monks came to town, I listened intently, even when language and accent were nearly impenetrable. I was on some sort of path to be sure, but I didn't know what it was or what it was aimed at. Words like "enlightenment" had no meaning for me. My overriding question had become simply, "What the fuck is really going on here?"

# Dope

Shortly after returning from Vietnam mutual friends introduced me to Joe Blanchard. Joe was in Special Forces and on leave before heading to Vietnam in a few weeks. I had just returned, and he had questions, one of which was where was the best place to get assigned. I told him the Central Highlands, and also told him about II Corps Mike Force, where I'd been. I did not try to sell him on it, but he seemed interested, and our conversations centered around Mike Force from then on.

Usually these conversations took place at the Corner Pub, a local bar that while I was in the Army had become the center of social life for many of the friends I knew from high school, and for many other folks from surrounding neighborhoods. After I returned, it became that for me as well.

The Pub attracted an interesting mix of people, and looking back it lives for me as a snapshot of the times. Among those bellied-up at the bar were adults from my youth—coaches, teachers, fathers of friends—who wanted to buy me drinks because of my military service. At the tables were families getting pizza with the kids, rabid Redskins fans watching TV, groups of young women out on the town, long-haired hippies who smelled of weed. Most evenings started at the Pub, where you'd either hook up with a woman, or with some guys and go carousing other bars looking for women. Ah, youth. As T.S. Eliot so shrewdly observed:

> Birth, copulation, and death.
> That's all the facts when you come to brass tacks:
> Birth, copulation, and death.

In Vietnam Joe volunteered his way into II Corps Mike Force, just where I'd been. It was a small unit with maybe 40 or 50 Americans assigned at the time, so this in itself was somewhat amazing. Plus, some of the guys I served with were still there, so Joe and I ended up having mutual Mike Force friends.

Understandably, when he came home we had a lot to talk about, and we became close. While he was in Nam I was doing acid and reading eastern philosophy. I also became a small time cannabis dealer, buying pounds and selling ounces, which in those days earned me enough to support myself without a job. Joe was not interested in acid or philosophy, but our Mike Force bond was strong and we got an apartment together. This put Joe at just as much risk as I was for selling weed out of the place, so I shared some of the profits with him.

One summer I decided to grow my own, to go for "the big score," and Joe decided to throw in with me. I rented a deserted 100-acre farm in Virginia with a livable house for $200 a month, and Joe and I planted an isolated meadow in the woods with weed. Periodically we'd spend a couple days and nights in the farmhouse and tend the plants as they grew.

As harvest time neared, Joe and I were having lunch in the house one day when a Virginia State Police helicopter descended into a cleared area near the house. We watched in horror as it nearly touched down, not fifty yards from the house, then for some reason lifted off again and disappeared.

We grabbed whatever personal shit we had in the house, jumped into my old baby-blue 4-hole Buick Roadmaster, and highballed it to the weed patch as fast as the pot-holed old logging road would allow. We frantically pulled up plants and stuffed them into the massive trunk until full, then filled the back seat tight, and still had to leave almost all of them. Then we barreled out of there and headed back to the city.

We had planned to do all the drying and curing at the farm, and bring back cleanly packaged weed to town. Instead, now we had a shit-ton of raw weed to somehow cure and dry in a second floor garden apartment in the D.C. suburbs. So we bought sun lamps for our closets and used them to dry the weed, which caused a strong distinctive odor to waft throughout the entire building and descend down to the parking lot.

This was the early '70s, when you could get major jail time for possession of a single joint, so if you think this is the most reckless, stupid thing you've ever heard, you may be right. If you keep reading though, you'll probably agree I managed to top it.

Eventually we cured and dried all the weed, which turned out to be of excellent quality, and my customers quickly bought it up, except for a stash we kept. This left us with a good amount of cash. It also left us feeling we had pushed our luck as far as we could in that apartment and that we needed to get out.

For a variety of reasons, moving to another apartment in town and doing the same things I'd been doing for the last several years did not appeal to me. I got the bug to hit the road. Joe had similar feelings, so we stashed our few possessions with friends and headed cross country.

Our plans, such as they were, included visiting Mike Force buddies, which we did. Our last stop on this nostalgia tour was Brownsville, Texas, where Pat Ireland, the team medic who initially treated my wounds, lived. Pat was later sent home wounded as well, and had a deep scar running the length of one thigh.

During our visit Pat took us across the border into Matamoros. I loved it. I loved the people, the festive atmosphere, and the relaxed attitude towards life Mexicans seemed to have, as opposed to the uptight, fearful attitudes of many Americans. I told Joe I wanted to head down into Mexico from there, and he agreed. A couple days later, however, he was no doubt regretting it in spades.

Entering Mexico involved a ritual of bribery, which we learned at the first customs stop. Basically, you will not be attended to by an official until you have the appropriate amount of money visibly in your hand. If you are uncertain what that amount is, you keep adding bills until they are accepted.

After the initial border stop in Matamoros, there were four more customs stops, every ten or fifteen miles or so, along a long road with no side roads. At the first one of these, I opened the trunk with money in my hand, the official gave something a token pat, closed the trunk and took the money. At the second stop, same thing. I was getting the hang of this.

Between the third and last stop, feeling relaxed and confident, I decided I wanted to smoke a joint. I had brought with me—wait for it—a pound of weed *into* Mexico. It was in a brown paper grocery bag, along with all my paraphernalia, stashed up in the springs under the back seat behind me. So I pulled over, opened the back door, raised the seat, took out the bag, grabbed a joint, put everything back and got on the road again, happily toking.

As we pulled into the next customs stop the Federales were waiting for us. El Capitan came to the driver's side of the car, and a lieutenant blocked Joe's door. I got out and started filling my fist with pesos. The Capitan went straight for the back door on my side, raised the seat, took out the bag, and started asking me questions in Spanish.

I smiled as best I could, said, "I'm sorry, I don't speak Spanish," and kept adding money to my offering. It seemed we were totally fucked.

Getting no answers from me, the Captain reached into the bag. Inside, there was a large bag of weed, plus pipes and other paraphernalia, and a couple film canisters full of roaches. His hand emerged with one of the film canisters. He shook it, listened to it rattle, and said something to me in Spanish.

I kept smiling and pulling out money, saying, "I'm sorry, I don't speak Spanish." He considered me for a long moment, then put the film canister back in the bag, rolled it up, and put it back in the springs under the back seat. Then he snapped the seat back down, closed the door, took my money and waved us on through.

I pulled away slowly, wondering if my heart was going to come through my chest. After several silent miles I said, "Joe, I'm so fucking sorry."

"Mexican prison. That close."

"I know. I'm really fucking sorry."

Further down the road we came to a small town and stopped at a traffic light. A cop walked over to the car and stood at my open window, speaking to me in Spanish. My mind raced. The Federales had called ahead, changed their mind, and now we really *were* royally fucked.

I smiled and said, "I'm sorry, I don't speak Spanish," but he kept talking, in a somewhat friendly way it seemed. Then I noticed he was holding tickets in his hand. He wanted to sell me tickets to something! I quickly gave him a fistful of pesos.

He smiled big and handed me the tickets, then pulled out a couple more for me since I had overpaid. The light turned green and he gave us a cheerful salute as we pulled away. Joe and I drove in silence for awhile, then as if on cue we turned to each other and started laughing our asses off, which continued off and on for many miles.

My take on what transpired is this: A Mexican who passed us while I was pulled over reported us at the next customs stop, saying he saw some gringos messing with their back seat. The Captain followed up on that, but luckily for us pulled out a film canister rather than the weed. My theory is that the Captain was asking me if the film was exposed or not before he opened it. I apparently did not seem worried about him having it, so he just put it back. It is said God protects two-year-olds and drunks. I guess that sometimes includes extremely stupid stoners.

Once in the interior of Mexico I thought about driving around the northern states in search of Yaqui shamans like Don Juan, but I

48

knew Joe had no interest in such as that, and besides, after the adrenaline overdose I had caused us at the customs station, I figured we could both use some R&R. So we headed west and drove down the Pacific coast, stopping in various places to enjoy the beaches.

Eventually we ended up in San Blas, which at the time was a sleepy little fishing village with a single old hotel, mostly vacant. One reason for this was the presence of *jejenes*, little sand flies that shared the beach with you on windless days. The town was a few narrow dirt streets with chickens and pigs roaming free, and women making tortillas in outdoor kitchens. I loved it.

We stayed a few months, and I felt more free and relaxed each day. In San Blas I got a taste of something I didn't know I was looking for—contentment. Here I was a nobody from nowhere and free to do or not do whatever I desired. But I didn't desire much. All ambitions and ideas that I should make something of myself in life faded into insignificance. I began making plans for how I could stay more permanently.

Joe, however, wanted to head home. And so we did. I told myself I would turn right around and come back, but I sensed that would not happen. The spell would be broken when I left, and once back in my old environment I'd be seduced into my old ways.

We threw away all our dope and paraphernalia in the desert before going through U.S. Customs, and cleaned out the car to make sure there were no roaches or buds hanging around. Damn good thing we did, too. Customs directed us aside to park in a special area where they went over the car with a fine-tooth comb. Two young guys leaving Mexico in an old car, one with shoulder-length hair (me), made us likely suspects. They literally picked up crumbs from the carpets and inspected them, hoping to find dope. Luckily, we skated.

That experience, plus the general oppressive feeling of re-entering the U.S., where all my responsibilities, obligations and personal identity awaited, formed a massive weight that descended upon me, triggering a depression I could not shake as we drove back to Maryland. I felt like I was entering prison.

# Erasing Personal History

I'd spent most of my money on the road, so once back my options for where to stay were limited, but a good friend let me live in his basement while I figured out what to do next. In those days there were a lot of people moving "back to the land," and that appealed to me greatly. I had no money to buy a place, so I started studying the want ads for cheap rentals, or ideally, caretaking opportunities.

The latter idea took hold to the point where I put an ad in the Washington Post soliciting a job as caretaker somewhere rural. I received a surprising number of responses, but they were all highly undesirable, like staying in an old trailer to keep rednecks from shooting out the windows, and I became discouraged to the point of giving up on the idea. Enter the hand of the Divine.

I got a call from a man who said he needed a caretaker for the house he planned to retire to eventually. I would need to mow the grass, and generally take care of the place in exchange for rent-free living. We made plans to meet and go check it out. He was an affable older man with white hair and a humorous spark in his eyes. I climbed into his Cadillac and we drove to his place near Hagerstown, Maryland, in the Appalachian foothills about 70 miles west of D.C.

I loved the countryside around D.C., both in Maryland and Virginia, and often took long drives alone down country roads to escape the city. As we approached our destination I was cautiously elated at the beauty of the area, but nothing could have prepared me for what awaited.

We turned down a narrow road and passed by a beautiful old stone house with an acre pond and a stream running through the huge yard. I said, "Wow, what a beautiful place," not realizing it was his. He just smiled, then turned into the driveway, which was flanked by two stone pillars with a wrought iron gate. "Glad you think so," he said. Obviously, I took the job.

I lived there several years, most of it with the woman who would later become my first wife, and pursued a back-to-the-land, intentional poverty lifestyle. We planted gardens, caught trout in the stream, hiked the mountains, swam in the pond in summer, skated on it in winter, raised chickens, and bought big sacks of wheat berries we ground into flour in a huge old cast iron general store coffee grinder we bought for $2 at auction. The flour came out course, but made good, if a bit dense, bread. I harvested apples from trees that had gone wild, and gleaned ripe tomatoes from a nearby commercial field left by laborers who picked only green ones for shipping. For money I found odd jobs and seasonal work, like pruning commercial fruit trees for five bucks a tree.

I also dived more deeply into spiritual matters—reading, meditating, staring off into space from my throne on the second story screen porch, and doing a lot of self-inquiry and introspection into my identity and core beliefs.

After being home several years, smoking dope, doing acid, dating hippie chicks, watching anti-war news, I had gradually become ashamed of being proud of what I did in Vietnam. Not ashamed of what I did, but ashamed of being *proud* of it, which I was, no matter how much I had to agree we had no business being there killing people who were defending their own country.

Regardless of the political and humanitarian issues, the war had given me the chance to become someone I liked being, and I struggled with how to keep him in my stateside life. I would later talk about this conflict—to myself and others—by saying that I'd been three men in my life: The one I was before I went to Nam, the one I was while there, and the one I was after I came back. And of the three, the one I liked best was the one I was in Nam.

This struggle between pride and shame became emblematic for me over the years as I began to see it in all aspects of my life. To live and act with neither pride nor shame became a goal of sorts, and I developed the habit of looking at myself through that lens. Was I proud of this action or aspect in myself? Why? Was I ashamed of this aspect or action in myself? Why? I was beginning to understand that the purpose of self-inquiry, of self-knowledge, was not to "fix" what you discover, but only to clearly see it. That is enough.

My self-image as an ex-SF soldier was probably still the strongest aspect of personal identity I had then. But in Hagerstown I had become obsessive about my reading of Carlos Castaneda books, and took to heart Don Juan's advice to "erase personal history" as a step to becoming a "man of knowledge."

So one day I threw away everything military I had, every memory of the war I possessed. Stuffed it all into a duffle bag and put it in a Goodwill bin—uniforms, two bronze stars, purple heart. Pictures of SF buddies, Montagnard friends, enemy dead. My green beret with camouflage silk liner sewn in by an old mama-san in Pleiku. The knife I carried. A vintage French cigarette lighter inscribed "Etoile" I took off a dead NVA, whose father (in my imagination) took it off a dead French Legionnaire in the 50s...

The only two pictures that survive are a portrait my mother insisted I have taken after I returned home, and a snapshot of me drunk in the A-camp commo bunker shortly after I arrived in country, which I had included in a letter back to the states. I never ordered any prints of the portrait, but my mother kept the proof copy, which years later I found among her things (p. 38).

I don't miss having any of the items I put in that Goodwill bin, except for one thing—a black wooden plaque mailed to me after I was sent home on the hospital plane. It was a plaque given to every soldier who served in II Corps Mike Force. If you were leaving under your own power after your tour, it was presented to you in person. If you were sent home wounded, it was mailed to you. If you were killed in action, your plaque was hung on the wall behind the bar in the Mike Force team house.

My plaque contained the Special Forces patch, U.S. and Vietnamese jump wings, the Combat Infantry Badge, the Mike Force insignia of a six-toed dragon, and a brass plate with the inscription: *To SGT Barton N. Marshall, from the officers and men of II Corps Mobile Strike Force.* That, I wish I had back.

The Castaneda books were a big influence on me in other ways as well. I resonated deeply with Don Juan's teaching that one must live life as a *warrior*, and with the possibility of eventually becoming a *man of knowledge*. Prior to discovering Don Juan, I was reading mostly eastern texts that spoke of a vague goal called "enlightenment," which was indescribable, not achievable through effort, and historically attained by the rarest of the few. Whereas the path to becoming a man of knowledge, while also attained by very few, was specifically described in a series of practices and "ways of being" that responded directly to effort applied. It was seemingly attainable by anyone willing to put in the work. And I was.

The spiritual adventure aspect of Yaqui shamanism was also a tremendous pull. I wanted to be able to transform into a crow or eagle, and to roam with power the magical realms Castaneda described. I considered Don Juan and his buddy Don Genaro my teachers and wanted to be like them. If putting my Army gear in a Goodwill bin was a step in that direction, so be it.

As best I could, I tried to duplicate the salves and potions Don Juan used from the sketchy descriptions in the books. I studied and learned to recognize the plants he hunted. I drank jimson weed tea and roamed the woods at night. My girlfriend referred to these doings as my "boogie man stuff," which carried over to her attitude about all my subsequent spiritual activities, an attitude that eventually undermined our marriage.

I was in a constant tug of war. I liked who I was, but in addition to Don Juan's admonition to erase personal history, most of the eastern philosophy books I was reading said the "ego mind" was one's greatest obstacle to Self-Realization, and that one's task was to move beyond it. One's personal story was irrelevant baggage that must be left behind.

I understood all this, at least on some level, and accepted it as valid. And so gradually, one small decision at a time, I moved away from my familiar idea of who I was and into the unknown. As part of this I decided to move geographically, to a place I'd never been, and to leave behind my relationships with family and friends.

And so my girlfriend and I packed everything we owned into my old International Travelall, and with $300 dollars in our pockets headed west for Tucson, Arizona. After all, that's where Carlos met Don Juan. Maybe I'd get lucky, too.

# Arizona

The Sonoran Desert is a magical place. It's a "lush" desert, full of all sorts of different species of cactus, shrubs and low trees. Roaming it put me in a state of mind that was exhilarating, and just being in that new environment filled me with a heady surge of enthusiasm and energy that manifested in every aspect of my life.

After a few months living in town getting the lay of the land, we rented a two-room adobe house in the middle of the desert with a statue of St. Francis on top. It was heaven. Just us, St. Francis, and the coyotes and Gila monsters. I took up running, and went on long meditative runs on deserted dirt roads to nowhere.

For money, I was able to get odd jobs. I also sometimes worked for barter or very low pay in areas of personal interest. I did landscape work for a tennis pro in exchange for lessons. I stretched canvases and mixed colors for an artist with cerebral palsy who painted by holding the brush in his teeth.

At some point, though, I realized I was going to need a steady income, so I started applying for entry-level and blue-collar jobs. Nobody wanted me. A common theme was that I was "overqualified," even though I had no qualifications whatever. I came to realize what they really meant was that I seemed like someone who would not stay interested in what they had for long, and they wanted someone who would stick around.

So I decided to try my hand at real estate. I got on with an office that helped me get my education and license, and went to work. In three months I sold exactly one property, and it wasn't even a house, it was an undeveloped lot. I think my commission was $150.

By this time we'd been in Arizona a year, which made me a legal resident and eligible for in-state tuition at the University of Arizona in town, which was $300 a semester—the same as my ill-fated foray at the University of Maryland years earlier. I didn't really have an interest in going back to school, but I started considering it. To add fuel to the idea, I had the G.I. Bill to use, which would pay me $350 a month to go to college, more than I'd made in any one month for a long time. After chewing on it for awhile I applied to UA, and was accepted. I have no idea why.

At first I majored in studio art, but the program took longer to complete than I had time left on my G.I. Bill. So I switched to English, took heavy course loads each semester, and graduated just as the checks stopped coming. While all that was going on, my girlfriend and I got married and bought a little house in a blue-collar neighborhood. She had found a good job while I was in school, but we'd since had a kid, which now kept her home. I was going to need serious income soon.

As an undergrad I'd gotten in good with a few professors and they suggested I apply for the MFA in Creative Writing program there, which happened to be one of the top programs of its kind in the country. They also said I could get a teaching assistant job that paid $3,600 a semester. Sold.

Two years later I graduated and was again in need of a job. By this time I'd been indoctrinated into the world of writers and professors and was mainly applying for entry-level teaching positions at universities around the country. My MFA in Creative Writing was considered a terminal degree in the field, which one could ride into a tenured professorship if you were also a well-published writer. So I figured I'd do some teaching while I wrote the Great American Novel, and see where that took me. I got a few offers, but they were for unappealing jobs at backwater colleges, and paid maybe $14,000 a year tops. Still, it was money, and my wife was pregnant again, so I kept applying for teaching jobs I might like better.

While I was in grad school, though, IBM had built a lab outside Tucson. It was a big deal for the town since it brought in lots of people making good salaries, and opened up opportunities for local folks as well. I didn't know a damn thing about computers, but I decided what the hell, maybe they need someone to write memos or something. So I applied. Turns out they were looking for technical writers, and I caught them at a time they had determined it was easier to teach a writer programming than to teach a programmer to write.

The first step of their process was to administer a Data Processing Aptitude Test, which I must have done well on because I was called back in. The interview process involved an entire day of being bounced around from one manager to another, as well as some of their team leaders, all of whom eventually asked me a similar question as they glanced over my resume, which was sketchy to say the least—though I'd done my best to cover for periods of selling dope and living in intentional poverty.

"Mr. Marshall, you're thirty-five and it seems you've never really had a steady job. Why should we think you'll stick around if you're hired?"

"Well," I said, "for one thing I'm married now, with a young child, and my wife is pregnant with our second."

This usually produced a smile and slight nod, as if to say, "Yeah, we got you. You ain't going anywhere."

I remember well the day I heard back from them. I was setting fence posts in the back yard and had my hands in wet concrete. My wife came to the door and said, "IBM's on the phone!" I rushed in and she handed me a towel. I composed myself and took a deep breath.

My plan was that if they called I'd play it cool, like I had other offers, maybe negotiate a bit about salary. I cleared my throat and answered.

"Hello?"

"Mr. Marshall? Hi, I'm with the personnel office at IBM. We'd like to offer you a job as a technical writer."

"Oh, okay. Thank you. What else can you tell me?"

"The starting salary is $23,500 a year."

"I can start tomorrow."

"Tomorrow's Saturday, Mr. Marshall. Monday will be fine."

Tucson, Arizona, 1977

# Householder

While living in Tucson, just after we bought our house, Joe came to visit for awhile. It was great to see him and I enjoyed introducing him to the desert and mountains I had grown to love. I suggested maybe he'd be happy here, too, and offered him our spare room while he got situated. But nothing seemed to engage him. Joe had always been a sort of "dark" character, who had difficulty finding joy in life, but he seemed even more distant and unreachable then, even in the midst of what I considered achingly beautiful natural surroundings.

After Joe left he took to calling frequently, in the middle of the night, while drinking. I would lay on the floor with the phone, fighting sleep, and talk with him until he hung up. This went on for quite awhile, until late one night I got a call I assumed was from Joe but wasn't. It was my brother Richard calling to tell me Joe had killed himself. He had run a hose from the exhaust pipe of his cherry red '62 Corvette to the interior and drifted into death with the engine running.

Joe's suicide propelled me into a flurry of self-recrimination. Why didn't I see it coming? Did I do all I could for him? Did I say something wrong on the phone? Was I a good enough friend over the years? Did showing him the things that made me happy in Arizona make more painful his own lack of joy?

But eventually I came to the end of it and learned to be at ease with the hole his absence left in me, a hole I came to realize also had to do with losing my last connection to Mike Force. In addition to being a great friend, Joe filled a unique spot in my character's life. My Mike Force persona was one I still clung to then with great tenacity, and because of our shared Mike Force experience, Joe and I held each other in a certain kind of regard that no one else ever could or ever will again.

I know Joe's death had nothing whatever to do with me, but I've never been able to shake the feeling that I somehow failed him. Even now as I write this, that feeling comes over me.

Not long after, I signed on with IBM. A few months later, our second son was born, and two years after that, our daughter. As grateful as I was to have the job at IBM, I considered it a temporary measure while I got my serious writing career underway. I remember telling a like-minded colleague at lunch my first week that

I'd do three-to-five, then I was outta here. I approached it like a jail sentence or Army hitch. Thirty years later I retired.

During those thirty years I did everything I could to get out of the corporate world and make my own way. I wrote screenplays, started side businesses, tried to get in on the internet boom... Nada. I shouldn't complain though. The money was decent, the promotions kept coming, and I was able to raise three kids and put them through college. After I'd been there a couple years, IBM paid for us to move to a lab on the east coast, which I requested to be closer to our families now that we had kids.

I had been ambivalent about having children, but my wife's biological clock was ticking and she really wanted babies. Once that first one was in my arms, though, I fell deeply in love and my children became the most important thing in my life — topping even my search for Truth.

They were 11, 9, and 7 when I met Richard Rose, the man who became my primary spiritual teacher, and began listening to him talk about how you had to be willing to give up everything for Truth. I saw that same theme reflected in other readings and teachings as well, and somewhere, maybe from Rose, I heard and internalized the prayer, "Whatever stands between me and Thee, take it from me."

I prayed it many times before it occurred to me that my children may be on the table. I was more than willing to take any necessary personal hits for Truth, but not my kids, no way. I did not stop praying the prayer, but I added an addendum: "But if you harm any of my children, all bets are off. I will die an alcoholic in the gutter before I make one more gesture in Your direction." Apparently, and thankfully, that was not a show-stopper.

Raising kids, as any parent will attest, is hard, sometimes achingly painful work. But it is also one of the most beautiful and instructive experiences a person can have. And too, for most people, it's the first time you love someone unconditionally, and significantly more than yourself, which in itself is an extremely valuable experience.

As a teacher, when I was holding weekly meetings, I was often asked by young men, and occasionally women, if, as serious seekers, I thought they should have children. Rose, who was a big proponent of celibacy on the path, would have advised them to postpone marriage and children until after Self-Realization. That's what he did, and it "worked" for him, so he passed it on.

That was not my path, however, and so over time I formulated a response to their questions that went something like this: "Raising children can teach you more about yourself, human nature, and the ways of the world than any other endeavor. But the price of that knowledge is sometimes high and you must decide whether you are willing to pay it. You may be tested in ways you never imagined, and pushed to the limits of your emotional and psychological capacities. Because of this, raising children can be a constant invitation to self-inquiry, if you're so inclined, and can become an integral part of an earnest seeker's path."

For me, it did indeed become an integral part of my path, but I was far from a detached observer. I was an activist dad who threw himself into every aspect of fatherhood and their upbringing, and for the most part I enjoyed every minute of it. There were definitely challenges and hard times, but they were far outweighed by joy, and yes, pride. I was far more delighted by my children's successes than I was by my own.

I am blessed with three incredible kids, Bart, Danny and Karen. Bart has a son, Jadon. Danny has two girls, Ameya and Anya, and a boy, Ayden. Karen has two girls, Emerson and Landon. My children and their families are the greatest joys of my life.

While raising our children, we lived on a cul-de-sac in a wooded suburban neighborhood with a creek the kids could play in. The cul-de-sac was often filled with neighborhood kids tearing around on Big Wheels or playing street hockey, depending on ages.

Two miles away was our swim and tennis club. It had three pools—a regulation 10-lane racing pool, a social pool with lounge chairs, snack bar, and diving boards, and a secluded pool with a huge waterslide I'd ride until my legs got too tired to climb the steps. There were 24 tennis courts, including 4 composition courts, which I loved because they were easier on my knee.

We had a golden retriever, Rowdy, a stray cat, Midnight, and a basketball goal in the driveway. Our neighbors were sociable and friendly—except for one asshole, but there's always one—and my wife and I were in a close circle of six couples who came to call themselves the "Support Group." We had frequent get-togethers, commiserating over wine and good food about our children and lives, and some of our kids were friends and teammates. It would not be an overstatement to say I lived a suburban cliché during my householder years.

I loved my home life, and was keenly aware how blessed we were, though I never completely assimilated. I was in it but not *of* it. My inner attention was always elsewhere, somewhere in the netherworld of spiritual aspiration, and even as I lived my blessings I was somehow also estranged from them.

Over the years my wife became increasingly intolerant of the time and attention I was giving to my spiritual search, and to the friends I had who were a part of it. Our relationship became less and less affectionate, and neither one of us was truly happy with the other. We were great at raising kids together, but had little else in common. I could not imagine what we would do or have to talk about without the kids, and increasingly my vision of my future did not include my wife. I knew that when the kids were on their own I would have to leave.

My last official act as a householder was to give Karen, our youngest, a beautiful, extravagant wedding. I put a lot of thought and effort into my father-of-the-bride speech, and it had the crowd alternately rolling in the aisles and dabbing their eyes. Karen later told me she felt like I was saying goodbye to her. I wasn't, of course, but I was on the verge of leaving her mother, and being the intuitive young woman she is, she sensed something was about to change.

During these child-raising years my IBM job became more and more suffocating. At about the twenty-year mark it got so bad my body would go into revolt as I walked towards the building in the morning. I felt like I was entering prison. The only way I made it to the finish line was to finagle my way into being able to work from home my last ten years.

All the while I remained obsessed with spiritual work. I read everything I could get my hands on that might open the door to Truth. I meditated regularly (sort of), and constantly prayed to be shown the way.

I even tried my hand at Christianity. When the kids were young my wife started taking them to church and Sunday school at St. Michael's Episcopal, and eventually I began to join them. I'd always had an aversion to church since I was a kid, and I found I still didn't like it. And yet, beneath all the pomp and poppycock there was, I don't know, something. When they stopped making me stand up and sit down every two minutes, inside I got very still. More often than not, I wept taking communion.

Later on I also occasionally visited a Trappist monastery in South Carolina, and would spend the weekend helping out with their chicken farm, and chanting psalms with the monks seven times a day. My favorite service was the one at 3:00 a.m. in the dark gothic cathedral with only candlelight. It was magical and moving, and often brought me to tears. But in the end, I still did not feel church held what I was looking for as far as actually finding Truth.

In 1989 I hit the wall on all spiritual fronts. My meditations were an exercise in impatience and frustration. I'd browse my hundreds of spiritual books and not feel like opening any of them. When I listened to spiritual teachers my mind wandered, and their words faded into a background hum.

So I gave up my search for enlightenment and resolved to be a normal person. I was 43 and for half my life I'd been dogged by the nagging sense that nothing was as it seemed. The desire to be one of the chosen few who knew Truth had been the driving force of my life. Now it was gone.

I still believed it was possible for ordinary people to know first-hand what Buddha and Jesus knew, but suddenly, without warning, I'd lost all hope that it was possible for *me*. Meditation, books, teachers… I'd done what I could and nothing happened. It was time to move on.

In a way I was relieved, like a burden had been lifted. But mostly it felt like shit, like not making a team you really want to play for. I slipped into a mood of sullen indifference. If God wanted me to make any further efforts in His direction, he'd have to give me a very obvious sign.

A few weeks later Cheryl came into my office with a flyer for a lecture. "We should go to this," she said. "It's tonight."

Cheryl's visits were the highlight of my day. She was the only person I knew at IBM who was even remotely interested in serious spiritual matters, plus she had a great ass.

I glanced at the flyer. *Five Years with a Zen Master: An American Businessman's Story*. She was right. If it weren't for my sour grapes attitude about being unworthy of enlightenment, it was just the kind of thing I'd go to. I tossed it aside.

"Some yahoo goes to Japan and wears a black bathrobe for awhile then hits the lecture circuit? No thanks."

"You never know. It could be good."

"I'm done with this shit. Burned out."

She looked at the flyer again, then pressed it into my desk like it had stickum on the back.

"I'm going. You should come."

I didn't. The next day she dropped by with her report.

"It was great. Just your kind of thing."

"Maybe next time."

"One of the speaker's friends taped it for broadcast on Cable Access. I'll find out when they're going to show it."

"I don't have cable."

"I'll tape it for you."

"Don't bother, I'm not—

"Do you have VHS or Beta?"

"Beta."

"Shit. I have VHS."

"Look, I appreciate the effort, but—"

"My ex-husband has Beta, though," she said, turning to go. "I'll get him to tape it for you."

"Seriously, you don't need to do—" But she was gone.

And so, despite my best efforts to avoid it, a month later Cheryl walked into my office, carefully placed a Beta videotape on my desk, looked me hard in the eye, and said, "Watch this."

65

# Mister Rose

That night after the kids were in bed I reluctantly slid the tape into my VCR, mainly because I wanted to be able to tell Cheryl I'd watched it and not have to deal with her nagging me until I did. The speaker's name was Augie Turak, and he was not talking about a Japanese Zen master, but an enlightened West Virginia hillbilly farmer he'd studied under named Richard Rose. It was an excellent talk, and the more I listened the more excited I got. By the end of it I had but one thought in my mind: "I have to meet this guy Rose!"

Finding Augie was the only way I knew to locate Rose, but he could have flown in from anywhere for the talk. On the chance he was local I looked him up in the phone book. His address was two miles away. I called, and he invited me to a weekly meeting he held at his house.

The following Friday I went. A table was set out with all the books Rose had written and I bought a copy of each before the meeting started. After the meeting Augie told me no one had ever done that before, let alone at their first meeting.

"They usually just flip through one or two of them and don't buy anything."

"They must not be serious about this shit then."

"Tell me about it. I've been holding these meetings for two years and all I get is curiosity seekers."

I continued to go to the meetings for a few weeks to build cred before asking Augie for Rose's address so I could write him. Rose wrote back and invited me to come up.

On the agreed upon weekend, I drove the nine hours to Benwood, West Virginia and parked across the street from Rose's house. Benwood is a depressing ex-coal and steel town on the banks of the Ohio River, with rows of dingy, soot-stained houses that might best be described as blue-collar gothic. Rose's house was one of these.

He answered the door with a welcoming smile and warm handshake. He was a short, stocky man in his 70s, with an open, round face and hooded eyelids that gave him a vaguely oriental aspect. I immediately liked him.

It was a cold day in March 1990 and Rose had two gas burners lit on his kitchen stove, which I came to find out was the only heat in his house. Once you left the kitchen, you might as well have stepped outside. On top of his ancient refrigerator sat a small black-and-white TV with aluminum foil on the antennas. It was tuned to a local news story about an ongoing trial. Rose took a last glance at it before switching it off.

"That guy is innocent, but he'll be railroaded into prison. Every judge in the state is crooked. Hell, every judge in every state is crooked," he laughed.

His kitchen table held an old iron typewriter from the '40s, and a stack of pages for a book he was writing, along with an array of used spiritual books being readied to send out to customers of his small mail-order book business. No one else was living there then, but in the early days, the house was full of seekers who Rose let live with him. He even moved his own things into a small storage room with a narrow iron cot, and gave his bedroom to someone else. That right there is all you need to know about how Rose lived his life, but similar examples of his selflessness and generosity abound.

Much of his fascinating story, as well as his teachings, is related in *After the Absolute* (realfacepress.com). Other books and essays about Rose and his work can be found on tatfoundation.org, searchwithin.org, and richardroseteachings.com.

Rose's life got off to a dramatic start. When his mother was pregnant with him his father shot and killed a man for accosting her in the street. Afterwards he turned himself in and went to jail. Rose's mother then proceeded to camp out on the steps of the governor's mansion in the dead of a West Virginia winter, stoic in rain and snow, and refused to move until her husband was set free. Faced with the prospect of a pregnant woman freezing to death on his front steps, the governor caved, and Rose's father was pardoned.

When Rose was a boy, he was put into an orphanage for awhile because his parents could not afford to feed him. He also had extra-sensory capacities that worried his parents. For instance, he knew someone was going to die soon if he smelled flowers in their presence, and he would tell them so, embarrassing his mother. But he was always right.

He'd had a lifelong spiritual calling since the age of six, when he filled page after page with the words, "Many are called, but few are chosen," and at the age of 12, he entered a Catholic monastery thinking it was the best way to find God. At 17, he left disillusioned.

That evening we settled into a comfortable rapport, and talked and drank tea for hours. By the end of it, I knew I'd found my teacher. He showed me to a room upstairs and gave me a sleeping bag and some blankets. My guess is it was about 35 degrees in that room. We said goodnight and I shivered myself to sleep.

The next day he drove me out to his farm in the mountains. A half-dozen or so of his students lived there at the time and were working around the place when we arrived. In the late '60s Rose had opened up his farm as an ashram and let anyone with a serious spiritual interest live there, and even build their own cabins in the woods. Later, he created the TAT Foundation as the legal entity for his teaching efforts, and held four gatherings a year at the farm. TAT stands for "Truth and Transmission."

It was rough going in the early days, and the local hillbillies didn't take too kindly to a farm full of hippies in their midst. They even shot at the house sometimes when they drove by. On one occasion Rose and some of the guys grabbed guns and shot back, wounding one of the attackers. Rose ended up in jail for it, but was judged innocent due to self-defense. One of the attacker's bullets had missed his young sleeping son by six inches.

Rose introduced me to the guys there that day and we chatted a bit, but he had something else in mind. He turned to me and said, "Let's take a walk." It was a huge property, mostly woods, and Rose kept up a steady stream of esoteric teachings as we walked, as if he never expected to see me again and this was his last shot at helping me. At one point, as we stopped to admire some intricate forest moss, I got up the courage to ask what I'd come to ask.

"Mister Rose, what do you see when you look at me? What's my greatest obstacle to enlightenment?"

He didn't hesitate. "Your greatest obstacle is your family. The majority of your energy is channeled in that direction and it's energy you need for the search. But there's nothing you can do to remedy it. You can't leave them. They are your sacred responsibility. Your work is to find your way in the midst of the turmoil of family life."

His words caused me to weep. It seemed an overwhelming task, and I said so. He stayed silent for a several moments.

"Think of it like this: Suppose one of your children had a rare fatal disease that could only be cured by the root of a single tree, but you didn't know what that tree looked like or where to find it. How hard would you look for that tree?"

"With my whole being," I said.

"Do that now for yourself," he said. "That child is your soul, and you are the only one who can save it."

# Vietnam to Zen

I continued to attend Augie's Friday night meetings, and at one he turned to me and said, "Bart, we never hear much from you. What's your background? What got you interested in the spiritual search?" I responded with a very abbreviated version of what you've read here so far. Augie's jaw dropped. "You need to give a talk."

In addition to his Friday night meetings, Augie also ran a student group called the Self-Knowledge Symposium, which had chapters at each of the three major universities in the area— University of North Carolina, Duke, and North Carolina State. The main reason he did all this was to find people who might be serious enough to want to work with Rose. His method of attaining visibility for his mission was to bring in speakers to give public talks, and to give talks himself, like the one I saw on the tape. Now he wanted me to give one.

I was not enthused. Going public was not my style. I've never been drawn to the spotlight, being naturally more suited to the anonymity of observation than the scrutiny of stardom. Add to that, while I was in this proposed spotlight I'd be talking about things most people would think were crazy.

I was what you might call a "closet seeker," in that few people in my daily life knew what I was up to. Besides being nervous about public speaking in general, I was concerned about blowing my cover. But I agreed, thinking what the hell, I'll be speaking to a handful of college students who don't know me from Adam in an obscure campus venue. What could go wrong?

One consideration, among many, I had not factored in was that Augie was a master salesman and publicity expert. He'd been an executive at MTV when it was getting off the ground, and had held a number of high-level sales positions elsewhere.

He gave me a gaudy title for my talk, "From Vietnam to Zen: A Green Beret's Story of Life on The Razor's Edge," and proceeded to market the hell out of it. He sent out press releases, had posters put up on every light pole and bulletin board around campus, and scheduled me for radio and newspaper interviews.

The Durham Herald-Sun gave my interview a front-page teaser headline above the name of the paper, and the complete front page of their Lifestyle section was devoted to it. The entire space above the fold was an extreme close-up of my face. You could count my nose hairs, I swear to God. So much for anonymity.

At each increased level of exposure I would console myself: "It's okay, nobody listens to AM radio." "It's okay, nobody pays attention to posters on light poles." As I drove to campus the night of my talk I told myself, "It's okay, only a few dozen college kids who don't know anyone you know."

When I walked into the room the first thing I saw was a crowd of 150. The second was a videographer set up in the center aisle. I asked him what he was going to do with the tape.

"Put it on Cable Access TV," he said. By this time I was pretty much punched out, but still managed a weak, "It's okay, nobody watches Cable Access," as I walked on stage.

While all this buildup was taking place I was working intently on my talk. If I was going to do this I wanted to do it as well as I could. Being a writer, I wrote the whole thing out in detail. My talk was basically a 20-page essay. My job at the podium was to try not to look like I was reading it. Lights, camera, action...

"My talk tonight is about philosophy," I began. "About war and Zen, personal power and philosophy. Not intellectual, pipe and spectacles philosophy. Philosophy in action. Philosophy as a means of penetrating to the core of life and reality — staring it in the face, unafraid, undaunted by clarity and truth. Philosophy as a means of ordering your life so that you gain energy and power as you go. Philosophy as expressed by a medieval samurai master, who said: 'You must concentrate and consecrate yourself wholly to each day, as though a fire were raging in your hair.'"

It was boffo. Some weeks later the tape aired on Cable Access TV, and for whatever reason they kept airing it several times a day for weeks. Nobody tuned in cable access on purpose, but everyone I knew eventually stumbled on it while channel surfing and watched because they recognized me. People at IBM stopped me in the halls. Suburban neighbors cornered me at barbecues. Team parents gathered around me on bleachers and sidelines.

What I found was that almost everyone was moved by it in some way, regardless if they had any spiritual inclinations or not. A colleague at IBM who was a retired Marine master sergeant left me a five-minute voicemail on my work phone, his voice cracking, saying how the Vietnam portion had made him understand his own experience, and the spiritual parts made him think thoughts he never knew he was capable of.

Self-Knowledge Symposium sold cassettes and CDs of the talk. Augie had me reprise the talk for other local universities, and several Rose-based spiritual groups around the country paid my way to come give the talk at their public gatherings. "Vietnam to Zen" was a bit of a minor phenomenon in a very small world of seekers, and sort of "put me on the map" as a spiritual spokesman, even though it would be another 14 years before I knew what the hell I was talking about.

Perhaps the most directly impactful result of the talk to me personally, however, was sometime after that—after I'd had a conclusive spiritual occurrence—when I was contacted by Bill Miiller (yes, two "i"s), who said he'd made and given away over 100 cassettes of "Vietnam to Zen" to friends and fellow seekers since he first got hold of it, but had never thought of trying to contact me until he'd recently seen something about me as a spiritual teacher on the internet.

We became email friends, and for several years after he kept inviting me to come out to where he lived in southern Colorado and talk to his Zen group. He was an ex-biker who became a Zen monk for 20 years and still held regular sittings in a circular adobe kiva he built  as part of his home. "I really think you'll love it here," he said.

I kept declining, until finally he said if I wouldn't come there, he would come to me. I was holding weekend retreats by then, and he said, "I hate flying and I never leave this valley, but I'm coming to your October retreat." He never made it. He got stuck in Atlanta and the next flight out would not get him to Raleigh until Sunday morning, the day the retreat ended. So he flew back to Colorado. When I heard this I resolved that if he invited me again, I would go.

He did, and in 2011 I went. I immediately fell in love with the physical beauty of the place, and with the friends I made. I've been going back ever since, and now own 30 acres there I plan to build on. You just never know what leads to what. Thank you, Bill. Thank you, Augie. Thank you, *Vietnam to Zen*.

Richard Rose, 1917-2005

# Taking Leave

For as important a teacher as Rose was in my life, I spent relatively little personal time him. I went to some of the TAT meetings at his farm each year, but probably only visited him alone three or four times in the five years I had with him before his Alzheimer's took over. Much of what I gained from Rose was not the specifics of his teachings, but his "way of being," and his meta-advice on how to be an effective seeker.

The specifics of his teachings I learned mostly from working on two projects: a book, *After the Absolute* (realfacepress.com), and a video documentary, *Mister Rose* (tatfoundation.org). Shortly after I met Rose and started coming to TAT meetings, I was included in conversations about the need for a good video about Rose. One thing led to another, and I took on the project with a friend, Matt Giovinetti.

We shot 30 hours of footage and edited it down to four—in the days of analog video editing. This involved meticulously logging every minute of every tape, and watching and re-watching every second during the painstaking editing process. Everything Rose said on those tapes I probably heard thirty times. Something had to have sunk in.

The book was a joint effort with one of his early students, Dave Gold, and is Dave's story about his time with Rose in the '70s and '80s, when Rose was at the height of his powers. It's the best introduction to Rose and his teachings available, and has also been responsible for inspiring many people to become more serious about their spiritual lives.

A big part of the project was us gleaning Rose quotes from more than a hundred tapes that had been made of his talks over the years, which was a great education for me. And of course writing and re-writing the book hammered things home.

By 1995 Rose's Alzheimer's was so advanced he was no longer an effective teacher, and my opportunity to learn from him directly had passed. Over the next ten years I would still visit him, but things were a lot different. On one visit his wife Cecy had him sorting coins to keep him occupied. I sat at the table with him. At one point he looked up and said, "You know, I used to have a group. I was the head honcho." Then he went back to putting nickels with nickels, dimes with dimes.

A couple times Cecy left me with him while she took a break to do errands. He was visibly distressed without her. "Where's Cecy?" he would ask every few minutes.

"Doing errands, Mister Rose. She'll be back soon."

He'd stand at the window to watch for her, and become paranoid about the cars parked on the street. "Who's car is that?"

"I don't know, Mister Rose. Just a neighbor."

I took him on a walk once. He moved with a slow shuffle and kept asking to go home. "Just a little further, Mister Rose. It's a beautiful day, isn't it?"

Eventually she had to put him in a home, and I visited him a couple times there. Once, there was a "party" for the patients, and Rose shuffled around with a Buddha smile serving everyone cake. At a later visit he had progressed past being able to speak coherently, but would still sometimes talk in what sounded like an alien language.

On this occasion I was sitting across from him at a table while he spoke softly in an unintelligible tongue. Suddenly he broke into perfect English and said to me, "You should be ashamed. You took the bait," then fell silent. To Rose, "taking the bait" meant falling prey to the seductions of the world.

I felt like I'd been kicked in the stomach by a mule. A memory flashed of a note a friend had passed on to me he'd received from Rose with a book order. He'd written to Rose that I'd been the one who recommended Rose's books to him, and Rose wrote back: "One publishes a thousand books to find the one-in-a-million. Bart is the one. A cool breeze on a hot summer's day."

I should have been pleased at the compliment, but all I felt then was guilt for not being what he thought I was—my opinion of my worthiness being considerably less generous than his.

And now, facing him across the table in a shabby state-run dementia institution, still ignorant as hell, I was overwhelmed with regret for being such a disappointment to him—and myself. There on the spot I solemnly resolved to live up to his expectations or die trying. Two years later, I disappeared in favor of the infinite clear emptiness of God. Less than a year after that, Rose died.

When I got word he was actively dying and not being given food or water, I considered going up. But it was a long drive and I had a lot of things to do. I might insert here that once you realize you don't exist and neither does anything else, death of the body—yours or anyone else's—loses most of its drama. Still, this was a man I revered above all others in my life…

Days pass. Email updates arrive. Rose grows weaker—not expected to live out the day. Every day for a week he is not expected to live out the day. Suddenly, without warning I jump to my feet. "What the hell am I doing?!"

It's a nine hour drive from Raleigh to Wheeling. The whole way I worry my epiphany has come too late, but when I get there Rose is still alive. Mike Casari, a Rose student of thirty-five years, sits in a chair at the head of Rose's bed. He's been there for three days and looks it.

"Broke down in three different cars getting here," he says. "But I made it." He steps out to give me some time with Rose.

Rose has been without food or water since he lost the ability to swallow. The final fast. His once-powerful body is frail, his face gaunt and drawn. His chest rises and falls with weak, labored breath. I put my hand on his shoulder and speak to him. His eyes open slightly. They are clear and deep. I feel, as I always have, that they see clean through me.

Late into the night Mike and I sit by the bed and catch up in low voices—trying not to disturb Rose's roommate, George, on the other side of a thin curtain. Sometimes our laughter gets loud.

"We keeping you awake, George?" Mike says.

"Yes."

"Okay, good. Just checking." They have become friends these last three days and developed a vaudevillian banter based on George's grouchy demeanor.

"Who the hell wants to sleep anyway?" George says. "Plenty of that coming up soon enough."

Sometime after midnight Rose's daughter Kathie and her daughter Julie show up. Julie is thirty and looks twenty. She wears a red T-shirt with a South Park character and the words: "Screw you guys, I'm going home." She carries a violin case, which she opens with some urgency.

Kathie gave birth to Julie alone, having left home to escape a strict father who once read her diary to investigate her virtue. ("All he found was page after page of how much I hated him.")

She bends now to stroke his head as Julie plays Mozart to break your heart on a 200-year-old violin crafted by a famous European who made only 25 instruments in his long life. Though priceless, it was sold to her for next to nothing by a master violinist whose fingers were blown off in war. Listening, you understand why he wanted her to have it.

In Julie's purse is a return ticket to Norway where she's taking a Master's in Ibsen and doing her thesis on Duke Ellington's version of Edvard Grieg's "Peer Gynt" — commissioned by Ibsen for his play. Her professors have refused to approve it — too obscure a connection to the literature, they said. "Screw you," she told them. "I'm doing it anyway." She also has her grandfather's eyes.

The night staff gathers in the hallway to listen as Julie moves from Mozart to bluegrass to Celtic paeans with effortless grace. Later they help us move Rose's bed into a large recreation room so we can have some privacy and be as loud as we want. We take full advantage.

"You're not leaving without a party, Grandpa," Julie says, kicking into a version of "Orange Blossom Special" we could swear makes Rose's foot move.

The staff brings us food and coffee throughout the night and can't stop saying, "If you all need anything, anything at all, please let us know."

Mike brings a white rose from a bouquet in the dining room and places it in a vase by Rose's bed. The bed is parked under a large window. A Madonna statue — the only religious object I've seen in the home — is being casually stored on the sill. Its outstretched hands now hover over Rose's head.

The next day an attractive young nurse named Erin comes in to check Rose's vitals. She touches him with great tenderness and shakes her head.

"What?" I say.

"No way he should be alive."

"He's always been strong."

She nods. "Still…" She starts to leave then turns back. "Can I get you a hot dog? We're having hot dogs today."

"You don't have to do that," I say without thinking. She's a nurse, after all, and has more important duties than waiting on us.

Her eyes flare. "I know I don't!"

I sense my mistake. She has been with Rose for years perhaps, monitoring his decline, unable to help. "Yes, please," I say. "A hot dog sounds good."

The others say yes to hot dogs and Erin leaves. Seconds later she is back. "I'm sorry I snapped at you," she says. "It's just that… I feel I'm part of the family, and... We're not supposed to cross the line. They teach us not to cross the line."

"It must be hard."

"I read one of his papers, you know. Somebody left it here." Her eyes light up. "It's how I *think*. What he says in there is how I *think*. I've never heard it said before... God I wish I could have known him." She takes a deep breath. "You want cole slaw, too?"

I nod. "The works."

Later she drives Mike and me to a gourmet coffee shop and buys us expensive drinks with homemade whipped cream. Her shift is over but she doesn't want it to end. It seems she is on the verge of returning to the home with us, but there is just no precedent for such a thing. "I'll see you tomorrow," she says finally, knowing it's unlikely.

The next evening Rose is still alive but his condition seems to have worsened. His breaths come further and further apart and Erin shakes her head when taking his vitals. Kathie, Julie, Mike and I stand around his bed, expecting every breath to be his last. It's the Fourth of July, and on the other side of the dark window behind Rose's head, fireworks burst continually in the sky. The perfection of the moment could not be greater as we wait. And wait. A half-hour later Rose's mouth opens into a gapping yawn. Not only is he not ready to go, he's bored with us making a big drama out it.

"Is there such a thing as a death yawn?" I muse.

"I don't think so," Mike says.

In the middle of the night Mike and I sit with Rose as Kathie and Julie sleep nearby. A caregiver comes in and stands at the foot of the bed. She's built like a linebacker, with short, slicked-back hair and a black dragon tattoo that covers most of one calf.

"First thing I always do when I start a shift," she says, "is come visit Richard." She pats his leg. "How you doing, baby?"

"Thought we were going to lose him earlier tonight," Mike says.

"He'll go when he's ready and not a minute before. It's his show." She pats him again then turns to us.

"Thought I was gonna lose one of my own tonight," she says. "Just come from the hospital. One of my boys—I got four boys— went through the windshield in a wreck and broke a phone pole with his body. All he got was bruised, though—he's a heavyweight boxer. Got the call and drove eighty-five all the way to the hospital, cop cars wailing after me. By the time I pulled in there was six of 'em behind me, lights flashing. I tossed my wallet on the seat and told 'em, 'Leave the ticket in the car,' then I run inside to my boy.

"He weren't the one driving. The boy driving's had eight wrecks in a year. His mother never liked him. Neither do I, but I feed him and let him sleep at the house some. A real annoying kid. I've had to stick a gun in his face a few times to get his attention. I got fifty guns, license to carry. My grandson's two years old and's got four guns — real ones that I give him. I love guns, love hunting. Went into labor deer hunting once but refused to go to the hospital till I got my buck. Got me one, too, then went on in and had the kid. Week later I was hunting again."

Mike and I are laughing hard and she's grinning big. "You're one tough momma," Mike says.

She snorts. "I'll tell you who's tough," she says, cutting her chin towards Rose. "That one there. I'm a hilly, raised in the hollers. I knew about him long before he came in here. Lots of folks did. He's a good man but he didn't take no shit."

She pats Rose again. "I'll be back in awhile, baby." At the door she turns to us. "If you need anything, anything at all…"

When the end finally came, five of us stood around the bed: Kathie, Tatia — another of his three daughters — Mike, Julie and me.

Julie said, "Does anyone have a Bible? We could read the 23rd Psalm. He loved the 23rd Psalm."

For some unknown reason I'd been moved to commit the 23rd Psalm to memory several months before. "I know it," I said, then began to recite:

*The Lord is my shepherd. I shall not want.*
*He maketh me to lie down in green pastures.*
*He leadeth me beside the still waters. He restoreth my soul.*
*He leadeth me in the paths of righteousness*
*for his name's sake.*
*Yea, though I walk through the valley of the shadow of death,*
*I will fear no evil, for thou art with me.*
*Thy rod and thy staff they comfort me.*
*Thou preparest a table before me*
*in the presence of mine enemies.*
*Thou annointest my head with oil. My cup runneth over.*
*Surely goodness and mercy shall follow me*
*all the days of my life,*
*and I will dwell in the house of the Lord forever.*

Rose took his last shallow breath, Erin checked his pulse at the neck, nodded solemnly, and that was that. The women, including Erin, cried. Mike and I stood on either side of him with a hand on a shoulder and silently said our goodbyes.

Kathie fished in her purse for her camera and handed it to me. "Get the three of us," she said.

The Rose girls composed themselves and got their smiles ready. "Dry your eyes," Tatia said. "This is for Daddy."

Rose had often said the difference between him and ordinary men was that they lived to live, he lived to think. The irony of him being taken out by a disease that slowly robbed him of his mind was not lost on all who knew him. But he saw it coming. Decades before his death he wrote this poem:

> *I will take leave of you*
> *Not by distinct farewell*
> *But vaguely*
> *As one entering vagueness*
> *For words, symbols of confusion*
> *Would only increase confusion*
> *But silence, seeming to be vagueness,*
> *Shall be my cadence*
> *Which someday*
> *You will understand.*

Kathie, Tatia, Julie

# Flight 99

Rose's greatest desire in life was to pass on what he had found to someone else, to facilitate Self-Realization in one or more of his students. He used to say, "If I can keep five lemmings from going over the cliff, and each of them can keep five from going over, my life will have been worth it, and the world might be benefitted."

But in over 30 years of active teaching and running spiritual groups none of his students ever woke up. Several years after he was out of it with Alzheimer's, though, unable to speak, living in a state-run dementia facility, things started happening for some of his former students, and happening fast.

The first to pop was Bob Cergol, who was one of Rose's early students, and had been with him since he was nineteen. Bob was one of the guys in a small spiritual group we had in Raleigh. There were only four or five of us, mostly ex-Rose students, who started meeting for dinner occasionally, then decided to be more regular about it and meet at Bob's house once a week.

Our pattern was to rotate who led the meeting, and when it was your turn you'd prepare something. One week when it was to be my turn, Bob called the night before and said, "Can I take the meeting this week. There's something I need to talk about."

His voice sounded a bit shaky so I didn't press him for details. "Sure," I said. "See you then."

At the meeting he told us he'd had a transformative spiritual experience triggered by a passage he was reading in some letters from Alfred Pulyan to Rose, which had been compiled and were being passed around by TAT members. It was obvious then as he spoke, and in subsequent weeks as his Realization matured in him, that this was the real deal.

Bob's Realization had a powerful effect on me. The most immediate was, "Holy shit, this really *can* happen to ordinary people. This gun I'm playing with is loaded!"

One of the things I loved about Rose as a teacher was that he was such a regular guy, not some swami on a throne. But on another level, he really wasn't so regular. He had capacities and strengths I did not attribute to myself, and while knowing him made enlightenment seem more possible than if my only models were Jesus and Buddha, I still did not put myself in his league.

But Bob? Bob I'd known for years and knew to be a truly ordinary guy. On some level I might even have thought I was "ahead" of him on the path. Which brings me to my second reaction: "Why him and not me? What's wrong with me? What am I doing wrong?" Bob's experience both gave me hope and threw me for a loop.

Three months later, Bob Fergesen woke up. Three months after that, Shawn Nevins. What the fuck is going on here? I was both happy for them (in a jealous sort of way), and depressed that in this frenzy of enlightenment goodies being handed out, I was being passed over by the Divine. What am I, chopped liver? I double-downed on my spiritual efforts and prayed it might soon be my "turn."

But several years passed and nothing else happened. Nobody else got enlightened, and certainly not me. I thought, "Well, those guys were all younger than me. Maybe I've aged out of it." By then I was 58.

In the early days of his teaching, Rose said that if enlightenment hadn't happened by age 30, hang up your spurs. Later, as all of his students turned 30 and beyond, he amended that to age 40. But he never upped it from there. He also spoke about enlightenment in terms of extreme trauma, saying things like, "They're going to have to carry you out on a stretcher," and, "You're going to walk through death and that takes some vitality," so I wondered if at my age I'd be able to survive it if it did happen.

I was 44 when I first met Rose, so I started off fighting the odds, and now, at age 58 I was at a crossroads. Give up completely, or make a Quixotic last assault. I opted for the latter, and in order to demonstrate the sincerity of my desire, I did things like getting my affairs in order, and destroying old writings I would not want others to see — as gestures saying, "I am prepared to die for this."

Then Art Ticknor, another long-time Rose student from the early days, had a conclusive spiritual experience — and Art was two years older than I was! And a few months after Art's experience, another TAT friend, Anima Pundeer, had a conclusive experience, although I did not hear about that until sometime later.

Art had been reading *The Little Book of Life and Death*, by Douglas Harding on an isolation retreat when his experience kicked in, and coincidentally I'd recently gotten an email announcing Harding's annual Gathering in Salisbury, England to be held that August. I knew Douglas' work and admired him as a teacher, but I

84

didn't really have the money for that kind of trip. The idea of working with him was too compelling to resist, however.

As the first day of the Gathering unfolded I was immediately disappointed. Looking around I judged my fellow attendees to be New Age lightweights. Before the meeting got started one woman announced to the room she'd appreciate it if no one wore perfume, as the smell disturbed her energy field. A bearded American man wearing Indian white linen loudly announced that he'd be doing yoga on the lawn at the end of the day and encouraged everyone to join him.

When the meeting got underway, Douglas, 95 years of age, sat in a wheelchair with his head drooped as members of his organization gave talks that were unimpressive. It seemed Harding at his advanced age was just a figurehead now, a marquee name that attracted people to an event that featured other speakers. I felt I'd foolishly spent money I didn't have to be trapped with people who were not as serious as I was, who did not have the spiritual background I did, who were my spiritual "inferiors."

When the current speaker finished up, she turned to Harding. "Douglas, would you like to say anything?"

Harding lifted his head and in a booming voice said, "Why, yes I would!"

From then on it was his meeting, and every day after for the four-day Gathering. We did his "experiments," drew self-portraits of our headless world view, and listened in rapt attention as he held us in thrall with profound teachings delivered in glorious Shakespearean tones. On top of that, over the course of the Gathering I literally fell in love with everyone there for being exactly who they were, to the point of feeling constantly on the verge of tears.

When the last day ended everyone said goodbye to Douglas and his remarkable wife Catherine, a beautiful French woman in her eighties who seemed to embody every aspect of the feminine at once: mother, lover, sister, muse... Most everyone was headed home that day, but my flight was not until morning so I waited until everyone had dispersed to say goodbye to Douglas.

Harding was an incredibly kind and loving man, and when we first met a few days earlier he greeted me like an old friend, as I'm sure he did everyone. "I feel as if I've known you for a very long time," he said.

It was with that kind of warmth we said goodbye to each other. Then suddenly, without warning, his arm shot straight up in the air, his eyes flared, and he shouted, "Simplify!"

I was so shocked I probably took an involuntary step back. I was too stunned to speak. My mind went blank. Harding's eyes stayed fixed on mine. His arm remained in the air, index finger pointing to heaven... I turned and staggered to my room.

Once there I sat in a small wooden chair and stared at the floor without thinking. I don't know how long I stayed that way. Then without warning my chest heaved and the dam burst on a gut-wrenching crying jag that would not let up. It was like a plug had been pulled and everything was pouring out, a painful retching of tears and emotion I could not stop or control.

When it was over I couldn't move. The floor between my feet was soaking wet. In the stillness I knew without a shadow of a doubt I would never be enlightened. My search was over. It had ended without reaching the goal. A great lightness came over me, a joy I had never known. My burden had been lifted. With all my heart I thanked God for all the gifts I'd been given and apologized for always wanting more. It was done. I was now as I'd always be and that was that.

In those days I was in the habit of carrying a small notebook in my shirt pocket. That night in bed I wrote:

*Stop looking and See. Stop searching and Be. There is only this view, here, now — nothing else. What is there to look for or find? What else is needed? What is it you think you want? There will never be a time there is more than this. Recognizing This as All ends the search.*

I turned out the light. The next morning was glorious. Salisbury Cathedral shone gold in the sun as I waited for my taxi. The driver was so friendly he continued our conversation long after I'd paid the fare. On the train I had no sense of time, of duration. Every so often I'd wonder if I'd missed my station — even though I knew I'd not slept or even closed my eyes. Everything was poignant, moving. I made one note:

*Young girl with pink hood sleeps with her head against the window, a strand of hair across her face. Pushing a cart up the aisle the refreshment lady says to passengers, "Excuse me, my love. Thank you, my love." My love... My love... An unshakable quiet overtakes me.*

I arrived early at the airport and enjoyed watching people, catching bits of overheard conversation. There was no sense of waiting. I was conscious of seeing with the "single eye" that Harding—and Jesus—spoke about, but nothing about that seemed remarkable. Everything was just *as it is*.

United flight 99 from London to Philadelphia was over half empty and no one sat near me or even in my view. I looked forward to the solitude. I took out Harding's *The Science of the 1st Person* and opened it. Reading failed to happen. The marks on the page produced no meaning. Out the window, magnificent cloud formations appeared. I searched for my questions and doubts. I couldn't find them. I was convinced I could live from here without further certainty. I made this note:

*The next step, if there is one, is learning to trust it, this seeing of the single eye. The eye of the one living thing. The eye of the One. Live it.*

At some point after that note, something happened. The first of what was to be a series of occurrences took place. I can't say what it was. I didn't seem to be present for it, yet there was no interruption of bodily awareness as far as I know—no break in the visual stream reporting my surroundings, for instance. I just disappeared without going anywhere. Coming out of it I discovered I was weeping. A great quiet followed.

This pattern repeated maybe six or eight times for the duration of the flight. Something would happen that did not register on the mind, then the body would weep, then thoughts and words would come—some of which I wrote down—then utter quiet.

It was not fragile. During the quiet periods I would get up to go to the bathroom, look around the plane at people. The stewardess would bring coffee. I'd take pictures of clouds and the birth of icebergs from Greenland glaciers. After each  episode I'd think it was over, then without warning I'd disappear again, then weep, and the pattern would repeat. Between episodes I took notes:

*What's different now? I trust It. I trust it absolutely. This in no way bestows a mantle of enlightenment – in NO WAY. I am in no way different. Only now I know where I am. I am the stillpoint of Now at the center of the universe, the portal through which Nothing becomes Everything. This is happening here, now, where I am – at the moment, in the seat of an airplane.*

*I am filled by the world. Literally.*

*I have been dealt with gently. No agony of death, no pain of realization. I've been overwhelmed with gifts and blessings until I crumble to dust under the weight of them. How can I deserve this? How can anyone? There is no way. NO WAY to learn enough, to become a good enough person, an earnest enough seeker to deserve this. It is a gift you cannot earn or ever deserve – and yet it is given.*

*I can't stop crying. Wave upon wave. What about Bart? Is he gone? Such quiet. Even these few thoughts are thin and distant, like faint echoes of thought. Attention is not drawn to them. To be empty is complete fulfillment.*

*The emptiness is here, right where I am. It is not an experience of emptiness being had by a non-empty being. There is only emptiness. Why is this not terrifying? Because inexplicably and impossibly it is emptiness that weaves the world.*

*It is. That is all that can be said. I can't find an "I" to say, "I am that I am." It is. I am not.*

*All the thinking about and talking about and writing about I have done has no place here. There is nothing to be said about it. There is no way to know anything about it. No explanation for it. No reason for it to be. It Is. That's all that can be said.*

*It is not vast. Everything is contained Here. But Here bends in an instant from my hand to the horizon with a flick of the Eye.*

*It is closer than close. It is inside itself.*

*I imagined the Void, the Absolute, to be a distance from me, as if it could be traveled to like a foreign country or distant star. It is nearer than near. It is in the center of my chest and it encompasses the known and unknown universe. There is nothing it does not contain. In the place you feel a heart, it is there. This is not a metaphor or an attempt at poetry. It is there, that close, all of it. There beats the pulse of Creation.*

*Your Eye is the only eye. This is true for everyone. How is this possible? It's not. And yet, there it is.*

*The Void is crystal clear. There is no distance between the seer and what is seen. No distance. None.*

*Nothing and Everything coexist in the same space in the same moment —*
*Now. How can this be explained? No way. Why try? Even if it could, what's the point? The information is not good for anything. I don't even want to know how.*

*Nothing is the very stuff of Being. The very substance of Creation, of Everything. Nothing is what Everything is made of. This is not a metaphor. It can be witnessed.*

*Each time I think the crying is over, the whatever-this-is is over, a new wave hits. Between episodes it is very quiet inside. A stewardess comes by with coffee. I take pictures of clouds and the birth of icebergs.*

*Any understanding I thought I had is gone. Not wrong, really, and maybe even somewhat correct as far as the mind is capable. But now, This. It's not the same thing at all. No understanding is possible.*

When we landed I stood and waited in the aisle to file out. The story of Buddha getting up from the Bodhi tree came to mind. It is said that after his enlightenment he got up from where he sat, walked a few feet away and looked back at where he'd been sitting. He sat back in the same spot, then got up and looked back again. He said, "This cannot be taught." I stared at the seat I had been occupying and agreed. How can you teach what cannot be grasped?

I felt shaky and disoriented, and was vaguely concerned about remembering what I was supposed to do when I got off the plane. I reminded myself about my connecting flight, and going through immigration and customs. I tried to "sober up" for what came next. I had doubts about my ability to do what people do, but was also in a state of faith and bliss. I trusted I would be well taken care of.

What followed was the worst airport experience of my life. The Philadelphia terminal was being remodeled and was a maze of visual confusion and chaos. Everyone but me seemed to know where to go, and was in a hurry to get there. I followed the crowd to the immigration and customs area, which was jam packed. By the time I finally got through, it was time for my next flight to board, but I had no idea how to get to the gate.

I also had to get through TSA re-check first, and got hassled about my computer and camera not being out of my bag. I said something angry to the guy and got hassled even more, increasing my delay. I ended up running to my gate and got there just as they were about to close the door. By the time I settled into my seat, I was "back."

In retrospect I imagine the Divine thinking, "We can't let him go out into the world like this. He's helpless. Let's give him a good shot of adrenaline and anger to vaccinate him." Later I remembered Rose's story about the aftermath of his experience. He was so distraught at coming back into the world he wanted to jump off a bridge and get back to where he'd been. But he stopped at a Catholic church first and knocked on the door, thinking a priest might be able to understand what had happened to him and help.

A fat friar answered and listened as Rose poured out his guts. Then he then narrowed his eyes at Rose and said, "How long since you've been to confession?"

Rose said, "I got so angry I wanted to kill him. But the anger pulled me out of it, and I was able to get on with life."

When I got home I immediately went upstairs to my attic study and stayed there several days, staring out the window. All I wanted to do was sit still and "Be." I had an almost uncontrollable urge to head for the hills and leave everything behind—job, house, family…

For about a month after my experience on the plane it was very much front and center. I was in a state of absolute inner freedom and bliss, and not any good for much of anything—the honeymoon period, I call it.

Then gradually the world crept back in and was slowly assimilated into my new way of being. For almost a year after that I lived in a magical state where everything went my way and bluebirds strew rose petals on the path before me. Being "enlightened" was a blast. Then, foolishly perhaps, but who can know, I had the thought: "I wonder how enlightenment holds up when things aren't going so great."

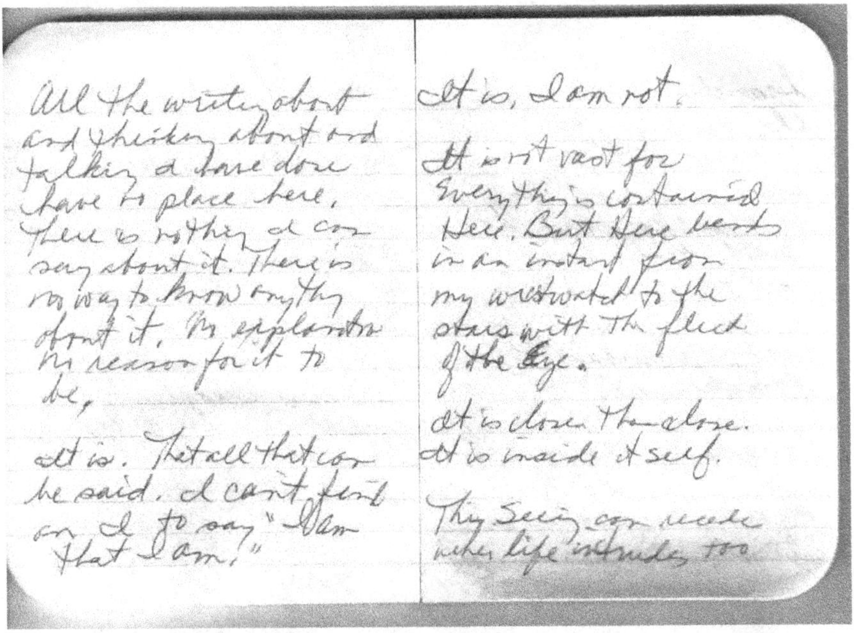

All the writing about
and thinking about and
talking I have done
have no place here.
There is nothing I can
say about it. There is
no way to know anything
about it. No explanation
no reason for it to
be,

It is. That all that can
be said. I can't find
an I to say "I am
That I am!"

It is, I am not.

It is not vast for
Everything is contained
Here. But Here extends
in an instant from
my wristwatch to the
stars with the flick
of the Eye.

It is closer than close.
It is inside itself.

This Seeing can reveal
other life in modes too

Douglas Harding, 1909-2007

# Orphaned at 60

Flight 99 was August 2004. In July 2005 Richard Rose died. Two months later, in September 2005, my father suddenly died. Six months later, in March 2006, my mother died. In a span of eight months, the three most important people in my life from the previous generation were gone.

I was presenting at a TAT meeting in West Virginia when my wife called to tell me my mother had been taken to the hospital with uncontrollable cancer pain. For the past year she had been mostly chair-bound, and told us all it was a back injury sustained while gardening. But no. Cancer. She was like that. So was my father. He once snuck off for a heart operation without telling us. Didn't want to worry the kids.

When I got to the hospital my mother's pain was still not under control. She was a stoic and a health fanatic who ordinarily refused to even take aspirin, but this was in another league entirely, and even the heavy drugs she was getting weren't touching it. The doctors decided the only option was an operation to remove at least part of the tumor pressing on her spine. While this was being determined, my brother and I alternated staying at the hospital with her at night, and driving my father the hour and a half back home to his bed.

One morning while I was at the hospital and my brother was home with Dad, he called to tell me he'd found Dad unresponsive on the floor of his room that morning, and that he was now on life support at the small local hospital. He had possibly had a brain aneurism, but who knows. He said the doctors were about to pull the plug on him because he had a do-not-resuscitate directive on file. I asked to talk to the doctor, and pretty much begged him to wait until I got there. He reluctantly agreed, saying he could lose his license. I drove as fast as I could.

When I arrived, Dad was hooked up to elaborate equipment that was basically the only source of life, if you can call it that. He was probably already gone, but the machines kept his chest moving, and gave the illusion of life. I asked for privacy. I told him he was a great father. I apologized for causing him trouble when I was young. I told him everything was okay and he would be free now. I recited the 23rd Psalm, as I had to Rose. Then the doctor came in, said time was up and hit the kill switch.

The problem now was how to tell Mom. Her surgery was scheduled for the next day, and if she was told Dad was dead we knew she would refuse it. So we didn't tell her.

They were inseparable. We always said we could not imagine one living without the other, and they said it, too. The day before, Dad had been sitting next to her hospital bed, with my brother Steve, my sister Marilyn and me sitting across the room. My mother said to him, "Remember how we planned to jump off the pier together when it came to this for one of us?"

Dad looked at his hands for what seemed a long time. Finally he said, "I'm not ready to go."

The next morning he was dead. Maybe just a coincidence, or maybe he changed his mind about trying to go on without her. He had already buried a son, and the thought of burying his wife may have been just too much.

Mom had the surgery and it did indeed relieve much of her pain. We let a day or two more pass without telling her, but she began to ask why Dad wasn't coming to see her. It fell to me to break the news. Afterwards, and for the next three days she lay immobile and unresponsive with her eyes closed, desperately trying to will herself into death. Sometime later she was admitted to hospice and sent home to die.

When I was making arrangements for Dad with the local funeral home, I had no real guidance from him about his wishes. I knew he did not want to be cremated, but the only thing he'd ever said about burial, partly in jest, was that he didn't want to be buried in the family plot, which had graves going back to the 1600's: "I'd like to be someplace where the grass gets mowed more often."

As a former Army major and WWII veteran he was entitled to a military funeral, and the funeral director suggested some state and local military cemeteries. I said, "What about Arlington?" He said it was very difficult to get into Arlington these days, especially a ground burial. I asked him to check anyway. He made a call while we were talking, and amazingly they called back right away.

When he hung up he said, "Who was your father?"

"As far as I know he was just a guy."

"Well, he's in. Ground burial. Full honors."

They can only do two full honors ground burials a day, due to the length and labor-intensive nature of the ceremony, so Dad was put in cold storage for a few months waiting his turn. When his time came, the funeral was beyond impressive. Horse drawn caisson,

94

marching band, speeches and sermons, 21-gun salute, the whole enchilada. I teared up a few times, and out and out wept when my sister was presented with the flag. The whole thing was immensely moving and reverent, and I was extremely grateful my father could have such an extravagant send-off.

But when imagining anything similar for myself, I had a visceral negative reaction. I realized during the proceedings that I was much more in tune with the sentiment expressed by Alexander Pope in the last stanza of his *Ode on Solitude*:

*Thus let me live, unseen, unknown;*
*Thus unlamented let me die;*
*Steal from the world, and not a stone*
*Tell where I lie.*

Mom refused to go to his funeral, even though we could have put her in a wheelchair and got her there. But she did ask me to tape it in case she wanted to see it later. So I did. And it turned out to be quite a moving documentary. Eventually she watched it. Three times.

I stayed with her while she was home in hospice the last six months of her life, and was attentive to all her basic needs. But I was not as attentive to her emotional needs as I could have been. She wanted me to be at her bedside, playing cards or watching TV with her—to spend as much time with me as she could before she died—and I did sometimes, but I really didn't want to. I'd often go to another part of the house to write or just be alone, plus I was still employed, working remotely.

She was basically bedridden, but one evening she got up and used a walker to shuffle to where I was to be with me. I felt bad and made a point to be at her bedside more often after that, but never really fulfilled her need, nor did I ever thank her for all she had done for me, or tell her from the bottom of my heart I loved her.

Near the end, when I was wiping shit from her ass and droppering heroin onto her tongue, she thanked me for all I'd done, and said I was "steadfast." I immediately felt ashamed for not being worthy of a more loving, emotional description of my way with her. But we'd never had a particularly close personal relationship, and those six months were a logical extension of that. Then too, I'd been a hospice volunteer for five years in the '90s and could be forgiven for taking a somewhat "professional," approach to her care. But regardless, to this day, not being more emotionally available to her during that time is one of the few regrets I have in life.

She died with her immediate family gathered around. I recited the 23rd Psalm and wiped away the black bile that oozed from her mouth. Hospice was notified, and within a few hours her body was removed, the hospital bed was taken away, and a nurse came to flush all her meds down the toilet, with me as the required witness. She was buried on top of Dad in his Arlington plot.

There's a subtle change in one's psychology when both parents are gone. While they live, there is always a small voice in the back of your mind wondering how they might judge this or that action you take in life. Their deaths bring a certain freedom you didn't realize you were missing, but also new responsibility.

You are now the reigning patriarch or matriarch of your family, and no longer have an older generation as counsel, nor do you have a built-in safety net. If your world collapses, there's no place you can go where they have to take you in.

And, of course, all the potential opportunities to tell your mother and father the tender things you never got around to saying, have vanished.

As Dad was getting older I had been visiting more often to help with upkeep of this place, but now I was the sole caretaker. I gratefully accepted the responsibility and drove the four hours from Raleigh every couple weeks to mow grass and take care of things. It was also a great opportunity to spend time alone, much of it on the screen porch, which offers one of the most picturesque views on earth, at least to me.

One night as I sat there watching a thunderstorm I got hit by lightning. I was sitting on an old metal glider, which has cushions, but my arm was probably resting on the bare metal armrest. It was a particularly dramatic storm, and as I watched, lightning actually hit the creek a couple times.

Then suddenly the world lit up like the sun had landed. The source was a blinding white phone-pole size bolt that appeared not 30 feet from me in the yard.

Simultaneously I was hit, and through no volition of my own suddenly found myself standing 15 feet away, vibrating violently, saying something like, GODSHITJESUSFUCKDAMN!

For a few moments I just stood there, not knowing if I was alive or dead. I ran my hands over my body and everything seemed okay. I checked myself in the bathroom mirror and saw no damage. As I stood there at the mirror, happily breathing, I was suddenly flooded with a feeling of high energy and euphoria that ended up lasting several days. I don't know if it was the thrill of survival or the result of having that much electricity light me up.

I checked around the house. The lightning had gotten into the wiring and blown up some small appliances and the telephone, but nothing major. I went back out on the porch and watched the rest of the storm, which by now had moved some distance away.

Over the next week or so I mentioned the incident to my kids during separate phone calls. They all asked the same question. "Do you have super powers now?"

It's said that once you've been hit by lighting you're statistically more likely to get hit again. Supposedly there's a park ranger who's been hit seven times. I keep this in mind now. I still like sitting on the porch watching storms, but I don't sit on metal furniture, and when lightning gets too close, I beat a hasty retreat.

*The Lanyard*, by Billy Collins

The other day as I was ricocheting slowly
off the blue walls of this room, bouncing from typewriter to piano,
from bookshelf to an envelope lying on the floor,
I found myself in the "L" section of the dictionary
where my eyes fell upon the word, Lanyard.
No cookie nibbled by a French novelist
could send one more suddenly into the past.
A past where I sat at a workbench
at a camp by a deep Adirondack lake
learning how to braid thin plastic strips into a lanyard.
A gift for my mother.
I had never seen anyone use a lanyard.
Or wear one, if that's what you did with them.
But that did not keep me from crossing strand over strand
again and again until I had made a boxy, red and white lanyard for my mother.
She gave me life and milk from her breasts, and I gave her a lanyard.
She nursed me in many a sick room, lifted teaspoons of medicine to my lips,
set cold facecloths on my forehead, then led me out into the airy light
and taught me to walk and swim,
and I in turn presented her with a lanyard.
"Here are thousands of meals' she said, "and here is clothing and a good education."
"And here is your lanyard," I replied, "which I made with a little help from a counselor."
"Here is a breathing body and a beating heart,
strong legs, bones and teeth and two clear eyes to read the world," she whispered.
"And here," I said, "is the lanyard I made at camp."
And here, I wish to say to her now, is a smaller gift.
Not the archaic truth that you can never repay your mother,
but the rueful admission that when she took the two-toned lanyard from my hands,
I was as sure as a boy could be
that this useless worthless thing I wove out of boredom
would be enough to make us even.

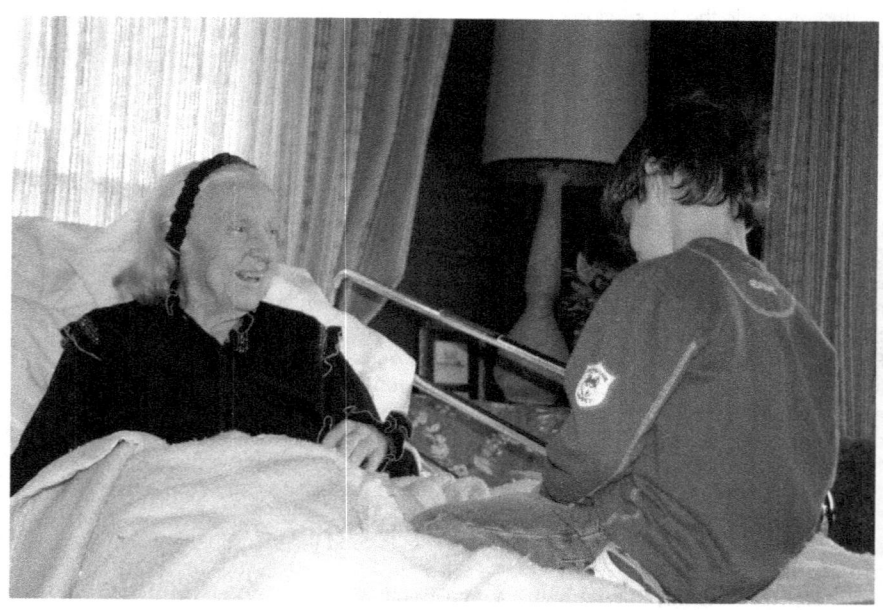

Mom rides as great-grandson Jadon controls bed remote

# Childhood

I grew up knowing I was loved. I've only recently realized, believe it or not, what a great gift that was — not just the gift of the experience itself, but as possibly having given me a leg up on the spiritual path. If one has not known that as a child, it may be more difficult to receive the experience later on of *being* Love, of being *God*.

One framework in which I sometimes describe the occurrence on Flight 99 is to say that I repeatedly experienced the trinity spoken of in Christian literature: the Father, the Son, and the Holy Spirit.

The Father, which cannot be experienced directly, was what I disappeared into. The Son was that which emerged, the one who had the "experience" of Truth and took notes about it in his seat.

The Holy Spirit, the Great Intercessor, the Christ, was that which imbued the Son with the capacity to enter the non-experience of the Father and emerge with enough residue of the encounter to know beyond a shadow of a doubt that "I and the Father are One."

While all this transpired, the mindbody of "Bart" was absorbed in an almost unbearable experience of pure *Love*, that quite literally crushed him to dust. I have friends who have had a conclusive spiritual experience that did not include this component of Love. I've wondered if perhaps it was offered, but they were somehow not able to receive it. I don't know, just a thought. "God is Love" is way more than a cliché, though. This I know.

I was conceived in Alabama before my father shipped out to the Philippines to be staged for the invasion of Japan. On the train back to Maryland, bawling her eyes out about her husband, my mother saw the newspaper headlines about Hiroshima. Nagasaki and surrender followed.

A million purple hearts were minted in anticipation of the invasion of Japan. Attacking a samurai, kamikaze nation defending it's homeland promised to be a fierce undertaking. But they were never needed. The one I got likely came from that batch.

Mom moved in with her parents, and we lived there for a year after I was born. Dad had to stay in the Philippines for awhile. When he came home he was able to get a row house in Greenbelt, Maryland, a low-cost, intentional-design, kid-friendly community built for returning vets. I lived there until 6th grade.

It was a place and a time when kids were king. The baby boom was in full swing, mothers followed the kindly advice of Dr.

Benjamin Spock on child rearing, and boys were allowed to pretty much roam free. "Be home for dinner," was about the only thing you heard as you went out the door.

I played Little League, walked to school weekdays and to the movies Saturdays, explored the seemingly endless woods behind our house, and won the Cub Scout soapbox derby two years in a row —

with different wheels each year. It was, in many ways, an idyllic childhood.

Mom's parents lived nearby in College Park, and often had me over to spend the night. Grandma Phillips doted on me, letting me stay up as long as I wanted, even sprinkling instant coffee on my ice cream to help me stay awake. My grandfather was head of the Zoology department at the University of Maryland, and had one of the big garden plots they provided for faculty. He would pay me sixty cents an hour, "A penny every minute!" he emphasized, to help him weed and pick, but he didn't care if I worked or not. It was just a bribe to spend time with him. He was a wonderful loving man and I would have gladly spent all the time he wanted with him for free, but I took the money. He died when I was 11 during a routine ulcer operation. Hospital error.

My other grandfather, Grand Bart, an equally kind and loving man, died around the same time from liver cancer. He was in his early sixties. As a kid I remember him coming into the house where I now live in tears because he had accidentally killed a nest of baby rabbits with the tractor sickle bar.

Mom and Dad had known each other since elementary school. Their families lived close to each other, and were connected in other ways. Mom had one brother, Fred. Dad had a brother, Choc, and two sisters, Babs and Berry. Choc and Fred were best friends growing up, and a few blocks away was the mansion where Fred's future wife, Alice Humphries, the daughter of a wealthy D.C. real estate mogul, grew up.

Our frequent family gatherings usually included both sides of the family, as well as family friends, and everyone seemed to truly

100

enjoy each other's company. Everything was an occasion for a party. My grandmother, who lived to be 96, was president of the Faculty Wives Club and arranged frequent social gatherings in that role, and I suspect she had a lot to do with the frequency of our family gatherings in those days as well. In this Christmas-season picture the men pose for posterity. Dad is the one in front:

Aunt Alice was glamorous and sexy, with a husky laugh and alluring walk, and as I approached puberty, I found my thoughts about her went beyond what might be considered proper. "Well, she's not my *blood* relative," I told myself.

Later on, when I was maybe 13 or 14, on a night my parents were having a party, I lay in bed listening to everyone's laughter, vaguely annoyed at not being able to sleep. We had moved to Silver Spring by then, and I had a large Washington Post paper route for which I needed get up at 4 a.m. to be able to deliver the papers on time and get ready for school. I always had a hard time getting up anyway, and took to putting my jarring electric alarm clock in an empty metal wastebasket across the room to force myself to get out of bed. When it went off I felt like I was being electrocuted over a loudspeaker.

As I tossed and turned that night there was a knock on my door, and before I could say anything it opened. Alice came in, tipsy.

"I'm out of cigarettes," she said. "Can I have one of yours?"

I wasn't about to be trapped into any confessions, and even suspected my parents had sent her in to suss me out. "I don't smoke," I said.

She sat down next to me on my bed. "Don't give me that. I know you do. I won't tell. Nobody even knows I'm in here." I held my ground and continued to deny it.

"Okay, be that way," she said. Then she kissed her fingertips and pressed them to my lips. "I love you anyway."

After she left, her perfume and the faint smell of alcohol lingered. I laid my hand on the bed sheet where her butt had been and left it there until I fell asleep.

Growing up in an environment where everyone loved each other and was always having a good time no doubt deeply affected my psyche. Life was safe, and adulthood would be fun when I got there. Most everyone in the family lived in the tidewater region of the Chesapeake Bay watershed, which billed itself as "The Land of Pleasant Living," and indeed it was.

As the saying goes, though, into every life some rain must fall. Later in life Alice left Fred for an old boyfriend, Don, she had reconnected with. They had been together while he was an undergrad at the Naval Academy. One time, as a joke, she had made a triple-batch of chocolate chip cookies using Ex-Lax as the chocolate, and passed them around Don's barracks. Everyone in the barracks was up all night, including Don, and some of them had to go to the infirmary. The next day Don and Alice were called into the commandant's office. Alice batted her eyes and nothing ever came of it. If you were Alice Humphries you could get away with shit like that.

After his divorce Fred moved to California and married a wonderful woman named Anna, then a few years later moved back to Annapolis to live in the house Fred and Alice had shared. Fred and Anna started socializing with Alice and Don, and the four of them often went out together. Anna was not thrilled about this, but

102

accepted it. One time at a family gathering, she leaned over to me and said, "Fred's still in love with Alice, but that's okay."

Don was a tall, ebullient extrovert, with a wide smile and a hail-fellow-well-met persona that left you thinking he must be the happiest man on earth. One day Alice came home from the store and found him on the basement floor bleeding out. He had cut his own throat. She called 911 and he survived. At subsequent family gatherings he always wore an ascot, but still exuded the same ebullient persona. Alice never again left him alone.

Fred and Alice had two daughters, Diana and Cindy. Cindy died of cancer in her early thirties. Diana lost Dawn, her only child at

the time, to a car wreck when she was 18. Dawn's boyfriend was also killed in the wreck. A double funeral was held for them.

My parents had four children, three boys and a girl. I was the oldest. Their middle son, Richard, was killed in a tractor accident on his land in the mountains at the age of 41. My parents were never again quite the same. Rich and I were six years apart, but as adults we became close friends, and would sit for hours on the screen porch where I now live, laughing our asses off at things no one else saw the humor in. I still miss him.

Uncle Fred and I had a special relationship. He was my godfather, and being extremely devoted to his sister, and having no boy of his own, he treated me like his son. When I was a kid visiting

Fred and Alice—ostensibly to spend time with my cousins—I most often found myself hanging out with Fred, sailing, chopping firewood, building shit, putzing around his garage.

Fred's last years were spent in a home for dementia patients. I did not go see him then. Diana said he would not be able to

recognize me, and I did not want to remember him like that. The Fred I knew was funny, and generous, and full of exuberant life. And now that everyone is dead, I can write it out loud: I loved him more than my father. Well, not more, maybe, I don't know, but with more heart. I loved Dad because he was my father. I loved Fred because he was Fred.

Summers we would go to Learla and Grand Bart's place, where I now live, on the Chesapeake Bay. They had 13 grandchildren, and often many of us were there together, with or without parents, sleeping in every nook and cranny of what was then a very small house.

I was the oldest, with Brooke close behind, only three weeks younger. Our lives have been subtlety connected ever since our joint baptism as babies, and during our summers together on the Bay, we took full advantage of the freedoms we were allowed, pushing the limits whenever possible. Brooke's brother Keith and my brother Rich were about the same age, and they hung out together. Sometimes we'd let them join us in whatever we were up to.

One summer Dad and Elliot, Brooke's father, decided to build us a diving board in the cove. Dad's uncle Cecil had built one when he was a kid, and now he thought we should have one, too. So one day they took Brooke, Rich, Keith and me in the skiff out into the Bay to search the shorelines for pilings that had washed up from big piers destroyed by storms.

We found four good ones, and lashed them together to tow home. Brooke and I straddled two pilings each and rode them like bucking broncos in the boat's wake and the chop that had picked up while we were out. "Be careful of those family jewels," Elliot called out to us. Rich and Keith lobbied mightily to ride the pilings with us, but were adjudged too young by the powers that be.

The diving board Dad and Elliot built was a work of rustic art, a double-decker masterpiece with high and low boards. The low board was short and stiff. The high board stuck out further to avoid the low board, and thus was springy, affording extra height and momentum. That structure became the centerpiece of our Bay experience for many summers.

Much later in life, Rich and I were sitting on the screen porch late one moonless night, drinking and smoking weed, when we heard a tremendous splash, like a rogue Orca had come into the Bay and breached in our cove. We grabbed a flashlight and went to check it out. On a dead-calm night with not a breath of wind, the diving board had surrendered to underwater rot and years of winter ice tugging at its pilings. It now lay mostly submerged, the high board pointing to the sky.

In 2019 Keith died in his sleep at age 68. He was to be cremated, and I suggested to Brooke that his ashes be scattered here, where I now live, in a place Keith dearly loved. Brooke seized on the idea and arranged a beautiful cousin reunion as a celebration of Keith's life. All of Learla and Grand Bart's surviving grandchildren came, some with their grown children, back to the place that held some of their most cherished childhood memories.

Keith was a physically powerful man who didn't know his own strength. He never married, nor did he range very far in life, choosing to live near his parents and work where his father worked. When Keith's ashes were scattered off the end of the pier, along with rose petals to track their path, they immediately drifted towards the property shoreline, towards the familiar.

But then they did a sudden about-face and headed out the mouth of the cove into the creek, and from there turned towards the wide waters of the Bay. From there perhaps they turned south and joined the Atlantic Ocean, and from there, perhaps, Everywhere.

Keith and Rich

# The Road Not Taken

Just before I was scheduled to report for Army basic training a woman I'd been recently seeing told me she was pregnant with my child. She did not try to put pressure on me, but it was obvious her preference was that we get married.

I had a clear vision and goal of becoming a Special Forces soldier, and marriage, though not a total show-stopper for that dream, was not remotely in my plans. The child's mother was a wonderful woman, but our relationship had been relatively casual, and I was not in love. Still, feelings of guilt and responsibility flooded in, and I became conflicted and confused. So much so, that I uncharacteristically asked my father for advice.

To his credit he did not try to steer me one way or the other, though I could detect he did not think I was ready for marriage, in the same way he didn't think I was ready for college. I was in the Army, which he saw as a key to me maturing into manhood, and he was glad of that, but one can be both married and in the Army, he pointed out, so it was not an either-or.

It was not a long conversation. Dad remained pragmatic and on-point, and did not diverge into a lecture about this being yet another example of my faults and failings. His final words on the subject were: "It's your life and I can't tell you what to do. But never let guilt rule your decisions in affairs of the heart." That advice has stayed with me.

I did not get married, and my child was put up for adoption. Her mother named her Kristine at birth, though that was later changed by her adoptive parents. For my whole life I have wondered about Kristine, how she was doing. Is she happy? Is she alive...?

Then in 2014 she wrote me an incredibly beautiful letter asking if I was her birth father. It is one of my most treasured possessions. The laws had changed in her state about adopted people being able to research their birth records. She found her mother, and through her mother found me. What followed was a love-fest of getting-to-know-you emails, which I also dearly treasure.

Even my other kids got in on it. They were excited to find they had another sibling out there, and started exchanging emails with Kristine. She and Karen particularly hit it off, and Kristine wrote to me in an email, "I love Karen!"

At some point, though, things got off track. Kristine had never wanted to meet in person, though I'd have flown to Timbuktu to meet for coffee if she'd said the word. We've never even spoken on the phone, though I very much wanted to. I always wanted more, and for awhile it seemed she did, too, but there was also hesitancy on her part.

Our emails started to take a turn in 2018, when I sensed a coolness, a distancing. When I asked her about it, it began to come out that she was angry at me for abandoning her, for not marrying her mother and raising her.

She had a wonderful childhood with terrific adoptive parents, and her current life is filled with success and blessings, but even with our newfound relationship, she has not been able to forgive me. "My adult self wants to see you and hug you," she said, "but my child self is hurt and angry." I understand this, and have even come around to thinking I don't deserve to have her in my life, no matter how much I might want it.

I tried for awhile to rekindle something, but my efforts seemed to further anger her. I couldn't say anything right. And so I stopped trying, at least then. I will continue to send her short, friendly emails now and again, hoping perhaps to get more than a short, cursory reply. But even if it's over for good, if she never wants to write to me again, what she has given me by letting me into her life for a brief time is one of the greatest gifts I've ever received.

If she ever wants to grab a coffee, though, or better yet, invite me to meet her beautiful family, I'm there. I love you, baby.

# Ladder Work

Rose used to talk a lot about the "Law of the Ladder." He said there was a ladder in every undertaking in life, and the ladder was pyramid in shape, with the widest rung at the bottom and the narrowest at the top. The financial ladder, for instance, has the hungry and homeless of the world at the bottom and the billionaires on top.

The spiritual ladder is the same way, he said. On the bottom rung are the ignorant masses ruled exclusively by animal nature, and on the top rung are those who have discovered their true nature as God. As a seeker, one needs to honestly place himself on whatever rung of the ladder reflects his current state. On that rung with him are his fellows, his peers. On the rung above are those he can hear and learn from, and on the rung below are those he can help and teach.

Rose advised working on all three rungs at the same time. Commiserate and exchange information with your fellows, learn from those who can help you, and help those who can hear you. If you try to reach too far up the ladder from where you are, you won't be able to understand what's being said. If you try too reach to far down, you'll be crucified.

Working with the rung above you comes naturally. Everybody's looking for a hand up. When one first steps on the spiritual path this is where they go—looking for help and teachers. Working with your peers is also fairly natural. We all like to shoot the shit with friends who are interested in the same things we are. Working on the rung below is where it gets more difficult. Now you have to give instead of get.

It was with this in mind that Rose advised his students to start groups of their own, to reach out to peers and those on the rung below. Augie was a prime example of someone who followed this advice, and there were many others. Rose said, "Don't wait until you're enlightened to teach. There are a lot of people who can benefit from what you have to say right now, even if it's to recommend a book they haven't read. Don't wait for anything in life. You might die tomorrow."

I never started a group intentionally, but as I mentioned, I was one of a group of friends who sort of backed into starting one as a way to avoid buying a restaurant dinner every time we wanted to get together. I was still attending those meetings before I left for Harding's workshop, and when I returned I found myself back there.

By this time we'd moved to a small room in a Methodist church that one of the members had arranged for $25 a month. For about a year Bob Cergol and I switched off leading meetings, then he lost his job and had to move to take another one. Now it was "my" group.

I'd always thought that if one got enlightened they automatically were drawn to teaching, or "passing it on," as Rose always said. Certainly Rose had this imperative in spades. It was not that way for me. My first reaction was to head for the hills and never look back. All I wanted was to just "Be."

But part of the momentum of my life was going to these meetings, and basically all I did was not stop. Next thing I know I'm being looked upon as a teacher, and talked about by some in the same breath as Eckhart Tolle and Adyashanti. It was not a role I sought, or was particularly comfortable with, and I guess it showed. I became known (in a very small circle) as the "reluctant guru."

The group started growing, and one of the members, wanted to create a web site for it, which he did. I was doing web sites for IBM at the time, so I later took it over. I'd speculated on a bunch of domain names in the late '90s and one was selfinquiry.org, so I used that, and we became Self Inquiry Group (SIG).

The group kept growing and one of the new members was Luke Roberts, an energetic, ambitious guy who wanted me to do a weekend retreat so his friends from out of town could come. I told him I didn't want to fill all that time alone, but if he got some other presenters I'd do it.

He did, and the weekend was a big success. It became an annual event and eventually we had six or eight awakened teachers at a single retreat. I was pleased they were successful, but my heart was not fully in it. Nor was my heart in the weekly meetings anymore.

I'd been doing them for 10 years by then, and there were 25 or 30 regulars, but I felt like I was just plowing the same ground, and that most of the people coming were not serious. They wanted their lives fixed, not Truth. It felt like I was a form of entertainment for them that lasted as long as the meeting, but when they left they did little on their own.

I never looked forward to meetings, but they always went well, and I left feeling good about them. But then my doubts and laziness would seep back in, and by the time the next meeting rolled around, I wished I didn't have to go. I wanted to stop but felt I had a commitment to the group, and I didn't know how to extricate myself.

About this time I started letting my second wife, who had had her own awakening — the day before we met, actually — co-teach with me at meetings, partly, I think, to take some of the burden off me. It seemed to go okay at first, but before long it became apparent it just wasn't working out. After doing it alone for so long I found it difficult to teach with her, and she complained about me being "overbearing." Also, the group did not fully embrace her, and attendance at the meetings started to drop off. She said the group made her feel like Yoko Ono — who was blamed for breaking up the Beatles.

Sorting this out while staying happily married — which was becoming increasingly difficult anyway — would have involved a lot of work and potential grief. Backing away from meetings and retreats I didn't want to do anymore anyway seemed an attractive option. So we quit doing meetings, and no more annual retreats were held.

I fought feelings of guilt about this, but kept telling myself I had a right to my own life. I envisioned my wife and I getting closer now that we were no longer living "in public." I started thinking about travel and us moving to another town. My desire to erase personal history and shed identities kicked in again. I didn't know where to go from here.

About this time my friend Bruce Rubin called with a proposition. Bruce is an Oscar-winning screenwriter, and had tried to help me break into Hollywood with my own screenplays. The closest we came to success with this was when he got a name-brand producer to consider my Vietnam script for a war movie he was planning. He said some nice things about it, but ended up passing.

Bruce and I met through a series of events surrounding a spiritual documentary in which I was interviewed, *Closer Than Close* (poetryinmotionfilms.com). We became good friends, and functioned as each other's teacher. He considered me his spiritual mentor, and I looked upon him as my screenwriting guru.

In his youth Bruce had a terrifying, life-changing experience on LSD that sent him backpacking around the world looking for spiritual teachers, even ending up with the Dalai Lama in India for a time. The Dalai Lama invited him to stay and be his student, but

Bruce declined, saying, "Thank you, but I don't think you are my teacher."

Bruce went on to find other teachers, most importantly for him, Swami Rudrananda (Rudi), a teacher in the lineages of Nityananda and Muktananda. Bruce also become a popular meditation teacher himself, giving frequent talks in his homes in L.A. and upstate New York, depending on where he was at the time—all of which are available on his website (brucerubin-class.com).

When we started holding annual SIG retreats, I invited Bruce to be one of the speakers, which he was for I think four or five of them, joking that he was the "token un-enlightened speaker" on the agenda. At his third or fourth retreat, however, that changed, when as he listened to another speaker, Paul Hedderman, the penny dropped.

He found me afterwards and I sensed he was different. He was beaming, and we just looked into each other's eyes for a few moments. Then he said simply, "It happened."

Now, a year or two later, he was on the phone with an offer I could not refuse. Bruce had a reputation in Hollywood as a "spiritual" writer, based on his movies, *Ghost*, *Jacob's Ladder*, *My Life*, and others, and he told me he'd been contacted by Sony Pictures and asked to create a two-hour pilot for a spiritual TV series. He asked if I would co-write it with him. Further, he said he was winding down his career and did not have an interest in being the head writer and showrunner if the series took off, but that he had confidence I could do it, and that he would always be available in the background.

I could hardly believe my ears.

"Jesus, Bruce, I don't know what to say."

"Just say yes," he said. "You're the reason I came to the end of my spiritual search. This is my gift back to you, and it pales by comparison."

I was overwhelmed. My chest tightened and I could feel my eyes filling up. Bruce is one of the most loving, generous people I know and I had become accustomed to feeling that in his presence

112

and on phone calls. As a mutual friend once said, "Whenever anyone meets Bruce, they want more Bruce."

But this was over the top. I actually felt uncomfortable being on the receiving end of this level of generosity from anyone. Plus, when I was writing screenplays I always just imagined someone buying it and taking it from there, perhaps at most consulting me now and then as it was being made. To be a head writer and responsible for creating multiple episodes of a long running series was daunting to the point of being downright frightening. But there was only one answer possible.

"Of course, yes. Jesus, Bruce. Thank you…"

And so we hunkered down and wrote *Shift*, an international adventure story of political intrigue and surreal inner landscapes, intertwined with the tectonic spiritual shift we both felt happening on planet Earth. We were pleased with how it turned out, and sketched out ideas for the first season's episodes as part of the package.

Bruce pitched it to Sony in L.A., and while they considered it my mind spun out tantalizing visions of running a writer's room, along with the requisite doubts and fears about my ability to take on such a task. But Sony sat with it long enough for me to become somewhat comfortable with the idea, and even look forward to the challenge. They called Bruce back in once or twice to ask questions and explore ideas, which increased my optimism, and by now, my excitement.

In the end Sony passed. I was disappointed, of course, but in another way it didn't seem to matter. Bruce's gift to me was complete in the moment he offered it, and working with him on the script taught me more about screenwriting and the movie business than I had gleaned in all the years I'd dabbled with it. Being a Hollywood showrunner, as heady as that might have been, would have just been icing on the cake. Pretty goddamn good icing, though.

As it turns out, I would not have been able to perform my duties as a showrunner anyway. Some number of months later, I contracted an undiagnosed brain infection, went insane, and was committed to a state mental institution.

Raleigh, North Carolina, 2012

# Brain Fire Madness

Sometime after leaving the Wednesday meetings, my wife and I started holding weekend retreats together, which ended up being quite successful. Outside the established pattern and expectations of the SIG meetings, we were able to settle into a way of teaching together that worked out well, both for us and for the participants. This success did not carry over into our marriage, however.

It had all started out so beautifully, magically, really, it's difficult now to see how it could have gone so wrong. Before we met I was actively having the thought, "I wonder what true love feels like." Because I didn't think I'd ever experienced it, not the love of poetry, song and myth, anyway. With her, I found out.

From kindergarten on I've always thought girls were pretty swell, and my twenties coincided with the sexual revolution and an abundance of newly liberated women. I was a kid in a candy store. But as often is the case with young men, I think, my womanizing was also a defense against falling in love, and being "trapped" in a relationship with one woman.

I got married when I was 31, and I loved my first wife, but it was more a "familial" love than a head-over-heels love. I actually had the distinct feeling I was being asked by the Divine to take care of her, and that we were "supposed" to be together. When I think of our children, and their children, I have to agree, and I am deeply, deeply grateful to her for all that she gave to me, and to them.

The woman who would become my second wife appeared in a flood of auspicious omens and synchronicities, and sent my heart into the stratosphere—not to mention stirring in me a lust I'd not known since youth. We fell deeply, helplessly, recklessly in love, and I was certain we'd be together the rest of our lives. I felt like we were living a mythic love story, and wonder of wonders, I was the male lead. It was exquisitely breathtaking uncharted territory.

For awhile our life together was beyond amazing, but of course that sort of intensity never lasts, and gradually we had to start dealing with those aspects of each other our fevers had caused us to overlook. Add to that, external circumstances seemed to conspire against us, and eventually my wife became constantly angry at me for things I'd done or neglected to do, large and small, real and imagined. I'd take it for awhile, then when I'd had enough I'd haul out my papa bear voice and back her up. It got to where we were having serious arguments almost every day.

While all this was going on I began to feel something was not right with me mentally. She had noticed it a couple months before I did, but I denied anything was wrong until I became virtually incapacitated by it. I had retired from IBM but was still doing contract work for them, and one day I realized I could not make any sense of what I was looking at on the computer.

It was work I could normally do with ease, but now I could not perform the simplest tasks. I would try, then become agitated and pace the house, then come back to the screen and try again to no avail. I could not even compose an email to tell them I would have to stop taking assignments, so my wife sent one for me.

She took me to the doctor, who prescribed drugs that didn't help. I became extremely paranoid and started hearing and seeing things that weren't there. I imagined cops were after me, watching my every move, waiting to pounce. It actually felt more like they were malevolent entities materializing as cops, but I never actually saw any entities or cops, real or imagined.

I didn't trust my wife and resisted everything she did to try to help me. I imagined she was in on it with the cops and was letting them hide in the house. I wouldn't take showers because I thought that's when they'd come out and I didn't want to fight naked. I'd stand stock still in the living room, frozen like a statue, feeling their eyes on me through every window, waiting to shoot me if I moved.

As all this transpired, I was in a heightened state of energy and awareness. At one point I didn't sleep for six or seven days straight. If my wife somehow convinced me to come to bed with her I would lay on top of the covers, fully dressed with my boots and parka on, and watch imagined laser sighting beams playing across my body all night, waiting for them to open fire on me if I moved.

On the coldest night of the year, eight degrees and a foot of snow, I went outside in shirtsleeves at 3 a.m. and pounded on the windows of cars parked on the street, convinced there were entity-cops hiding inside. I wanted to get the confrontation over with. When they wouldn't come out I raised my arms over my head and lay face down in the snow in surrender. When they didn't come for me, I got up and walked the perimeter of the yard round and round, wondering what it felt like to freeze to death. I decided to find out.

All the while my wife kept coming to the door every few minutes, trying to coax me in. Finally, my legs stopped working and

I collapsed. Somehow she got me moving and helped me crawl inside. My limbs were frozen stiff and my voice did not work. As I lay on the floor thawing, I was flooded with a feeling of absolute elation. Taunting death was exhilarating.

Understandably, she'd had enough. She took me to UNC hospital and I was admitted to their psych ward. My first night there was spent in a rubber cell with a rubber bed without sheets or pillow. The next day I was moved to their regular ward, where I stayed some number of weeks with the other crazies.

My only task there, other than swallowing God know how many drugs, was to fill out a menu sheet with what I wanted to eat the next day. There were very few choices, but every day I struggled mightily with that sheet, unable to decide the simplest things. Eggs or pancakes? Ham or meatloaf?

I'd repeatedly get up and pace the room then come back to it. Orderlies would ask if they could help but I'd refuse. I was determined to do this. Hours passed. Finally they would come to take it from me and in desperation I'd check, "Chef's Choice."

I did not get any better but they sent me home anyway. It was a small ward and they needed the room, plus, I think, they had no idea how to help me.

I didn't last very long in the free world again. My next stop was Rex Hospital, a regular general hospital, where for weeks it seemed they ran every medical test known to man on me. I refused to eat. I had imaginary pains and illnesses. I lay in bed all day and was unresponsive. I prayed for death, and told my wife, "I'm ready to take my hands out of the gloves." I was put on 24-hour suicide watch and never left alone.

I was convinced my wife would not take me home with her when I was discharged, so I kept asking her to bring me my hiking boots and parka, because you need good shoes and a warm coat when you're homeless on the street. A couple times she brought them in to placate me, but wouldn't leave them there. A good deal of whatever thinking I was capable of in those days revolved around making plans for how I would live on the street.

Then one day she asked me, "Will you sign over medical power of attorney to me?" I said no. I still did not trust her and even suspected she might somehow be responsible for my illness. Also, I was so out of it I didn't really understand what was being asked, plus I was like a two-year-old in those times, saying no to everything—food, needles, tests, visitors…

"If you don't," she said, "you'll become a ward of the state and I can't help you."

"No."

The next day I was handcuffed and put in the back of a professional transporter's black Camaro, plexiglas shield between us, and driven two hours to the state mental institution at Thomasville, North Carolina. There I was put in a small room with a cot and a toilet. The door closed.

Rex Hospital garden, 2015

# Bartonella

The whole time I was in Rex Hospital getting tests, my wife kept asking them to test me for Lyme disease and other tick-borne illnesses like Bartonella and Babesiosis, but they would not do it, or perhaps did not even know how. She'd had Lyme disease herself, and while her symptoms were mild and nothing like mine, the literature showed that tick-borne illnesses can attack anywhere, including the brain.

"Well if you won't test him, just start him on antibiotics and see if it helps."

"We can't prescribe drugs until we know what he has," they said. Catch-22.

One day a young doctor from another country was in charge and she asked him if she could wheel me down to the out-patient facility and have my blood drawn. He said okay, but get back as soon as you can.

So she had my blood drawn and had them send it to a lab that specializes in tests for tick-borne illnesses. She got the results back while I was in Thomasville. They reportedly showed that my levels of whatever markers they look for with Bartonella were off the charts, but I never actually saw the report itself.

Meanwhile at Thomasville I kept getting worse. Every day my pill cup had more pills, and they never seemed to be the same ones as the day before. I was so out of it I didn't even know how to wash myself. The only shower on the ward was in the day room, so you had to take all your stuff and a fresh gown and go there. I'd spend an hour trying to put together what I thought I needed to make the trip. When I got there, I'd put it all down and not know what to do. I knew I had to turn on the water, but then what? I'd pick up everything and go back to my room.

One day they took me to the "other side" of the asylum, where the permanent residents lived—as a first step to sending me there, probably. I was taken to a day room with maybe 30 other disheveled zombies and we were each handed a grubby Christian songbook. Then they tried to get us singing hymns. No one was watching me, so I left and tried to go back to my room, but I had no clue how to get there. I wandered around for what felt like hours and ended up in a deserted maintenance area. I sat on the floor and prayed for death. A janitor found me and took me to my room.

119

I don't know how long I was in Thomasville—weeks, maybe a month, maybe two months, maybe more. But one day my wife shows up with some clothes and says, "I got you out." She had seen what was going on with my meds cup and threatened them with lawsuits for HIPAA violations and using me as a guinea pig for all sorts of untested drugs. They caved. She's a fierce warrior woman, which was great when she was on my side, but not so great when she turned against me.

Back home she put me in the shower and washed me. As she was drying me off I saw myself in the mirror for the first time in months. I'd lost 50 pounds, from 175 to 125, and had the body of a holocaust survivor. I had no idea who was looking out at me from that mirror.

The next day she took me to a Lyme doctor, who took only cash and worked under the radar to keep from losing her license. Treating tick-borne illnesses then was not tolerated by the insurance industry or medical establishment. The doctor joked about my name being Barton and me being driven mad by Bartonella, and put me on multiple black-box antibiotics with instructions to take them for a year.

In Thomasville I had been given six Electro Convulsive Therapy (ECT) treatments, and the Lyme doctor told us to keep doing them as an outpatient at Duke hospital because they also helped kill the Bartonella bugs. They used to be called electro-shock treatments, and are what the Jack Nicholson character was given in *One Flew Over the Cuckoo's Nest*. These days they anaesthetize you first, so I was unconscious and never felt anything. Afterwards they'd give me peanut butter crackers and orange juice. I had six more treatments at Duke before refusing to continue. I could feel them stealing my memories.

Larry Inderbitzen, a friend who is a psychiatrist, and who followed what was happening to me closely through my wife, later told me he didn't think I ever had a tick-borne disease, but that my madness had been triggered by a certain kind of depression, the name of which I forget, and that it was the ECT that saved me, not the antibiotics. I don't know. I never had any sign of a tick bite that I know of, but I'd recently been in tall weeds on a farm in Ireland. There's also some evidence that tick-borne illnesses can be sexually transmitted and my wife had had Lyme.

Another couple friends speculated it was an entity attack. My children, who had grown to hate my wife during all this, thought she

120

had poisoned me, and in fact secretly had the hospital test me for a evidence of that, but none was found. So who knows. The bottom line, I guess, is that the Divine wanted me taken down, and so I was. The means doesn't much matter.

It would make a nice story to say that the experience of all this brought my wife and me closer together, but the opposite happened. After probably saving my life, or at least keeping me from being permanently institutionalized—for which I will be eternally grateful to her—once I was home she went on the attack again. I don't know why, but I guess she had her reasons. I was still too far out of it to understand most of what was going on. Among other things, I suppose, I was definitely not the man she fell in love with, and nursing a recovering lunatic was not what she signed up for.

In my weakened state I didn't fight back much and that seemed to embolden her even more. It would get so bad I'd lock myself in the second bedroom—which had become my room—to try and get away. She'd unlock the door with a coat hanger and renew the attack.

One day she came at me with a butcher knife and cocked it above my chest with fire in her eyes, shouting, "I'm going to kill you so fucking dead!"

I just stood there, impassive, aware of thoughts and calculations running in my head at lightning speed:

*Before she brings the knife forward she'll probably cock it back further, giving me time to catch her wrist. If I miss or she's faster than I think, she probably doesn't have the strength to drive it through my breastbone. If it slips past the breastbone and pierces my heart, well, that's just how I'll die.*

I didn't much care one way or the other, and for no particular reason I smiled. It pushed her over the edge. She slashed the knife forward and stabbed the upholstery of an ornate antique chair next to her, a chair she cherished, an inheritance from her beloved aunt who loved her like a daughter.

I watched with quiet indifference as she stabbed and stabbed and stabbed until her shoulders slumped and she stopped, the knife buried deep in the chair. Wisps of batting drifted aimlessly above her, and a few pieces settled gently in her long hair, which had fallen quite beautifully in strands across her face, like a Japanese anime heroine.

I knew I had to leave.

ART(C)SAKIMICHAN.DEVIANTART.COM

# Standing Rock

In addition to getting deathly ill and going insane, most every other aspect of my life fell apart during my second marriage. So much so, that by the time I left I was flat broke and deep in debt, with a credit rating at the bottom of the toilet. I was homeless, physically ravaged, and my self-confidence was long gone. I was estranged from my children, and whatever standing I may once have had as a spiritual teacher was up the flume.

Just the thought of packing my things and getting out of the house was physically intimidating to me, but I was determined. I stopped taking my meds, and that helped give me a little more energy. I found a place that would sell me a camper shell for my truck on credit, because I didn't know if maybe I would be living in it. I gave a bunch of clothes to Goodwill so I'd have less to pack. But I knew in my weakened state it still would take me several days to gather even what little I had—books mostly—and the thought of doing that with my wife nipping at my heels the whole time was exhausting to contemplate.

Then I got a break. She went on a week-long trip while I stayed with her dogs. I was able to pack all my things at a pace my body could tolerate, and put all of it except what I was immediately taking with me into a small storage unit. As soon as she got home, I told her I was leaving. If it hadn't been for the dogs, I'd have already been gone. She pitched a fit and tried to stop me, but I was already in motion.

As I backed out of the driveway she appeared at the side door and threw a bottle of wine at my truck, cracking the windshield—a small price to pay for freedom. It bounced off the glass and rolled down the hood slowly enough for me to notice it was the most expensive bottle we had, being saved for a special occasion. I wondered if she took the time to choose it for dramatic reasons, or if it was just the first one she happened to grab.

Four hours later I pulled up to the front door of a secluded waterfront farmhouse on the Chesapeake Bay—my favorite place on earth—and let myself in with my key.

I'd been coming there my whole life and just the act of driving down the long lane always brought me immense peace. My great-grandparents had built it, my grandparents, and then my parents had lived there in retirement, and now I was hopeful I could live there, at least for awhile.

I had inherited it jointly with my two surviving siblings. We had a loose agreement that it would remain available to the whole extended family, and none of us would live there permanently. Nevertheless, I was hopeful they would be okay with me staying there until I got back on my feet. They had homes, I didn't.

I settled in and began to heal. At first I slept a lot. Then I started walking around the property and doing small chores. I caught fish off the pier and cooked them on the grill. I took the canoe out and paddled hard to begin rebuilding muscle. Evenings I sat on the screen porch and sipped scotch. I rejoined the living.

But I was not the same. Having been brought so low gave me a deep visceral connection with the truly needy and downtrodden of the world, and in many ways they were my alter-selves. I *was* that man sitting on the sidewalk with the begging cup. I *was* that bag lady sleeping in a cardboard box. And with all my heart I wanted to somehow help.

It was about this time that the DAPL pipeline protest in Standing Rock, North Dakota was increasingly in the alternative news. Native tribes from all over the country had gathered there in solidarity against an oil pipeline that was about to be run *under* a reservoir that was the only source of water for an entire reservation. (What could go wrong?) Arrayed against them were military units and sheriffs departments from five states, equipped with urban warfare tanks. For reasons I can't fully explain, I felt I had to join them.

So in late 2016, a couple months after I left my wife, I put an air mattress in the back of my truck, bought an extra-heavy sleeping bag and a Mister Heater propane heater, and headed to North Dakota. I also threw in some spare winter coats and the contents of my pantry. The protestors were digging in for the winter and needed all the supplies they could get.

The military had blocked off the bridge and other ways to get to the site, but I eventually found my way in. I parked and camped and joined in the work, but I was unprepared for the effect the cold would have on my weakened body.

One night there was a big confrontation between the protestors and the military at the bridge. I had tried to get there on foot but got lost in the dark. By the time I found my way back to my truck I was exhausted.

The next day the news was not good. The military had opened up with water cannons in 15-degree weather, and were firing tear gas canisters and other hard objects. One young native girl got a broken arm. Another lost an eye. Part of me felt guilty for not being there. A larger part was grateful I never made it. No telling what a water cannon in sub-freezing weather would have done to my body.

By this time the cold had taken its toll and I was getting weaker. At 3 a.m. one bitter night I had to take a shit. I walked thirty yards to a deserted area and squatted in the dead grass. Afterwards I could not stand up. I had to fall forward and crawl to my truck where I could pull myself to my feet.

Inside, I fired up the heater and wrapped myself in my sleeping bag as I sat in meditation, body shaking, mind on fire. I had come with visions of working side by side with like-minded souls for a grand purpose. Now all I wanted was to be in a warm house somewhere, anywhere.

When my friend Bill heard I was going to North Dakota, he'd said as long as I was out west to come by his place. At the time I told him I didn't know how long I'd be at Standing Rock, but now I knew. Not much longer.

A couple days later I left Standing Rock with my tail between my legs and headed for Bill's. On the way, I stopped in Granby, Colorado and spent a few enjoyable days visiting Bob Fergesen. At Bill's I crashed on the couch in his kiva, joined the meditation sittings he held four times a week, and caught up with friends. It was just what I needed after Standing Rock. Soon, though, I realized that what I really wanted was to go home.

There was a snowstorm predicted and Bill wanted me to stay until it had come and gone, but I longed for home and decided to leave right away and be ahead of it. Silly boy. On a long stretch of deserted road in New Mexico I hit it head on.

Visibility was near zero, but there was no place to pull over, and the next civilization was 100 miles away. I basically had no choice but to inch ahead, flashers on, and hope for the best. My tires were worn and should have been replaced before my trip, and I repeatedly had to correct for skids. It was the most nerve-wracking driving experience of my life.

But eventually I got through it, and out of the worst of the storm. Near Santa Fe I turned east and headed into Texas, where the sun began to come through and I was able to relax my death grip on the steering wheel. Three days later, I was driving down my lane, enveloped by that familiar peace it always brought me.

Inside the house, I lit a fire and poured a scotch. I thought about Standing Rock, and the brave souls who were wintering there. I fought feelings of defeat and guilt about my time with them, but there was no denying I was at this moment exactly where I was supposed to be.

I had tried to be a social justice hero and failed miserably. Or, to shine a different light on it, I was shown in no uncertain terms that being a social justice hero is not why I'm here.

# Anguilla

A few months after returning from Standing Rock I got a text from my friend Brent: *Would you be in on an all-expense paid trip to a five-star hotel in the Caribbean for a week?*

Brent had come to a retreat my wife and I held before I got sick, and had signed up for the next one, which we had to cancel because I was descending into madness at the time. When my wife was sending refunds to those who had paid, Brent told her to just keep his. He stayed in touch while I was healing and even flew in from Chicago once to visit.

I texted back: *Is this a trick question?*

It wasn't. He was one of the top salesmen in his company and had qualified for their annual reward trip. He and his girlfriend, a former Miss Virginia, had just broken up, and he was offering me the "plus one" spot on his invitation.

*If you don't come, I'll be going solo, which seems a waste. I'll just tell them you're my mentor, and that you work at IBM, which is one of our biggest customers.*

I thought about it for a microsecond or two, then: *Shitchyeah.* Later that evening I burst out laughing at the extreme contrast of my Standing Rock experience and what the Divine had just dropped into my lap. "Who writes this stuff?" I wondered out loud.

The hotel was the Four Seasons in Anguilla. Marble floors, shower the size of a small bedroom, hot tub on the balcony overlooking the ocean…

Every day was a pool or beach party with lavish food and open bars. Every night when we got back to the room there were matching expensive gifts waiting for each of us—monogramed bathrobe, crystal whiskey decanter with *Marshall* etched on it, an ornate bottle of the most expensive rum on the planet…

For a few days I took it all in and indulged to the max. "So, this is the good life everyone talks about," I thought. "Not bad. Not bad at all." But that sort of thing is not sustainable, at least not for me. How much food can you eat? How much alcohol can you consume? I realized—though it was not really a revelation to me—that even if I were rich enough to afford this sort of lifestyle, it's not what I would do with my money.

Before coming on the trip I researched Anguilla, and one of the bits I came across was that a reggae musician named Bankie Banx lived there, and that he owned a beach club called the Dune Preserve where he played, and where other musicians came to visit. Bob Dylan and Jimmy Buffett had even come to play with him. I resolved to make it a point to go hear him while I was there.

But now I was over halfway through the trip and I hadn't moved on that. I tried to interest Brent in taking a cab with me to Dune Preserve that night, but there was a "special" party he didn't want to miss, so we planned to go the next night.

When the next night came, the trip organizers revealed that we would all be bussed to various local restaurants for dinner as a change of pace. I still wanted to go see Bankie, but didn't want to abandon Brent for the evening, so we went.

The bus going to the best restaurant was full, as were a couple others going to the more desirable places. The bus we were assigned was half empty. We all joked about being on the "D-list" bus, and I was vaguely disappointed that in addition to missing Bankie, I wasn't even getting a great meal as compensation. The restaurant we ended up at was mostly empty, and the meal, while good, was not memorable.

Afterwards Brent and I walked down what seemed a deserted beach, then noticed the lights of a tiki bar and headed for it. We sat at the bar and I ordered a scotch.

Not much later a car pulled up and a few local men got out. Two of them sat at the bar, but one sat on a low split-rail fence right behind me, not five feet away. I recognized him from his pictures online. We exchanged nods.

"Are you Bankie?"

" I am."

He had brought a drink with him in a rocks glass.

"What are you drinking?" I assumed rum because, Caribbean.

"Scotch," he said. On an island where rum is king, he drank scotch. My man.

"Can I buy you one?"

"Sure, mon."

And so we sat there drinking scotch, Bankie and me, and we hit it off like we'd been friends a long time. In a parallel universe or previous life, maybe we were, who knows. After a couple drinks he left with his friends, saying, "Come to the club."

The next evening was the big "finale" party for Brent's company. It started before sunset on the beach, and was beyond extravagant. Beautiful women in sequined G-strings and huge feather headdresses walked around on stilts. Name-brand bands played on the bandstand, scantily-clad waitresses circulated with trays of food and colorful rum drinks, open bars if you didn't want rum...

I had a great time, but as the evening wore on I was ready to head out to Bankie's. Brent had agreed to come with me, but he had settled into a conversation with his boss, and his boss's boss, and I had a hard time pulling him away.

Eventually we got into a cab and headed for the Dune Preserve. It was on the other side of the island and took longer to get to than I expected. That, plus the delays at the party, got us to Bankie's late. Bankie was in conversation with some customers, but we saw each other and exchanged nods. I asked the bartender when the next set was and he told me Bankie was done playing for the night. Shit.

The Dune Preserve is right on the beach, and looks like it washed up in a shipwreck, which it has, just not all at the same time. It's cobbled together with scraps of most everything imaginable. We ordered drinks and Brent apologized for making us late.

"Not your fault, man. Those guys are your livelihood. I just really appreciate you inviting me along for all this. I wouldn't be here at all if it weren't for you." We clinked glasses.

About then Bankie steps on stage with his band and starts playing. His style is sort of folk-reggae with a little jazz thrown in. Some have characterized him as the Dylan of the Caribbean. After his set I told him how much I enjoy his music. "Your bartender told me you were done for the night. I'm glad he was wrong."

"He was right, but when I saw you come in, mon, I knew I had to play for you."

We sat on a ratty couch and picked up where we'd left off the night before, with scotch rocks and a joint he produced from nowhere. We talked for a long time that night, about how his arrest for possession of a joint in Barbados had led to him being "stuck in paradise" for 11 years, which led to the development of the Dune Preserve, and to the Moonsplash Music Festival he held every year.

I threw in some stories about how some of the worst things in my life led to some of the best. I also told him about the serendipitous events that led me to be at the tiki bar where we met. He said he hadn't wanted to go out that night but his friends talked him into it. We clinked glasses and agreed you just never know what leads to what.

Bankie and Bart, Dune Preserve, Anguilla, 2017

# Mexico Redux

At the time Brent texted me about going to Anguilla, I was in the midst of trying to climb out of a deep financial hole. I've never thought much about money in my life. No matter how strapped I was I always seemed to have enough, though it did have the frustrating habit of showing up just in the nick of time, for which I was extremely grateful, of course, though I'd occasionally complain to the Divine, "It would be nice to have a buffer if you could manage." But that has not been the case for me, either financially or in most other things. My life has stubbornly continued to exhibit the truth of the saying, "God is never late, but he's seldom early."

The pursuit of Self-Realization had been my priority since the age of twenty-two, and there just didn't seem to be room for more than one obsession, hence money always took a back seat. I've made numerous attempts over the years to accumulate enough to be free of money concerns, but I've never been driven to be wealthy, nor have I had a head for it.

Staying at the Four Seasons and indulging at the lavish company parties re-fueled my desire to be financially independent, while at the same time showing me that living the high life was not that attractive. I felt more at home with Bankie in the Dune Preserve.

My renewed interest in money, however, started me thinking about it in different ways, and opened me up to becoming more proactive about acquiring it. It was in this frame of mind I first heard about bitcoin and cryptocurrency from my friend Keith Conway, a couple months after returning from Anguilla.

Initially I was highly skeptical, and completely intimidated by the complexity of buying some. It took me six weeks of research into all aspects of it before I bought my first coins. I felt compelled to understand the technology behind it, as much as I was capable anyway, and studied everything I could, from Satoshi's original white paper, to online technical lectures, to YouTubers with investment advice. I didn't have much capital to work with, so when I finally jumped in I tended to buy large amounts of altcoins that sold for way less than a penny each, looking for a home run if one should go to a dime.

At one point in January 2018 things were looking good in cryptoworld. My modest portfolio had gone up 4,000% in six months and if I'd got out then I could have built a house on my Colorado land. But I let it ride, and after some number of months it was under water. Crypto is a roller coaster with wide swings, and that same portfolio is now up 500% as of this writing. Most of the coins I bought are still alive, so I think of them as lottery tickets that never expire, and if one of them should catch fire, who knows.

My interest in crypto currency led me to research money theory in general, and in particular Austrian economics, which promotes an unrestrained free market with little or no interference from government. It emphasizes complete freedom and sovereignty of individual property rights, as well as the abolishment of central banks and a return to the gold standard. Not surprisingly, it's fiercely opposed by mainstream economists, who call it "anarchist economics," and barely acknowledge its existence.

Cryptocurrency, and its threat to fiat currencies and central banks, fits in quite nicely with this anarchist economics, which led me to look at anarchy in general, and I discovered it most closely describes the political instincts of my character.

Anarchy is not the chaos in the streets scenario that mainstream media pushes. It literally just means, "no rulers," so of course the current rulers—and the media they control—sell chaos as the nightmare consequence of such freedom. The truth is, when rulers are absent, problems disappear. People cooperate, organize themselves for common goals, and take care of each other. Leaders emerge, of course, people who are willing to take on more responsibility, but there are no kings, no dictators, no governments, no rulers. Another word for it is "voluntaryism," and what it boils down to is individual *freedom*, something that has been a driving

force for me my whole life.

All of these thoughts were in play when I heard about Anarchapulco. Anarchapulco is the brainchild of Jeff Berwick, a balls-out rabble rouser for freedom, and an early adopter and proponent of cryptocurrency. It's a large gathering of iconoclasts, anarchists, financial outliers, counter-culturists, spiritual seekers, and red-pilled researchers of all stripes held in Acapulco, where Jeff lives as a Canadian ex-pat. The more I read about it the more I knew I had to go. And so in February 2018 I flew to Acapulco.

I'm not a big fan of flying anymore. I hate TSA, for one thing, and I'm old enough to remember when flying was fun. The stewardesses were attractive and friendly, the food was decent, and friends and family could come to the gate with you to say goodbye, and wait for you to disembark when you returned. Now, on U.S. airlines and in U.S. airports in particular, I feel like a prisoner being transported from one facility to another.

On my American flight from Raleigh to Houston I sat next to a guy who asked where I was headed. When I told him he said, "I hear it's really dangerous to visit Mexico." Government propaganda at work. At the time the U.S. State Department was issuing warnings about the dangers of visiting Mexico, partly to punish Mexico for something or other, and possibly even to try limiting the attendees at Anarchapulco, not realizing, perhaps, that people interested in Anarchapulco are the least likely folks on the planet to give a shit what the U.S. State Department has to say about anything.

The flight attendants were an arrogant gay guy and a frumpy middle-aged woman, who seemed put out when I asked for a full can of ginger ale, like it was coming out of her paycheck or something. By contrast, on my Aero Mexico flight to Acapulco, the flight attendants were beautiful, friendly young women in stylish uniforms and red pillbox hats. Three kinds of beer were among the complimentary beverages offered. As many as you wanted.

In Mexico City the line for immigration was incredibly long because a couple jumbo jets had just landed from Japan. I had plenty of time before my next flight so no big deal, really, but after an hour or so I was ready to have it be over. Just about then an attractive woman in her fifties opened the tape in front of me, gestured me and a few others nearby to come through, then hooked it back up.

I followed her to a place where they had kiosks to do what I was waiting for. She did the kiosk entries for me, asking me the questions. When it came to whether I was in a group or single, I said "Single." She looked at me with a twinkle and says, "Single? Why?" I said, "Divorced." She smiled big and said, "Oh. Divorced. Well, you're in Mexico now. We'll take care of you," then winked.

On the train to the other terminal, sitting across from me, I shit you not, was the most beautiful woman I've even seen, either in real life or in movies. Think Catherine Zeta-Jones in "Zorro," but twice as beautiful. Long raven hair down her back, a face that proves the existence of God, and a smile that would melt rock. She was wearing a skin-tight, multi-colored body suit that looked painted on her centerfold-perfect body, with so much cleavage her nipples were barely covered. I fucking love Mexico.

Anarchapulco was an amazing, and in many ways, life-changing experience. In addition to an impressive lineup of speakers on the main stage, there were numerous other tracks in smaller rooms, with speakers on everything from alternative medicine, to international finance, to the occult, to deep state tyranny, to cryptocurrency.

The best part, though, was meeting and talking to other attendees during meals and evenings at the bar. Everyone was deeply into some aspect of alternative culture and thinking, as well as having an overall understanding of the truth about what's really going on in the world, and the criminals who run it. Everyone was red-pilled to a high degree, and I felt I had found my tribe. I went again in 2019.

My time there in 2018 also included an all-night *ayahuasca* ceremony, and a second night tripping on the *jaguar*, a powdered entheogen from the sap of a South American tree. Anarchapulco was held in a beautiful beachfront hotel, and these plant medicine ceremonies took place in one of it's conference rooms. It was not an ideal setting for these sorts of journeys, but an excellent shaman was in charge, and his team did a good job transforming it into a ceremonial space.

The first night was ayahuasca. It started at 9 p.m. and went until 7 the next morning. The first two cups were given to everyone about 45 minutes apart. The third cup was offered individually if you wanted it. After that, every hour or so the shaman would say, "If you would like another cup, you can come up." I always went. Six cups in all.

The experience for me was very visual—lots of phantasmagoric imagery that showed me where the ayahuasca artists get their inspiration. My inner world was filled with incredible beauty that would morph into grotesqueness and back again. It all had a cartoon quality, though, so no matter how terrifying or beautiful the image was trying to be, I could not take it seriously.

I did not receive any profound revelations or insights, and physically I was uncomfortable the whole night. The room was over air-conditioned, and I'd only brought a towel to lay on. The floor was carpeted, but still hard on my aging bones, and I never threw up during the trip so my stomach hurt the whole time. When the shaman said it was over and I was rolling up my towel, though, I had the sudden urge to puke and barely made it to the nearest bucket. I threw up violently six times, once for each cup I drank.

The second night also started at 9 p.m. and ended about 4 a.m. Same conference room, same shaman, same ceremonial ambiance. But the medicine and experience were quite different. We had to pair up with a partner because only one would be doing it while the other sat by for support. A young woman, Stacy, asked if I would be her partner. She was experienced with plant medicine, she said, and particularly loved mushrooms, but her boyfriend, Ernesto, was not into it at all and had not wanted to join her that night.

The *jaguar* is administered by the shaman blowing the powder up your nostrils through a reed, then you lay down with eye shades and off you go. It's an incredible journey that affects people in wildly different ways. Some folks screamed in terror, some laughed uncontrollably, many just reached out a hand to their partner for reassurance and comfort. Stacy said I never moved a muscle during my trip, but inside I traveled far. During her trip she looked like she was having continuous orgasms, and later told me she'd lost her fear of death. Afterwards, there was much hugging around the room no matter what one's journey had been.

At breakfast the next day Stacy saw me and called me over to her table, where Ernesto and I developed an instant rapport. I learned that he and Stacy were well-connected entrepreneurs in the crypto space, and their businesses even included ATM machines for crypto currency.

I had become by then quite good at researching and analyzing altcoins, and I related to them what I'd been up to, and that my modest portfolio was up 4,000% in six months. Ernesto was impressed, and suggested I start a fund for friends and friends of friends who had no idea how to get into crypto, which was still quite intimidating then. He even said he'd put me in contact with some people who could help.

We stayed in touch after Anarchapulco, and I did indeed start a crypto "hedge fund," Willow Creek Investments, named for the creek than runs across the back of my Colorado land. My friend Jeni made me a gorgeous website, complete with realtime performance tickers of the ten paper funds I created—all of which were outperforming bitcoin and the total crypto market by wide margins. This, and Ernesto's help with contacts, gave me enough cred and visibility to be invited on conference calls with heavyweights in the crypto space.

I never got to the point of actually taking investments, however. In the wild west of early cryptoworld, there were no regulations about who could open and manage a crypto fund, but there were lawyers and stockbrokers on these calls talking about coming regulations that would have precluded my participation. Plus, as my hubris subsided, I realized that no matter how good I may or may not be at picking altcoins, I was extremely ill-suited to be responsible for other people's money. All this coincided with the continued slide in cryptocurrency at the time. I gradually came to my senses, took down the website, and politely declined participation in future conference calls.

While at 2018 Anarchapulco, I also met Dr. Diego Navarro, who specializes in administering a healing and deep cleansing protocol involving a number of procedures and methods not available in the U.S. At the time I was still concerned that the Bartonella bugs, or whatever had invaded my body and drove me insane, may not all have been destroyed, and were perhaps capable of regrouping for a future attack. After talking with Diego at the conference, and in a number of emails and Skype calls afterwards, I decided that his protocols were my best shot at getting rid of any bugs still alive once and for all.

The process involved four 3-hour sessions a week for a period of five weeks, and included such things as ozone IVs, neural therapies, hydrocolonics, and small placenta implants in the fat tissue of my stomach—a sort of poor man's stem cell therapy, which he also offered but was out of my price range, even though it was less than 10% of what you'd pay in the U.S.

I can't imagine what such a long series of treatments would cost in the U.S., if indeed they were available, but Diego quoted me a total price of under $900 for everything, which even I could afford.

His clinic is in a town near Sayulita, one of a dozen picturesque small beach towns on a 100-mile stretch of coast known as the Riviera Nayarit, which also includes the town of San Blas, where I had visited with Joe and wanted to stay. It all added up to a trip I knew I had to take, and so I booked with Diego for that June.

Upon hearing about my trip, my friend Mark asked if I wanted company for a couple weeks. I said, sure, of course. One of the few constants in my life has been my friendship with Chuck

Bunce and Mark Levy. We've known each other since 7th grade, and have been in and out of each other's lives ever since.

Somewhere along the way, after we had wives and families, we took up fishing as an excuse to get away and get together. We've fished up and down the east coast and southeast from the Mid-Atlantic to New Orleans to Key West, and have traveled as far as Baja California, Mexico in search of piscean glory. Over time, as our peccadilloes and misadventures mounted, we dubbed ourselves the *Idiot Sportsmen*.

It's a rare gift to have close friends you've known for over 60 years. We are well aware of that, and of the fragility of all things. The older we get, the more often we get together. One of Mark's brothers recently discovered the color picture of us shown here. We are on our way to senior prom, 1964, thinking we were the coolest dudes on the planet. I'm on the left in a gold tux jacket, Chuck in the middle in purple, and Mark on the right in neon blue. The picture was taken by my girlfriend, Stephanie, Chuck's sister, who later broke my  heart when she dumped me for a guy who looked like Elvis.

So anyway, Mark was in the midst of some domestic turbulence and a little R&R in Mexico sounded good to him. We made arrangements to arrive on the same day and meet in the Puerto Vallarta airport. Whereupon we rented a car and drove to the house I had rented in San Pancho, about 30 minutes from Diego's clinic.

I had seen pictures of the house on Airbnb when I rented it, but the actuality of it was staggering. Three bedrooms, two baths, huge modern kitchen, garage, dipping pool, and a blue tile dome worthy of a Spanish church. Plus, a gardener and maid every few days. Cost: $32 a night. Granted, it was off-season,

and the owner was running a special because she was just getting started with renting it, but still...

A day or two later I started going to my appointments with Diego, during which Mark read pulp novels while sunning himself like a lizard on the balcony by the dipping pool. Late afternoon we would walk to the beach for a swim, then back to our dipping pool for a rinse-off before dinner.

Being off-season the restaurants were mostly empty, so the staff was always glad to see us. At night we often sat on the balcony watching fantastic lightning displays, but it rarely rained, which is typical for that time of year there. A month or two later is monsoon season, and it rains every day. Mornings we would walk a couple blocks to a coffee and pastry shop owned by Priscilla, who lived for many years in San Diego, but had moved back to San Pancho because she liked it better. Can't say I blame her.

Mark and I also chartered fishing boats and had incredible days on the water. The captains cleaned our catches for us and we'd take filets to our favorite restaurant, the Barracuda, where the cook was a master at preparing them in deliciously unexpected ways. Good times.

After Mark left I continued with my clinic appointments for another few weeks. They were not always the most pleasant experiences, but Diego and his charming nurse Elsa were wonderful, professional, and never in a hurry. I always enjoyed their company. One of the treatments was colonics, of which I had five, and by the end of them I surely must have had the cleanest intestines on the planet.

Elsa administered them, and the day before one would give me a mischievous wink and say, "Colonic tomorrow." Oh boy. They are not much fun. I rarely looked at the clear tube on the wall that was carrying all the waste material away, but occasionally Elsa would nudge me to look at stuff she thought was interesting, like a huge white mass moving through. "Mucus," she said. Once I think I may have spotted a couple of pop-beads I swallowed as a kid.

I spent a lot of time on the beach, and walking around the narrow streets of San Pancho. I love that little town, and if I'd had the money I probably would have bought a small house there before I left. Who knows, maybe someday I still will.

It was also during this period that I started writing the book you now hold. I'm not sure what prompted that, but it just started happening and came out in a rush. Something about being alone in a foreign country at age 72, perhaps, sent me on an inner journey over where I'd been, and where I now found myself.

Being in San Pancho gave me a clear space — with no hooks or reminders of who or what I was to myself and others — to view and tell my story with an objective clarity and disregard for how it might go over with readers.

Ever since Flight 99 I've known that someday I would need to write my seeker memoir and my "finder" teachings, but it always loomed as a somewhat unpleasant obligation, as something I "owed" to others, as a daunting task that required more effort and enthusiasm than I could muster. In San Pancho, though, I started seeing it as a *recapitulation* project, as a part of my self-understanding and healing — as the spiritual and emotional counterpart to the physical healing I was undertaking with Dr. Navarro. The floodgates opened.

Even with years of self-inquiry and introspection behind me, I have been amazed at what I've learned about the Bart character, and the recurring patterns of his life, while writing this book. As I would remember a story or vignette, I'd often be hit with the thought, "Jesus, there's *that* shit showing up again," and I'd realize that the program running in this mindbody is absolutely consistent, manifesting the same characteristics and tendencies decade after decade, in myriad different situations and guises.

There is nothing to be done about this really. Nothing that should be done. This is the boat I was born into, a gift from the Divine. My purpose in life is not to make it a better boat, or to outfit it with lavish amenities, but to sail it to the far shore as it is.

In later chapters we'll be looking at things one can do to possibly improve one's chances of arriving on far shore in this lifetime, but none of those things are necessary. You are now, at this very moment, everything you need to be to receive Eternal Life instantly. The mechanism is simple: Just stop pretending you're separate from God. Truly, *Thou art That.*

# Realface Press

*What was your face before your grandmother was born?*
*What is your real face?*
— Zen koan

One evening while I was sitting at Rose's bedside as he lay dying, Mike Casari offered me a few spiritual books he'd brought with him. I wasn't really in the mood to read, and had in fact, after Flight 99, lost most of my interest in reading. But I politely accepted, and casually looked them over. One was printed in India, and was oriented "sideways," so that you opened it like a jewel box rather than a cabinet. The title was *Ashtavakra Gita*, and this particular edition also replicated the hand notes Ramana Maharshi had written in his own copy.

Somehow, in all my years of seeking, I had never encountered the *Ashtavakra Gita*, and I opened it with great curiosity. I began reading and was amazed. In short poetic verses it elucidated Truth better than I had ever seen it done before. But I realized as I read that what I now brought to my reading — in the aftermath of Flight 99 — allowed me to see what many others may not be able to see in it. It was translated by someone with English as a second language, and who I doubt had a personal experience of Truth, so in subtle ways it did not convey what I saw in it as powerfully as I imagined it might.

After reading for awhile, I took out a notebook and began jotting down "my" versions of a few of the verses. I liked the process, and was pleased with what I saw appearing in my notebook. After an hour or so I set it aside and returned to just sitting quietly with Rose. But sometime after I was home, I picked it up again and stuck with it, until a few months later I had completed my own version. My method was to gather together all available versions of it, both print and online, and work with them until my version of each verse took form. I liked how it turned out.

I created a PDF and sent it to Mike since he'd provided the catalyst. He ended up printing copies and spreading them around. It eventually got loose on the internet and became popular with those who found it, and I began to be contacted by strangers who had read it, and who were effusive in their praise.

This, coupled with the fact that I had thoroughly enjoyed the process of translation/versioning, led me to tackle a second ancient spiritual text, *Tao Te Ching*, which has been deeply embedded in my psyche since Ria DeFato read it to me on my first LSD trip. This led to translating other ancient texts until finally I published six of them as a book, *The Perennial Way*, then added four more and published *The Perennial Way: Expanded Edition*.

During this time I became aware that there was no text that contained only the words of Jesus, like there was for Buddha and the other masters I was translating, so I began creating one. In addition to five of the books in the New Testament, there are 20 other ancient Christian texts that contain quotes attributed to Jesus, and I wanted to include them all. It took six years of working at it off and on, but finally I published *Christ Sutras: The Complete Sayings of Jesus from All Sources Arranged into Sermons*. This led to other translation/versions like *Bhagavad Gita* and *The Emerald Tablets*, and I am now about two-thirds through doing the same thing for the Bible, which will be published as the *King James Reader's Version*. I also have a good start on the *Quran*.

My plan there, in addition to publishing them separately, is to publish a boxed set, *The Abrahamic Gospels*, which will consist of the Jewish *Tanakh* (Old Testament), the Christian *New Testament*, and the Muslim *Quran*. These three religions have been in conflict with each other in one way or another for millennia, yet they all spring from the same well, in the same part of the world, and their origins can be traced to the same prophet, Abraham — a man who was about to kill his son because a voice in his head told him to, when the voice said, "Never mind, just testing you."

I'm not a fan of what these religions have perpetrated upon humanity, and have an active aversion to much of what is taught in their names, but their influence on world history and culture is incalculable, and hidden deep within them are nuggets of Truth. Regardless, for whatever reason, I feel I'm being asked to create the clearest, most accurate, most faithful — and hopefully most poetic — version possible of the core texts of these religions, so that they can speak directly to the reader without any need for "expert" commentaries and agenda-driven interpretations.

As I work towards this goal, I've also published four volumes excepted from my version-in-progress of the Bible: *The Torah*, *The Book of Psalms, Poetry and Wisdom of the Old Testament*, and *The Four Gospels and the Gospel of Thomas*.

I've also edited and published relatively recent spiritual books now in the public domain that I believe are worth dusting off

142

and keeping in circulation, and have compiled the letters of Alfred Pulyan to Richard Rose into *Letters of Transmission: The Enlightenment Method of Alfred Pulyan.*

What I have not done, other than a small book of poetry, *Verses Regarding True Nature*, is to publish any of my own writings, nor have I published my "seeker story" as many teachers do — until now. It's not an overstatement to say that for sixteen years I've been avoiding writing the book you now hold. One of the main reasons for my reluctance is that I considered my personal story inconsequential, and any spiritual perspective I may have to offer, inferior to what has already been said and written better.

What changed my mind about doing this book was helping my friend Mike Snider write his story of seeking and finding Truth. Mike had done a podcast with Shawn Nevins about his story, which was truly excellent, and I encouraged him to make it into a book. At first he was even more reluctant than I am about mine, but I was persuasive, and as I heard myself trotting out all the reasons he should do it, I knew someday I'd have to eat my own cooking.

"Whatever I have to say has been said a hundred times better by others," he demurred.

"Yeah," I said, "but everybody says it different. Nobody else can say it like you can." Even as I spoke the words I could feel them cutting both ways.

Mike finally agreed, and we spent a year working on, *The Triune Self: Confessions of a Ruthless Seer.* Working with Mike on his book was an absolute joy. We sent dozens of drafts back and forth in emails, and Mike came for several extended visits where we could work together on the book in person, with plenty of time left over to sit on the porch, laughing and talking and "looking way off," as Mike calls it. I truly hated to see the project come to an end, but we still visit each other for a few days of profundity and belly laughs from time to time, even though we are separated by an 11-hour drive.

While it's certainly true that every person on earth is one-of-a-kind, some people are way more one-of-a-kind than others. Mike Snider is definitely in this category, and then some. Mike is world-class one-of-a-kind. He can make you laugh till your sides ache doing nothing but being himself, then come out with something so clear and true it brings tears to your eyes.

His gift for humor and effortless flair for storytelling — along with being a national champion banjo player — has provided him a good career. He's been a fixture at the Grand Ole Opry for decades,

143

still appearing most weekends unless he's playing somewhere out on the road with his string-band. He was a popular guest on a lot of talk shows on The Nashville Network until the channel got bought out, and was a regular cast member on the long-running TV comedy show *Hee Haw*.

I first met Mike on one of the rare occasions he agreed to talk to an audience of spiritual seekers. He was a speaker at one of our SIG retreats, along with a number of spiritual teachers who gave excellent talks of the satsang variety.

Then Mike got up there in farmer overalls with a banjo slung over his shoulder and laid into a roaring good tune, after which he quietly put the banjo in its case and proceeded to give one of the best talks of any kind I'd ever heard. One minute I was laughing so hard I about fell out of my chair, and the next my heart was breaking with the piercing profundity of his simple words.

And so, now I will add *Becoming Vulnerable to Grace* to the Realface Press memoir section, alongside Mike's *The Triune Self*, and Dave Gold's *After the Absolute*. I sincerely hope it contains a phrase here and there that may be of help to others.

Yet as I see myself write those words, I feel compelled to add that in my experience there are no "others." There is only One, and whatever "I" do is only in service to the One, which in turn does not care a whit what the imaginary thought-form called Bart does, or what effect it may or may not have on any imaginary others.

Still, I seem to have no choice but to act as if my actions matter, and to consider others in all I do. When this single eye of emptiness is in receipt of others, that is who I am.

# The Persistence of Identity

On a recent visit here Phil Consonery, who had seen me a few times during the long healing process after my illness, said now that I was finally "myself" again, he and other friends joked about me being "Bart 2.0." It struck a chord. My experience is definitely that I am not the same person I was before going down the rabbit hole of madness. It also prompted me to think in those same terms about other "stages" of my life.

Bart 1.0, the adventurer, held sway until a week before his 22nd birthday, when he was blown up and propelled into an infinite clear blackness that felt like Home.

Bart 2.0, the seeker, was in charge for the next 37 years, until the occurrence on Flight 99 revealed his true nature to be the infinite clear emptiness of God.

Bart 3.0, the teacher, tried for ten years, in his own somewhat clumsy and reluctant way, to help others realize that they, too, are the infinite clear emptiness of God.

Then in 2015, at age 68, illness and insanity rendered all three versions helpless and incapacitated. Virtually all identifiable aspects of the Bart character identity vanished. He became, one might say, Bart 0.0.

Recovery was slow, both physically and mentally, and it was not until September 2016, when I left my second wife—along with the house and town where the trauma had transpired—that a deeper healing began to take place, a healing that continues today.

The essential Bart characteristics of the previous three stages have been restored to "Bart 4.0," and I am now being taken into new territory. It feels as if there is no end to it, and that perhaps there might be a Bart 5.0 if he lives long enough.

Once I landed here on the Bay my body gained strength and my mind began to clear. Memories came back. I started writing again. For my whole life, this has been the one place on earth that felt like home, and now I am privileged to actually live here. The route taken was circuitous and sometimes dramatic, but here I am, right where I've always dreamed of being.

It's a place where my roots go as deep as they can in this country, unless you're a native. In the 1600s the king of England gave a 5000-acre land grant to an ancestor, and where I'm living now is the last 25 acres of it still in the family. It borders the property with the original plantation mansion, which is in the Virginia Historic Registry, and is now owned by a delightful couple who planted two thousand apple tress and operate a ciderworks there. She's a former Miss Texas, and the entrepreneur behind the business. He's a recently retired admiral. His wife says, "He used to command 30,000 men. Now he works for me."

My grandmother was born in that mansion, and when my great-grandfather was a boy there, invading Union troops commandeered the place and cooked his family's livestock in the yard. My heritage on my father's side is what's called FFV—First Family Virginia—meaning my family tree is heavy with name-brand ancestors from early America and the Civil War. Supreme Court Chief Justice John Marshall is my four-greats grandfather, and in less direct relationships, I can claim as kin Thomas Jefferson, Robert E. Lee, and George Washington's mother.

And in my own lifetime, this place has been deeply embedded in my psyche. I've been coming here since I was an infant. I've sailed its vast waters and explored its labyrinthine shorelines. I've worked with my uncles fishing their pound nets and delighted in the swirling silver bounty. I've bush-hogged

the fields, planted gardens, gathered oysters, pruned the orchard, and sold my modest catches of crabs for $3 a bushel to the big Buy Boat that used to come into the creek on its circuit around the Bay.

Summer mornings I'd get up before dawn to take a skiff out fishing, and Learla, my grandmother, would already be in the

kitchen making me breakfast on the wood stove, her long hair, usually in a braided bun, brushed out and flowing to her waist. This place holds some of my most beautiful and sacred memories, and is tightly woven into my backstory and personal identity.

And for that reason it is constricting. As cherished as it is to me, it subtly but powerfully insists on defining and limiting something that cannot be defined, and has no limits.

Erasing personal history does not mean rejecting it. I love the Bart character, and I gratefully accept the mantle of heritage, nostalgia and responsibility that comes with living on this property. I truly love it here. But when I'm in the high desert, for instance, at the base of snow-covered 14,000 foot alpine peaks, with 360 degree views and hundred-mile horizons, I'm nobody in the middle of nowhere, and that more closely reflects my Being.

The whole insanity thing, and being taken down to zero on every level was a reset for me. Prior to all that, the Realization that occurred on Flight 99 had been somewhat successfully assimilated into Bart's life and character. That is no longer the case. I have no idea how big this is or how destructive it may continue to be to the last vestiges of individual identity. But I say bring it on.

I got the answer to my question about how enlightenment holds up when things aren't going well. It holds up just fine. Even during the worst of my madness, True Nature was unfazed, unmoved, supremely indifferent. It offered no comfort to the little man in the cell. It did not say, "I am here for you," and in fact offered no help whatever. It was just Here, saying, "I AM you."

And Bart "knew" that more than ever in those darkest times. Concern for the fate of the body disappeared almost entirely, and the truth that the body is a burden as much as a gift stood out in stark relief. The mindbody known as Bart was a tangle of pain and confusion, no more to be cherished than a worn-out glove, and life was, as Rose often characterized it, a nightmare. I don't think there was a time during my madness I would have taken my own life, even if the means had been available, but I do know I lived with the constant prayer that it be taken from me.

Now, True Nature is more a part of my daily experience than ever. Illness and circumstance took away large chunks of my remaining identity attachments, and in their absence True Nature shines evermore clearly. Being taken down so hard has also made me even more grateful for the immense gift of this life, illusory though it may be, and the hand of Grace that guides it. I revel in every blessed minute of it—the good, the bad, and the butt-ugly—and I sincerely hope there's more to come. But when it's over, it will not be missed.

Chesapeake Bay, August 1954

Chesapeake Bay, December 2019

# Useless Effort Well Spent

At this point in the book we've pretty much come to the end of my story, which, as much as anything, is offered to give you the chance to decide if I'm someone you think worth listening to on the subject of Self-Realization, which, for better or worse, I will be expounding on in the following chapters. There's a Zen story Rose liked, where the student runs to the master, saying, "Master, I found an enlightened fish. What should I do with him?" The master said, "Eat him. He can't teach."

Rose, of course, was totally committed to passing it on, and I assumed that if I were ever "conferred with high office," that level of commitment to teach would come with the package. In my case, however, it did not. I wanted to head for the hills and never be heard from again. I understood and resonated with the Hindu yogis who hide in Himalayan caves.

But that is not my milieu, so rather than be an enlightened fish, eight months after Realization I found myself giving a talk at a TAT conference. In the intervening 16 years I have given many talks and held many meetings, and as I think about it now for this writing, none of them have wandered far from the things I emphasized in that first talk when "enlightenment" was fresh and new. First thought, best thought.

I tend to be a sort of nuts and bolts guy. I try to point out strategies that can be followed, things that can be practiced, rather than descriptions of what might be found. I'm not much interested in describing to you what it's like in Montana, but I'll try to draw you a map so you can go there and see for yourself.

This is not really possible, of course. As Rose said, "There's no recipe for a lightning bolt." Every person's path is unique. It's as if the Divine devises a special maze for each of us—specifically designed for our character and state of being—that we must find our way through to Truth. There is no guidance whatever available for how to navigate your particular maze. That's for you to figure out, mostly by trial and error. But there are some guidelines, some meta-principles, for how to navigate mazes in general, as well as some potentially helpful practices and investigations.

In the following chapters I talk about these things from my perspective, in a framework I call *Strategies for Self-Realization*. Keep in mind as you read, though, that none of these strategies will work.

Enlightenment is always an accident, always an act of Grace. The task of the earnest seeker is discovering how to become vulnerable to Grace, or as Rose put it, how to become accident-prone.

There are, of course, teachers who say there is nothing that can be done and no one to do it. This is absolutely true. But overwhelmingly, enlightenment happens to people who have put great effort in that direction. Those who have had a conclusive spiritual occurrence will tell you that nothing they ever did worked, but most would agree it is somehow important to *try*.

Even the teachers who preach there's nothing one can do are teaching an implied path: "Keep coming to my retreats and listening to me tell you there's nothing you can do until something happens for you." Because if there is truly nothing that can be done, one might ask, why are they talking at all?

Pure non-dual teachings of "nothing to do and no one to do it" are best reserved for those who have already beat their heads against the wall for years trying to do it themselves. Then they may be primed for a fortuitous release, a surrender that opens the door. Telling that to seekers who are new to the path, however, or who have only been giving it a lick-and-a-promise, is not helpful in my opinion. For them, maximum effort is most appropriate.

Like everything else in the spiritual arena, it's a paradox. So, to do or not to do? As my mother used to say, "Which way would you rather be wrong?"

I think there *is* a possible "path" of pure non-effort, but it is by far the more difficult way. If you choose it, you must not-do *everything*, not just spiritual work. You can't stop spiritual seeking and devote yourself to video games or fantasy football and expect enlightenment to happen. But if you drop completely out of life and live alone in nature with no desires—not even for enlightenment— then maybe the gift will be given. But if you are doing it hoping for enlightenment, it's just another kind of effort—which may end up resulting in enlightenment, but it will not have been a path of non-effort. There's no ducking the paradox.

Yes, there are cases where enlightenment hits seemingly out of nowhere, to people who have not been on a spiritual path, at least not in any traditional sense. John Wren-Lewis' realization came as a result of being poisoned by a thief in Thailand. John Davis was a homeless alcoholic sleeping in cemeteries, when one night amongst the gravestones he had a visitation and all was revealed.

But these "paths" are not prescriptive. You can't advise a bright-eyed seeker to become an alcoholic and sleep in cemeteries, or to find someone who will slip him poison unawares.

Another case of this type was my friend Jim Burns. Jim was a contemporary of Rose's and came to TAT meetings once in awhile. He had shown up out of the blue at a TAT meeting in the early days, and launched into a two-hour rant that careened back and forth between profundity and madness. Rose later told the guys at the farm he thought Burns was enlightened, so a few of them would sometimes drive the 60 miles to Jim's place in Pittsburg to hear more from him. A small group formed around Jim for awhile and the meetings were taped. Later, some of the highlights of those tapes were complied into a book, *At Home with the Inner Self* (tatfoundation.org).

Jim struggled with mental illness his whole life, and was in and out of institutions for much of it: "I wore out a hundred psychiatrists!" He could not hold a job, and for his whole life lived on various government programs that barely supported him. His mental illnesses compelled him to become a student of his chaotic mind, and he said that sometimes as he studied it, his mind would try to run away, to disappear, but that he'd reach out and pull it back.

"Then one day," he said, making a grabbing gesture with his fist, "I reached for it and *missed*." What he was left with was his True Self. But here again, Jim's "path" is not one to be recommended.

Jim was born with a withered arm, but it didn't slow him down. He rode motorcycles, and drove a stick-shift pickup with the vanity license plate: AGONY. He had a miserable childhood, with abusive parents who hated him because of his deformity. When he talked about them his voice would rise, his face would get beet red, and his ears would stick out, making him look like Yoda. "If they weren't already dead," he'd roar, "I'd murder 'em!"

Jim became a good friend, and many years ago I spent several days with him in his tiny Pittsburg apartment, along with TAT friends Shawn and Kendra, video taping him. I just used my home video camera, and set it on a tripod facing him while we talked and asked him questions. I ended up with about 25 hours of tape, and made VHS copies for Jim, who was interested to see how it came out, but I never edited the footage into a documentary as I'd planned.

In the ensuing years of moves and divorces, I've lost track of what happened to the originals. I think I included them in the boxes of the raw footage for *Mister Rose* I gave to TAT, but I'm not sure.

Maybe someone will run across them someday and do something with them. I hope so. There's some good shit in there.

The picture shown here is a portrait Jim had taken. He had a framed copy of it visibly displayed in his apartment, and I think for him it shows the stable, well-adjusted man inside that never had a chance to be in charge of his life.

I was in Colorado visiting Bob Fergesen after leaving Standing Rock when Kendra called to tell me Jim was on his deathbed. She had been a great friend and helper to Jim for many years, and tried mightily to get me to come to Pittsburg to see him before he died. "He asks about you," she said. "He loves you." I didn't go. Two-thousand mile drive. Nowhere near a major airport. Still weak from my own bout with insanity and my ordeal at Standing Rock. I had plenty of "reasons." None of them have kept feelings of regret at bay, though. I loved him, too.

Everyone is on some kind of path, spiritual or otherwise, and no matter what path it is, it makes sense to give it your best shot. Whatever you lay your hand to, do it with all your might, and all that. It is in this spirit I offer what I hope is useful counsel for those who seek Truth. It is an approach that assumes effort, while recognizing that Grace tends to happen only when all one's efforts have failed.

The following chapters are not meant to be in any way prescriptive. There is no formula or methodology for this. You are on your own. All I've tried to do is spend some time talking about things that were a part of my path, and that may be worth thinking about as you find your own way.

Godspeed.

# Energy, Rapport and Transmission

The concept of *transmission* was a big part of Rose's teachings, and one way he tried to set the stage for it was by sitting in *rapport* with his students. The process is to sit quietly in a circle, eyes open, and look around at each other—really *look* at each other, getting an intimate feeling of who these "others" are, and inhabiting a common ground that is neither you nor other. This process creates an energy greater than the sum of it's parts.

For those interested in studying and practicing rapport, Phil Consonery has written, "Guidelines for Rapport," which is available on searchwithin.org.

Rapport sittings were a frequent occurrence with Rose, and everyone looked forward to them with great anticipation—as well as a healthy dose of fear. Rose said he could see the energy circling over the heads of those gathered, and sometimes he'd direct that energy by pointing to an individual, who would then get hit with it and have some kind of experience. Most of these experiences were relatively minor in nature, but one proved to be much more dramatic, and was the stuff of legend by the time I met Rose.

Rose students were overwhelmingly male in those days, but a few women came around, mostly wives or girlfriends who came to keep an eye on their men. One such woman was Jane Slater. She had no interest whatever in spiritual matters, but had come with her husband, Chuck. When time came for a rapport sitting, she went into the kitchen.

During the sitting the energy got high. Rose later said he was about to direct the energy to Frank Mascara, but at that moment Jane appeared in the doorway with her cup of coffee. Rose very off-handedly said, "I see you got into the sugar bowl." Boom. The energy hit her. She dropped to her knees and started crying uncontrollably. Rose sat on the floor with her. Between sobs she kept saying to Rose and her husband, "I see you, but you're not there!" This went on for quite some time, and Rose, never one for sentimentality, later said, "She left a puddle of snot on the floor the size of a washtub."

Rose didn't hear from her after that until a year later, when she showed up on his doorstep one rainy night, looking like a wet cat. "I've been running from you," she said. "But I don't know what to do anymore. My life is in ruins. I don't know what life is for."

They talked late into the night and the next morning she left. He never heard from her again.

Not long after my experience on Flight 99, Mike Casari asked me if I could transmit, and if so, would I transmit to him. I felt around inside. I was empty. I had nothing to transmit. The occurrence had not given Bart anything, let alone something he could magically transmit to others. What then, I thought, is all this business about transmission in the literature? I began thinking about it deeply.

In the Zen tradition, the word *transmission* is used to denote the passing on of enlightenment from the master to the aspirant. It is a misleading word, however, in that it implies a sender and a receiver—an energy transference in which enlightenment flows from someone who "has" it to someone who does "not have" it.

It conjures up ideas of an ever-vigilant Zen master spotting the precise moment a student is ready, and with a word or glance zapping him into enlightenment. Or perhaps of the master on his deathbed, summoning his most worthy student to "receive transmission" in a secret ceremony and succeed him in the lineage. These are the images of story and myth, and have elements of truth, but they do not get at the essence of the phenomena of *transmission*.

Enlightenment cannot be *taught* like mathematics or language, or mastered with *practice*, like sports or music. The Zen master's task is more akin to helping someone born with no sense of humor suddenly break into an uncontrollable belly laugh. Or to trigger in a self-absorbed ego-maniac a spontaneous experience of unconditional selfless love. One never makes "progress" towards this sort of thing. It could happen at any moment, or never. And so when Truth stands revealed, it is said *transmission* has occurred.

Within that metaphor, however, it is more accurate to say that transmission is occurring *always*. God, Tao, One, Source, Absolute—whatever we might call it—is in an unceasing state of transmission. The invitation to accept that transmission is constant—there are no secrets! Awakening is when *reception* occurs, although this, too, is misleading because there is no *receiver*.

God's eternal state of transmission is a standing invitation to receive that may be accepted at any moment—but not by the ego-identity. The ego-mind—even one that has spent years seeking enlightenment—treats the invitation to receive transmission as a threat, as "the hound of heaven." As long as ego is in control—or believes itself to be—the hound is successfully kept at bay. But if ego is dethroned for even a moment, the hound is upon it, and its name is Grace. Invitation accepted, transmission complete.

Knowing the ego-identity to be the guardian of the gate, the Zen master—with the permission and complicity of the aspirant—goes about the business of undermining and attacking its authority in subtle, and sometimes not-so-subtle, ways. This is the *entire* work of true Zen. There is no teaching or practice, no zapping, no secret wisdom imparted with words—or rather, whatever there is of this is only used in service to the true purpose. The Zen master is up to one thing only—the maneuvering of the seeker's ego-mind into a sufficiently vulnerable position that it might falter just long enough for *reception* to occur.

The master transmits nothing. He does not "have" enlightenment himself—no one ever does—so what could he transmit? He is a midwife, a facilitator, an awakening therapist.

All rests with the seeker, the aspirant. Source is as unavoidable as air. It is the very space you now occupy. How near to you is the place you peer out from? How far from it can you stray? To "see" it where must you look? To "know" it where must you go?

As a teacher I've had people tell me they had an experience as a result of our conversations or emails, and I have witnessed transmission/reception taking place in person, but I take no credit for any of this. At best I may help undermine support for the entrenched beliefs and untruths a person carries, allowing Truth to take a shot at him or her, but Bart does not *have* anything he can transmit. *Reception* is a wonderful thing to witness, though.

In 2009, after our first SIG retreat, I was driving boxes of unused food to the food bank, and Elisa Graca, one of the participants was riding along. In response to her questions I was rambling on about spiritual stuff when she suddenly "got it." Her demeanor changed and she held up her hand, as if to say, "Hush." We drove in silence the rest of the way. At the food bank she did not get out of the car, but just stared through the windshield as I unloaded boxes. On the drive back she said something had happened that changed everything. She was ebullient.

In 2012 my friend David Newman invited me to do a weekend workshop with him at Omega Institute. David is a well-known kirtan musician (davidnewmanmusic.com), and his idea was for he and I to alternate sessions. During his session he would lead kirtan chanting, and during mine I would babble on about spiritual matters.

It actually worked quite well, with the participants being whipsawed between the love-and-light of David and his music, and me tossing out confrontational hand grenades. At one point I noticed Jenny Clarke, a Raleigh friend in our SIG group, laying on the floor watching an ant. After the session she wandered in nature the rest of the day. It had happened for her. Her spiritual search had come to an end. A year later, David had his own spiritual realization, which he recounts in his book, *The Timebound Traveler*.

In 2013 at a retreat my wife and I were holding in Asheville, North Carolina, two of our friends, Yvette Om and Erica Bleznak, woke up. It happened for Yvette in the evening when she was alone, but it occurred for Erica right in the middle of a session, and you could see it happening as it came upon her.

At the April 2019 TAT conference a large group of us were sitting in a rapport session that lasted about a half hour. Afterwards I was standing in conversation with some folks when I heard my name called. I looked up and saw Mike Gegenheimer, a Rose student from the early days and current TAT president, still sitting where he'd been during rapport, bent over in his chair, weeping. Someone near him had called me. I immediately knew what was happening.

I sat down close in front of him, knees to knees, and his weeping became uncontrollable. "The absence!" he said. "There's nothing but *absence*."

We sat there for quite awhile as he went in and out of crying jags, interspersed with the only words he seemed capable of: "This *absence*... There's nothing but *absence*." His body was vibrating with violent tremors.

"I can't stop shaking," he said. "This energy..."

I stood him up and hugged him with a vice-like grip. The tremors subsided. "That helped," he said, then sat back down and bent over in tears. "The *absence*..."

The room started filling up again for the next conference session, so I helped Mike to his feet, and walked him to a smaller empty room. As soon as he sat down a new wave hit him, and the pattern continued for quite some time. In between episodes he would ask me what was happening to him. I would only say, "You tell me."

Eventually things settled down for him and I sensed my usefulness was at an end—if indeed I was useful in the first place. I got up to leave and suggested he stay in the room alone for awhile, which he did. When I saw him later, he was beaming.

And so these things do indeed happen when energies combine and multiply each other in a conducive environment. As Jesus said, speaking as God the Father, "Where two or more are gathered in my name, I am in there in the midst of them."

**

That was the end of the original chapter. But because Mike's story was highlighted, I sent him a draft of the chapter for his comments. Reading it triggered memories of further details, which he sent me. He had also previously sent me a paper he wrote about his experience, which is available on searchwithin.org.

Because Mike's realization so obviously and dramatically illuminates the trinity of "energy, rapport and transmission" that is the focus of this chapter, I have consolidated what Mike sent me into the following account of his experience in his own words, and with his permission am including it here:

The April 2019 TAT meeting agenda was inspiring, including speakers Bart Marshall, Paul Hedderman, Norio Kushi and Paul Rezendes, with Phil Consonery leading rapport sittings.

Early Saturday before his talk, Bart and I caught up, and he asked if I prayed. He reminded me that realization comes from outside the mind. The prayer is for the Truth, and the answer is not in the mind. Bart noted as he does in his talks and writings, "Be careful what you wish for," and "Strap on the seat belt." Later that evening Paul Hedderman pounded away in his talk about what he calls "selfing," emphasizing that the self does not act as it thinks it does. Rather, thoughts and action proceed first, and the mind takes credit for it.

Afterwards, I spoke to Norio about a partial realization I'd had 43 years prior, and we talked about the "space between two people" being a creative space, where things can occur that are beyond the mind. I was reminded to just observe the feeling of rapport, and to absolutely trust the feeling of that "creative space." Somehow, the next morning, doing so invited Grace.

The first session Sunday was a rapport sitting. A lot of energy was in evidence. A pole was in the way between Bart and me, so I could not see him visually, but I could feel intense sustained energy coming from that general direction. What was absent and unseen seemed more real to me than what appeared present.

The energy built in intensity. With absolute trust, abandoning all mental reservation, I followed the feeling of rapport "inward" with all those present... Then suddenly, Grace intervened. The biblical phrase, "rending the curtain of the temple" points at what occurred.

My mind, which had been stubbornly hanging on to the belief that it could figure out the Truth, simply released. It was the proverbial unclenching of the fist. What remained was Total Absence, Nothingness, Absolute Emptiness, the Void. I did not exist. Only Total Absence.

I wept uncontrollably. Energy came in waves, and ran through my body, arms and legs like a live electric current. The few people sitting nearby were uncertain what to do. One of them offered what she thought was a comforting comment of mutual understanding, but it only revealed with absolute clarity the abyss between the mind and Awareness. The sadness of this was overwhelming. There is an abyss the mind cannot bridge to what IS.

The shock and sadness of total absence was devastating. Nothing mattered. Across the room, I heard someone mention Richard Rose, and it was immediately obvious to me that Rose never existed, that I never existed—that the world as seen through the mind never existed.

I knew that if Bart were to see me, he would know immediately what was happening. Grace intervened again, and someone pointed him my way. He came over and sat with me, and I knew he was feeling what I was experiencing.

The energy and Awareness continued in waves. I had no urge to think, simply to accept whatever was happening. No more questions. At various times, lines from sutras (oddly enough translated by Bart), and Rose's *The Three Books of the Absolute* passed through with new meaning. Each time it seemed the waves of energy were over, they would come again—intense Awareness, energy, total absence. IT was not done with whatever was to be revealed. Emptiness prevailed. This continued for about an hour.

Bart steadfastly stayed with me, and his presence helped. The best I can articulate it now, is that it was a live example of true Friendship, what Rose describes in his poem, *Friendship*: "Both of us had been to this same place..."

The room started filling up again for the next conference session, so Bart helped me to my feet, and we walked to a quiet library room upstairs. On the way, each step I took was as if stepping into Nothingness. In the library room, the intensity and frequency of the waves of energy, Awareness, total absence continued, then gradually became less frequent and less intense. At one point someone walked through to a restroom that was off the library, and it was like watching a stuffed puppet move through the scene.

Bart and I sat in silence for awhile. At one point I started to get up, then realizing there was nothing to do, I sat back down. I said to Bart, "There's nothing to do," and we laughed like two madmen.

As the Awareness and energy began to lessen in intensity and frequency, Bart left to allow space for solitude. After awhile, I rejoined the meeting and sat in the back corner of the room. When Paul Rezendes finished his session, the last of the day, he came over to see how I was doing and mentioned we could talk later. The compassion and love in this simple gesture began another crescendo of Awareness and energy. Out of exhaustion, the mind and body resisted slightly, and the energy did not again become overwhelming — yet Awareness remained. When the self is gone, only Awareness remains.

In retrospect, nothing "happened." Only a false belief in self was *taken away* by Grace, and All that IS was revealed. No one was there or ever was there — not me, not Rose, not anyone. I intimately understood what Rose was pointing to when he wrote "All that remains is All" in *The Three Books of the Absolute*.

Having heard many talks over the years seeking to convey the perspective of realization, I've realized how little good it does to talk about it unless it inspires action. We are not what our mind believes itself to be. For each person, what it is about their presumed identity that stands in the way of seeing what IS, is likely quite different — different from what needed to be subtracted from me, or more accurately, seen through and taken from me, and different from the path of others whose accounts one might read.

There is a great paradox here, which makes no sense to the relative mind. I can't express fully the mystery of Awareness and Absolute Emptiness. Both exist forever, in an Eternal Moment. Nothingness, just as Awareness, defies words. Many words have been written and spoken for something so simple, something the mind simply cannot understand. Bart addresses this paradox in his book, *Verses Regarding True Nature*. The 29th verse provides great insight into this paradox:

*Why is there something rather than nothing?*
*Awareness.*

*Presence, Life, Aliveness, God...*
*It has many names.*
*Timeless, ever new —*
*It can be called Eternal Life.*
*There is no reason or explanation.*
*It just is.*

*It is not ancient — it arises only Now.*
*It is not distant — it is nearer*
*than you are to yourself.*

*It is the substance of Void*
*and Everything is made of it.*

And so I just want to say to those seeking to know the Self, the Truth, there is hope. Your efforts are not in vain. There is a subtractive path that involves working on yourself, and with others. There is no formula. There is nothing to fear. It is always there, waiting, present in every moment, waiting for an opening of Between-ness where Grace might intervene.

May Grace befall every seeker who seeks Truth without reservation, who seeks Truth for its own sake.

— Mike Gegenheimer

# Between-ness

Do we have the capacity to become who or what we want to be? Is life a tightly scripted play we can only watch unfold, or does the individual *will* have the power to change directions and outcomes — and if so, what are the mechanics for this?

There are two main things I think worth studying. One is how to wake up from this dream we call life. The other is how to get what we want within it. As it happens, the formula for both is the same. It's a formula we might say for *aligning will and destiny*. By *will* I mean the personal will, the ego-will that says, "I want this, I don't want that." By *destiny* I mean the sense we have that life and events unfold according to some higher will or imperative — call it God's will or karma or whatever — that often seems to operate with total disregard for personal will.

When you get right down to it scientifically, how much actual free will, how much real *choice* can I possibly have? I was born into a life situation with strict definitions and rigid boundaries (white male American b. 1946 to middle class college-educated parents, etc.). My body and brain, talents and intelligence, are dictated by DNA. My thoughts and moods are highly influenced by chemicals secreted autonomically, and by the events that swirl around me. And when I look closely, it seems I have little or no control over the happenings in my life. Even when I think I'm taking decisive action, I get the feeling it's only because events have conspired to make it impossible for me to do otherwise.

And yet, there is a persistent feeling that my thoughts and actions do have an effect on the paths and outcomes of my life. And this feeling is supported by the great teachers in history. In the opening verses of the *Dhammapada*, for instance, Buddha says:

> *The experience of life is created by mind.*
> *Thought precedes experience.*
> *If one speaks and acts with a clouded mind,*
> *suffering follows, as the wheel of the ox-cart follows the ox.*
>
> *The experience of life is created by mind.*
> *Thought precedes experience.*
> *If one speaks and acts with a clear mind,*
> *contentment follows like a faithful shadow.*

In this chapter we'll take a new look at the age-old debate of free will versus predetermination, and examine the possibility of a subtle interplay between the two that can be mastered by the individual and directed towards any end—from worldly wealth to spiritual enlightenment.

If the great teachers are to be believed, what we experience as lack of free will, as fate, as destiny, is the momentum of our habitual thoughts, beliefs, fears and desires—what could be called *karma*—which is incredibly powerful because it's like a breeder-reactor on autopilot. Though we are caught in its grip, we're not aware it is the mechanism of our fate, and so we make no effort to control or manipulate it.

Our conscious efforts to improve our lot in life are limited to actions in the outer world—work, education, connections... All of which are important, but are they the actual cause of the results and outcomes that manifest? Or do things happen "by themselves" in accordance with an unseen mechanism, and we just take undeserved credit or blame for them?

If destiny is truly driven by our thoughts, beliefs, fears and desires, perhaps addressing it at this level is worth the effort. Perhaps this is where we have maximum leverage. But how is this done? The method is simple but not easy—change the mix. Cultivate right thinking, challenge limiting beliefs, overcome blocks and fears, weed out extraneous desires. As a part of this effort, it's also important to learn how to *hold your head* as you work with this mechanism, and as you live your life.

There's a place between caring and not caring, between desire and indifference, and if you inhabit that place with humility and power, your will and God's will become one and the same. Richard Rose called this state *between-ness*, and I've not found a better term for it. It is difficult to understand intellectually, and attempting deliberate practice is like trying to nail mercury to a table, but when one stumbles onto it, magic happens.

Between-ness is the intentional manipulation of the thought stream as it passes through so as to influence Creation in your favor—to perceive the subtle workings and come into alignment with them. It's a tool of the illusory *separate self* to get its way. It taps into the laws that govern the mechanism of the dream of Creation, and so could be called miraculous. It is an extremely subtle and elusive skill, not easily mastered, but its principles have been discovered by people in every century from all parts of the earth, and used to influence their dreamworld circumstances.

A master of between-ness can manifest very quickly, and people call it a miracle. Jesus was a master of between-ness. All the *siddhis* — the powers listed in the *Yoga Sutras* — are examples of what can be accomplished by mastering between-ness. Patanjali called it *samyama*. The principle is simple: An unconflicted intention with no countermanding beliefs, given 100% attention in a state of between-ness will manifest immediately. Truly, you can move mountains.

One does not need to be a master, however, to benefit from employing between-ness, especially if we don't expect instant results. Most of us are not interested in moving mountains — they look fine just where they are — but acquiring things like more money, the perfect mate or an exciting job may be of great interest. Employing between-ness to these ends is just as effective, though usually the manifestations appear more slowly — at a pace our constricting belief systems will support.

Everything in Creation is equally miraculous. It is only when something crosses a certain threshold of speed or credulity that we acknowledge it as a miracle, and we don't believe we ourselves are capable of causing miracles. If I voice my desire for a certain job and the phone immediately rings with an offer out of the blue that exceeds my wildest dreams, that might be more than my belief system can accept. But if I go on interviews and get the same job, that I can accept — even though it is no less a miracle.

Everyone is living the exact life they want right now. Based on the confusing mix of beliefs, fears and desires you are presenting to the Divine, the life you are now living is the only possible manifestation that takes them all into account to the exact degree they are felt. This mix of beliefs, fears and desires has created a momentum in your life that is difficult to manipulate, but it can be done. Challenge beliefs, confront fears, focus desire.

Between-ness can also be used in the pursuit of Self-Realization — in the attempt to *wake up* from the dream. When used for this purpose Rose called it *Ultimate Between-ness*.

After Self-Realization the (former) person lives in what could be called a state of "permanent" between-ness. Your preferences remain much the same, but you have less desire to push for them or try to make them happen. You still root for things to go your way, and do whatever work is required on your part, but you'd much rather have what you're "supposed" to have, than what the character thinks it wants.

Destiny is a symbiotic process. My job as an apparently separate entity is to desire that which I feel is in my best interest and work to achieve it. This is step one of between-ness. Step two is to have faith, have confidence that my desire will indeed become reality. Step three is to hold in my heart deep gratitude for everything I have right now, before my desire is fulfilled—to be grateful for everything *as it is*.

This leads to the fourth state—*indifference* as to whether my desire ever comes to fruition or not, to surrender to "Thy will be done." At this point one of two things will happen. You will either get what you intend to have, or you will be shown that your intention is not in your best interest—is not in alignment with your highest destiny. Either outcome is equally valuable. Many times I've ended up being extremely grateful I did not get something I thought I wanted—and learned a lot about myself in the process.

And so, living in a state of between-ness does not necessarily result in the character getting its way more often. Because in this state one realizes that what "I" want and what God wants are not different. God's will has become my will, and my will has become God's will. It all comes back around. I may have discovered the formula for getting anything I want, but along the way, also discovered I only want what God wills that I have—what best serves my highest destiny and purpose.

One who has discovered his True Nature as the infinite clear emptiness of God is not surprised by this.

"But how is all this possible? How can my thoughts and intentions influence the workings of the manifest world?" It's possible because there is no difference between thought and world. Creation is thought on display, nothing more. It has no substance whatever. The world is a thought-movie projected into a cloud of clear smoke. The point from which you imagine you are viewing and experiencing it is the projector. Behind the projector—the nothingness behind your head—is the Source, the Absolute, the Void. That's how close this stuff is. It's all happening right where you are and nowhere else.

All of this—the world, the universe, all appearances—has no substance at all. None. Or, you could say it has the substance of thought, because it *is* thought. This is why and how your thoughts create your world. They are one and the same thing. There is no

164

difference between a thought and an object. They are made of the same no-stuff. All experience is thought-experience. Nothing is actually happening. The world, the universe we experience, is not a "real" world of separate solid objects, but rather a virtual world transpiring in appearance only.

Intention, Confidence, Gratitude, Indifference. This is the formula for Between-ness. It's a way of holding your head that allows the ego-self to participate in the manifestation/projection of the world, and to some degree influence it. It is an ephemeral, indefinable state that must be *felt*, that must be learned by literally *feeling* your way into it.

But how?

## ULTIMATE BETWEEN-NESS WORKSHOP

At the September 2007 TAT Conference the theme was "What am I Becoming?" My session there was a workshop I called, "Aligning Will and Destiny: The Effect of Intent and Between-ness on the Manifesting Mind." It was a hit with attendees, and at their request I later wrote up my notes into a transcript entitled, "Ultimate Between-ness," and made it available online. I've heard from many people since then that it has been of great help to them, and so I'm including it here in slightly modified form:

**

The question this weekend invites us to ask is, "What am I becoming?" It's a good question, a good seed for self-inquiry, but as with any question or statement, we should look at the assumptions it's based on before we address it on the level of content or meaning. In this case there are two key ideas to examine. One is contained in the word "I," which of course invites the question, "What is 'I'?" The other is the concept of "becoming," which implies a movement or evolution from one state to another.

The highest teachings tell us that the concept of "I" is a false idea, a mis-identification that vanishes in the moment of Awakening, and that the universe this false "I" experiences is but a *seeming*, a mirage, a dream playing out in the timeless, changeless *presence* of pure Awareness. And You are That. You are pure Awareness. You are already and always All That Is. What could you possibly become?

So in the realm of who you *really* are, the idea of movement or evolution has no meaning. Any ideas of becoming must therefore necessarily take place within the illusion, and be experienced by the "false-I," the dream character.

But false or not, this dream character is complex beyond imagination, and has a tremendous desire to improve its lot and "become" more than it perceives itself to be. It wants to become successful, admired, courageous, rich, happy... Sometimes it even wants to become *enlightened* — to discover its True Nature.

But how much, if any, control does this vague collection of thoughts we call "I" have over its dream life? Is the dream mechanism rigid and fixed, or is it possible for the dream character to bend it to its will?

What we're going to do today is experiment with a certain way of *holding your head* so that your desires become manifest in your life experience. Richard Rose referred to this as *between-ness*, which is as good a term as I've heard for it. Rose sometimes spoke of between-ness as living "without fear of failure or hope of gain," which in a way says it all, but we've got 90 minutes to fill here, so we can't just leave it at that.

Between-ness can be used to get anything a person wants in life, from the most mundane to the most exalted. As an experiment, Rose even used it when playing poker to get the cards he wanted dealt to him. He also taught that between-ness could and should be employed as a means to Self-Realization. In fact, he said, "Finding Reality will only take you as long as it takes you to master between-ness." Used in this way he referred to it as *Ultimate Between-ness*.

I never really understood the concept of between-ness, and as a seeker I never consciously employed it. But as some of you know, three years ago I had a Realization that ended my seeking, and in the time since then I've come to the conclusion that what finally did the trick was that somehow I stumbled into a state of Ultimate Between-ness, and that this state proved magnetic to Grace.

Which is not to say that in any way I caused it to happen. Realization is always an accident, a gift that has nothing to do with worthiness or effort. And yet it seems there is not a total disconnect between desire and actuality. In fact just the opposite. An intense, unconflicted desire for Truth may be the single most important component of the spiritual path.

Between-ness is a unified state that is difficult to describe without breaking it down into composite elements that can be talked about individually, but it is much more than the sum of these elements. It is also much simpler than it seems when we dissect and describe it—so don't get lost in details. What we're after today is to get a taste of a complete *way of being* that we'll call *between-ness*.

Mostly I'd like to focus on the practical aspects—how to feel what it is, how to live it in daily life. But if we have time we can also touch on the mechanics of it—what's going on behind the curtain, so to speak.

As we talk about the various aspects of this mechanism it will be helpful to have a specific desire in mind to work with, rather than trying to retain the principles in the abstract. So let's do that now. Pick a desire you want fulfilled. It can be anything—a specific object, money, health, lover, Truth, anything.

Some of you may have a burning desire on the tip of your tongue, others may not be so sure. Regardless, let's take a few minutes to sit quietly and ask: "What do I really want?" This is not an invitation to choose a deeper or more esoteric desire, although that may happen. The important thing here, as in all self-inquiry, is honesty. Pick something that has real juice for you. Pick something that seems out of reach at the moment, but not out of the realm of possibility. Something you have the *capacity to receive*.

As you ask, "What do I really want?" fully expect to get an answer. Wait for it. And as you listen for an answer be aware of your mental state—your *expectant stillness*. Bob Fergesen calls this the *listening attention*. It's a good thing to become aware of and employ.

Also, as a desire surfaces, think about whether it may be a symptom or example of a deeper desire—whether there is a more basic underlying desire, or perhaps a bigger meta-desire that better expresses what you really want.

*Now write down your desire as a complete sentence starting with the word "I."*

### Intention

I've broken between-ness down into four elements so that we can talk about the subtleties of it more specifically. They are: Intention, Confidence, Gratitude and Indifference.

The first order of business in fulfilling your desires is to know what you want and ask for it—to have a firm *intention*. When employing between-ness your intention should be clear, simple, focused—no complicated caveats or if-then-else's. Be absolutely unequivocal in your desire. If you find yourself feeling a bit uneasy, perhaps even afraid that you might get what you want if you threw all your powers at it, that's okay. Perfectly normal. Good information to know, isn't it? That you are afraid of success in the area of your greatest desire? Any chance that might be why it ain't here yet? Maybe dissolving that fear is the highest and best use of your time.

When Rose was experimenting with between-ness playing poker, he always said out loud what card he wanted. "Steinie, deal me a jack," he'd say, and Steinie would deal him a jack. So let's hear what you want. *[Everyone speaks their desire out loud.]*

Great. Now let's refine the wording. Everyone's sentence began with the words, I *want* such and such. So the first thing I'd like you to do is use the word *intend* instead of "want" in the sentence, and change the grammar to make it work. Notice that your desire immediately shifts into a higher gear. I can say "I want to be rich" for years and never feel moved to do anything about it. But saying "I intend to be rich" implies a commitment, charts a course. Do you dare *intend* to have your deepest desire fulfilled?

But it's also important to edit out of your intention any implication that the fulfillment of it is *up to you*. In other words, rather than say "I intend to earn a million dollars next year," say something like, "I intend that my net worth increase by a million dollars by the end of next year." This does not mean you should do nothing to help it along, but it places the emphasis properly. It subtly acknowledges a higher power and puts the heat on that higher power to come through with the goods.

This may be a good point to address the aspect of *action*. Setting aside for a moment the question of whether or not our actions actually cause things to happen, it's important to note that at the very least, our actions influence our thoughts, our *way of being*, and so should be consistent with our deepest intentions and desires. All the horses should be pulling in the same direction.

Once you put forth a firm intention, your actions must henceforth be in line with your intention. Your actions will not be what brings it about. It is happening here, now, in the *thought*, but you must act in alignment with the thought, do what you think you need to do to make it happen. *Work as if it all depends on you, pray as if it all depends on God.*

Actions create acceptable explanations for what comes about "magically." They also strengthen your capacity for confidence, for certainty of outcome. What really is happening is that the object or experience of desire is manifesting spontaneously out of thin air, as it

168

were, but that is unacceptable to your belief system and so there is the need for an acceptable cover story — *action*.

Next let's get rid of any vagueness in your intention. Make it precise, specific. Make the meaning unavoidably clear, unequivocal. No wiggle room or caveats. Make it direct, simply stated — a mantra not a dissertation. If you get the wording exactly right on a deeply felt desire, it might give you a chill or emotional reaction, maybe even scare you. That's a good sign, a sign you're getting close to the bone. Okay let's read them again. *[Everyone speaks their revised intention and they are discussed individually.]*

Some common things to look for in streamlining your intention include hidden negatives and constricting prescriptions. For instance, in an earlier session today someone's intention was, "I intend to experience loss gracefully." While that may be a noble sentiment and a valuable practice, it is not a good intention because it contains a hidden negative. In order for that desire to be fulfilled, *loss* must continually be introduced into that person's life.

Constricting prescriptions in an intention can be very subtle. For example, someone said they intend to double their salary. But that has the hidden prescription of having the money come via *salary*, which implies a *job* (which in this case he disliked). What he really wants is twice as much *income* — no matter where it comes from.

The entity or force we are addressing with our intentions — call it God, Higher Self, Universe, whatever — is very literal. Be sure to ask for exactly what you want, with no room for misunderstanding. This, of course, requires that *you* know exactly what you want, which is really the essence of it.

Another intention — a common one in the TAT environment — is the intention to "awaken," "become enlightened," "have a realization," "know Truth," "get a final answer," that sort of thing. It's an especially tough one to word effectively because, unlike intending to have more money or better health, with this one we have no idea what we are really asking for, or how it relates to the "I" who is asking.

But if we get it right, if we intend this with power and immediacy in a way that speaks to our deepest yearnings, we may feel it as if for the first time — no matter how long we've been at this thing. In one of our earlier sessions this happened for a long-time seeker, who began to weep as he heard himself speak it out loud in no uncertain terms.

Okay, so now you have a clearly stated desire or intention. At this point you need to look at whatever might be countermanding your desire. This requires more time for introspection than we have in this setting, but on your own, think deeply about the roadblocks you yourself have set up to prevent the fulfillment of your intention. Consider also your *capacity to receive* what you say you desire. Is your internal and external life in alignment with the fulfillment of this desire? Has the ground been properly prepared?

The thing is, you are already getting exactly what you want in life, whether it seems like it or not. We all have hundreds of desires, large and small, many of them in conflict with each other in one way or another. Plus we have a whole set of fears (which are really just desires felt in the negative, and vice versa) thrown into the mix. And so, given this morass of cross-collateralized, conflicting fears and desires, the Universe is generating the only life experience that resolves and incorporates them all to the degree each is felt.

This is the source of your "destiny." On the one hand it has tremendous, seemingly insurmountable momentum and we feel helpless in its grasp. On the other, we notice it seems to respond to even small changes in the fear/desire mix.

You are right now living the only life possible given the current mix of your fears and desires. In order to alter or streamline destiny by force of desire, by force of will, you need to not only have a focused intention, but to see clearly what you are doing to sabotage yourself and prevent it from happening. Confront fears, limit desires. The world will open its arms.

## Confidence

Which brings us to the second element of between-ness: *confidence*. Other words that are just as good or better for this are *faith* and *certainty*. They all point to the same thing. If you harbor secret doubts about the mechanism, or have misgivings about your worthiness to receive, or ability to handle it when your desires manifest, it will slow things down to the degree of that doubt.

If, on the other hand you have 100% faith that your desire is going to manifest, and 100% confidence in your capacity to receive, then it's full speed ahead.

The message here is, don't just hope you get what you want, be certain it is coming. Your attitude should be that once you intend it, it's a done deal. Case closed. It's on the way. Intention and faith go hand in hand. Together they are like the good seed. Gratitude and indifference make up the fertile ground.

## Gratitude

To live in a state of gratitude is not always an easy thing, but there is no more powerful practice for getting what you want from the Universe. In keeping with the occult dictum, "As above, so below," the principle involved is easily observed on the human level. To whom would you rather give a new toy, a child who always thanks you and loves everything you give him, or a child who looks at everything with disdain and always wants something different?

In the practice of between-ness we feel gratitude on two levels. One is tied to the faith we have that we are in the process of getting what we ask for. We are so confident it is on the way that we're already grateful for it.

The other is an immense gratitude for our life, the world, and everything in it *just as it is*. This doesn't mean we necessarily go around being consciously thankful all the time, even though that's a good practice. When you see beauty in "ordinary" things, notice a small kindness, experience love, joy, or a sense of connectedness— these experiences include unspoken expressions of gratitude. The opposite is to live in a state of constant worry and complaint, which unfortunately is all too common.

So, we can begin to see what an incredible balancing act we are talking about with between-ness. On the one hand we are dissatisfied enough with our current state that we have an intense yearning, a powerful intention to improve it. While at the same time we feel overwhelmingly blessed to be experiencing things just as they are.

You could call this *dissatisfaction without complaint*. It's okay to want more, to want things to be better. But that's no reason to piss and moan about your life as it is, or to engage in recreational angst about all the bad things that could happen. For one thing, it's unnecessary wear and tear on the body, but more to the point here, it's counterproductive to the fulfillment of your desires.

## Indifference

In the confluence of desire and gratitude there is a quiet spot untouched by either—an island of high indifference. Desire and gratitude flow by, but you remain unmoved. It is a place where you honest-to-God don't care. A place untouched by anything this world has dished out or offered. A place where you know beyond a shadow of a doubt that none of it matters anyway. You could also call this *acceptance* or *surrender*. There is not even a thought of desiring or being grateful. Intention and gratitude run in the background while the mind is clear, and indifferent to outcome.

Intention, confidence, gratitude, indifference. Between-ness. If I were to recommend one thing to study, practice and master in life it would be this. Whether you want to be rich or enlightened or both, this is where your efforts are best spent.

Do not be discouraged when the world does not immediately start obeying your whims. You are at the helm of an oil tanker under full steam at sea. Direction changes happen slowly. Your ship won't turn on a dime. But with practice your life will increasingly come into alignment with your topmost desires, and sometimes—if your beliefs can accept it—mountains will move.

### The Playing Field

If what we are saying here is true—and the highest teachings all report that it is—then we must ask ourselves, "What is the nature of a reality that operates on, and supports such magic?" I mean, we are talking about spontaneous creation, creation "on demand." To say the least this is inconsistent with what we've been taught to believe—that we are born into a vast pre-existing universe of separate solid objects that have evolved to their present state over billions of years.

Again it is the teachings of the masters that provide the best source of information on how to think about this, where we should look for the truth about Creation. In the first verse of the *Tao Te Ching*, Lao Tsu tells us:

*That which can be perceived is not the timeless That.*
*That which can be named is not the nameless One.*

*The source of heaven and earth is without form or substance.*
*Naming creates the ten thousand things.*

*When desire is absent, the mystery is obvious.*
*When desire occurs, creation unfolds.*

*Mystery and creation arise from the same source.*
*The source is emptiness.*
*Void within void. The realm of Tao.*

Rose sometimes spoke of this Totality of Tao as being *Mind*. To talk about it he divided Mind into three aspects, but it exists as a singularity — *Mind*. The three aspects are *Manifested* Mind, *Unmanifested* Mind, and *Manifesting* Mind.

Manifested Mind is everything you experience as life, as the world — including *yourself*. It is mind-stuff made perceivable by the body and senses — which are also just mind-stuff. In terms of your immediate experience, Manifested Mind is what you perceive to be "before" you right now — everything you see, hear, think, believe and perceive. Everything. But, *That which can be perceived is not the timeless That*.

The "timeless That" is Unmanifested Mind. It is Source, Void, Emptiness, Absolute, No-thing. In terms of your immediate experience it is "behind" you. The "back of your head" is blown wide open to the Absolute, the Source, the Unknowable. It's that close.

What "projects" appearances *in* Source is Manifesting Mind. In terms of your immediate experience, it is located at ground zero of your experience of "Here." You could say it is behind the eyes, or in the heart, or in the solar plexus — wherever you experience *I Am*. This is Manifesting Mind — the light, the projector.

Everything you seek is *Here*, at no distance from *You*. *You* are the Source of All. *All That Is* is happening right now, right where *You* are and nowhere else. *You* are the One Awareness. There is no other.

But how is it possible for a dream character to "know" this? How can it witness its own non-existence? It is a question that has importance only in the dream. All that is important to know is that, inexplicably, somehow it *is* possible, and that nothing separates the dream character from this realization other than its own refusal to *See* what eternally stares it in the "face."

Since my experience, people have asked what I think is the key, what I would recommend as a practice and so on. I've heard myself say many things in response, not all of them consistent with each other — at least not on the level of words. Partly this is because my responses are specific to the person asking, and to what comes up in the moment.

But mostly it's because I have no idea what works. Nothing works. Each person's path is absolutely unique — though what is "found" is always the same. Nothing we do as dream-character seekers can possibly cause Realization. The mechanism is just not in place for that.

A few weeks ago, however, someone replied to an email I had sent, asking about what I'd said. And as I re-read what I'd written, I realized it came as close to what I think about "success" in the spiritual search as I have been able to articulate:

"I think the key is intent. If a seeker's intent is to become the Truth at all costs, then it will happen. All the reading and practices we involve ourselves with are useful only to the extent that they build this intent. If a burning desire for enlightenment is not present, no amount of meditation and practices will help. If it is present, no meditation or practices are necessary.

"Paradoxically, this burning desire for Truth can't be a reaction against a life we object to and are dissatisfied with. It must be in conjunction with an immense gratitude for what we have been given, with a "surrender" that asks for no divine rescue or special mercies. When a person who wants Truth more than life falls in love with *what is*, it happens."

"Man is asked to make of himself what he is supposed to become to fulfill his destiny."

—Paul Tillich

# The Single Eye

Jesus said, "Unless you become as a little child, you shall not see the kingdom of God." What did he mean by this? Children have many attributes. Which of them was he referring to? What aspect of child-ness was he recommending we acquire?

For me, this becomes more clear if we use the word *infant* in the quote, and expand it slightly to, "Unless you see the world as an infant sees it, you will not see the kingdom of God." I also think of this quote as being tightly related to another of Jesus' sayings, "If thine eye be single, your whole body is full of light."

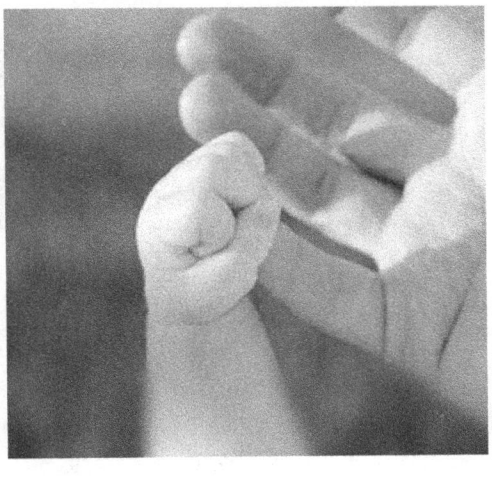

An infant has no sense of "me" and "not-me." When it opens its eyes, a world appears. When it closes its eyes there is no world. Its experience of the world is contained entirely in a vaguely circular viewfinder of sight, like looking through a spyglass that encompasses the entirety of its peripheral vision. This is the *single eye*. Whatever comes into that view, *exists*. When the object goes out of that view, it does not exist. The infant has no concept of what is in receipt of that view — no sense of self, or eyes, or head — and has no thoughts about anything not in view. Its experience is of being an emptiness that is quite literally *filled by the world* — a world of *light*.

As adults we are in receipt of that same view — emptiness filled by a world of light — but we were taught early on to accept and believe an alternate explanation for our perceptions. We believe beyond a shadow of doubt that we in fact do have a head, even though we've never actually seen it, and that our visual perceptions come to us through "two blobs of jelly in a meatball," as Douglas Harding says.

"But, but, I've seen my head," we protest. No, all we've ever seen is reflections that come into view as part of the world that fills the emptiness of the single eye. Our "head" only exists as part of the "external" world. We only and forever see the world from a first-person point-of-view (POV), that does not include a face or head. Where we believe those to reside, we experience clear emptiness, though we argue mightly that they do in fact exist unseen, despite the in-your-"face" evidence to the contrary.

For some children the programming does not take hold right away. Someone told the story of telling his three-year old daughter to go wash her face. When he looked in the bathroom later, she was on a stool washing the mirror where her face appeared. Another little girl was looking at a yearbook of her preschool class. She recognized every picture except one—hers. She said, "I've never seen that girl at school."

The teachings of Douglas Harding point directly at this truth of our situation, and use it as an entry point to Self-Realization. It is a very powerful teaching that can be experienced intellectually, experientially, and spiritually. On the intellectual level, after I'd denied it for awhile, I eventually had to admit that, yeah, I've never seen my actual face or head, only so-called reflections of it in mirrors and shiny surfaces "out there" in the world. "Ha ha, isn't that funny. But just because I can't see it doesn't mean it's not there."

The first time I "got it" was reading an article by Harding in which he said, "Look at your hand. Are you in your hand, or is your hand in you?" Before I looked I "knew" the answer to this silly question. But when I did look I was struck dumb by how wrong I was. It was instantly and viscerally obvious that my sense of "I" was not in that skin-bound morass of bone, sinew, blood and muscle. "I" was the *view* in which it was appearing! I exclaimed out loud, "I'm not in this body!" My wife looked over at me from the couch and shook her head. *There he goes again...*

On a later occasion, I was having dinner with a friend when this truth displayed itself even more dramatically. Suddenly, in mid-conversation, my experience of the world left my "head" and traveled around the restaurant, perceiving things from a variety of angles and perspectives. It was exhilarating and fascinating, but also a bit disconcerting, and after a short time I felt I really should be getting back. Wouldn't want to forget the way, you know. Instantly I again became confined to my "head."

On Flight 99, while I was in the throes of "enlightenment," I was headless emptiness filled by the world the entire time, and in the years since, it has settled in to become my constant experience. Whatever fills the emptiness of the single eye, is what "I" am.

When I talk about this to others, I frequently use the metaphor of video games, particularly first-person "shooter" games, where all you see is the weapon moving through an ever-changing world of targets. The face and head of the shooter is never seen, and in fact there is not even any code for "shooter's head" in the game.

The pictures used here are from a game called "Mirror's Edge," which is a first-person POV game without weapons. The protagonist is Faith, a courier who maneuvers through an urban landscape with exciting parkour moves, and you only see what she sees from her POV. This is our experience as well—absent the parkour moves for most of us.

The only way we know what Faith looks like is when we see her reflected in a shiny surface coded into the game. This, too, is our common experience. We carry around in our mind a vague idea of what we "look like" based on reflections and photographs that only exist in what we believe to be the "external" world. We have never seen, and never can see, the thing itself. Those who have no spiritual curiosity might shrug this off an as anomaly, as an amusing trick of perception, but totally logical because as everyone knows, "I"

exist *in* my head and *behind* my face, so of course I can't see them. Those who are on a mission to discover Truth, however, might see in this very profound conundrum an invitation to further investigation.

The video game metaphor is also useful when discussing another related aspect of "reality," what I call *creation on demand*.

Every culture has it's creation stories and myths. In the so-called civilized western world of today, there are two main competing creation stories. One is Genesis, in which a god who is both all-powerful and simultaneously quite flawed and petty, creates the world and man out of nothing in six days, then is so exhausted he has to take a day off. The other is Evolution, in which a mysterious Big Bang kicks things off and billions of years later man magically evolves from pond scum to the intelligent wonder he is now.

Let me tell you a couple different stories, or *alternate explanations*. And as you scoff and sniff at the preposterousness of them, I invite you judge these two widely accepted stories with the same skepticism.

In one story the world is a computer program, a simulation, a multi-sensory holographic virtual extravaganza of monumental proportions and complexity. The computer, of course, is not a metal and plastic box, but rather, the entirety of the energy field and plasma that "fills" the Universe. Interestingly, the simulation theory is beginning to be proposed by Elon Musk and other tech luminaries.

In the second story, the world exists only in the *imagination of God*, and life, as the old song says, "is but a dream." This is the story that most closely tracks with my experience.

The first two widely accepted stories posit a physical world — an infinitely old, infinitely vast universe of tangible material objects separate from each other—a world of fixed dimensions and strict rules about what is and is not possible. The second two stories describe a virtual, intangible world of infinite possibilities that can morph and change, appear and disappear on a dime. *Creation on demand.*

In a way, these two alternate explanations are not different. If, as we have been discussing, God is Everything and Everything is

178

God, the energy/plasma computer running the simulation is God, and so perhaps we can say that what we are calling "simulation," is simply the mechanism of God's imagination.

In the Bible we find this:

*In the beginning was the Word,*
*and the Word was with God,*
*and the Word was God.* – John 1:1

Since this is obviously a pre-language paradigm, we can safely substitute the close synonym *sound* for *Word*. What creates sound? Vibration.

In the original Greek version of the Bible the phrase translated as *in the beginning* also means *at the foundation of everything*. And what has been translated as the *word*, is more literally the *verb*, which is related to vibration, as in re*verb*eration. So an alternate, and perhaps more accurate, translation of John 1:1 would be:

*At the foundation of everything is vibration,*
*and vibration is of God,*
*and vibration is God.*

Not coincidentally, this lines up nicely with Nikola Tesla's famous quote: "If you want to find the secrets of the Universe, think in terms of energy, frequency and vibration." And so we might imagine that the concept of vibration in John also includes energy and frequency, and that what we call "God" is this trinity of energy/frequency/vibration, and that it is not only present in every nook and cranny of the universe – of all universes – but that it is in fact the thing itself. God is not *in* everything, God *is* everything. There is *only* God.

There is a common science experiment where sand is placed on a vibrating metal plate, and the vibration causes it to form into a pattern. Any slight change in the frequency of the vibration

changes the pattern. Might this be a clue to the mechanism of Creation? Energy (electricity in this case), frequency, and vibration.

How do the *single eye* and *creation on demand* relate to each other? Again, let's look at the video game metaphor. Nothing actually exists except as a possibility in the code, and the player of the game only sees that part of the code activated by the headless single eye of the protagonist. Everything else in the game only exists as a *possibility* in the code. When the protagonist "enters" a room, that possibility manifests, and when he leaves that room, it "goes away," back to just being a possibility in the code. The room does not continue to exist while awaiting his return.

Is this different from our experience of life? When I turn to the right, a certain view happens. When I turn to the left a different view happens. Is the view on the right still there when I'm looking left? It is impossible to validate through experience that it is. No matter how fast I spin around, I can never experience what's "behind" me.

Our direct, first-person experience is that the universe operates as creation-on-demand, just like a video game. But we reject our direct experience in favor of an unprovable belief in an infinitely old, infinitely vast universe of solid separate objects that exists whether anyone's looking or not.

Seriously, though, what all-powerful Creator in its right mind would opt for such a high-maintenance solution, when it has the power to just "make it so" whenever needed? When it can imagine the world into being with the barest glance?

Seeing the world as a pre-existing solid "reality" that exists whether I look at it or not, is not seeing the world as a little child sees it, and thus, according to Jesus at least, is not perceiving the kingdom of God.

My experience is that Creation expands in the direction of looking, and when I'm not looking it disappears. Is your raw *experience* — absent all beliefs — different from this?

My experience is that where my "head" supposedly exists, is actually a wide circumference of emptiness roughly defined by my "peripheral vision," and that this emptiness is filled by the world. Is your actual *experience* — absent all beliefs — different than this?

By the way, objections that you can feel your face and head with your hands, or vaguely see your nose out of the corner of your eye, are easily handled in the code. Our crude, man-made virtual reality games do this quite convincingly, in fact.

This "new" way of seeing — or more accurately, admitting what you've always seen but denied and explained away — does not come easily, and is especially difficult to arrive at through thinking alone. So Douglas Harding devised a series of what he calls

180

"experiments" to bypass thinking and possibly trigger the sudden perceptual shift that makes it all self-evident. I'm not going to go into these experiments here because they are well-documented in Douglas' books, and in the work of his students, like Richard Lang, all of which I highly recommend.

As I mentioned in the "Flight 99" chapter, the conclusive spiritual occurrence that happened to "me" on the plane was preceded by spending four days with Douglas and his experiments. Needless to say, I'm immensely grateful to have encountered him and am a huge fan of his work.

Shortly after my experience I wrote him a "thank you" note (talk about an understatement), which, as I said in the letter, fell as far short of the mark as an arrow shot at the moon. But I did the best I could, and it began a correspondence between us that lasted until his death a few years later, then continued on a bit afterwards with his wife Catherine.

Like Rose, Harding was totally committed to passing this on, and his work has contributed to the awakening of many seekers. As a tribute to Douglas, and hopefully as a helpful goad to you, I will end this chapter with his last word to me in person, which I think applies nicely to the transition from the old explanations of existence to the single-eye/creation-on-demand explanation:

Simplify!

182

# Self-Inquiry

*Know Thyself.*
— Oracle of Delphi

As spiritual seekers we commonly think and say that what we're up to is "looking for answers." We have become suspicious of the standard explanations taught by science and religion of who or what we truly are and how we come to be, and now we have questions. This is an essential element in a serious spiritual search, and one that is missing from the mindset of the vast majority of the population.

Most people believe what they've been told in school and church and other approved institutions, and by all manner of "experts" paraded out by mass media. They live in a state of belief and have no questions. So to arrive at a place of doubt where you begin to seriously question all you've been told, is to take a quantum leap beyond the hypnotized masses.

Enlightenment is not possible in a state of belief. Beliefs build a rigid, constricting paradigm that is a formidable barrier against Truth. Truth will not squeeze itself into *any* paradigm of belief, no matter how high-minded, profound, or anchored in tradition and scripture. The surest defense against Truth is to think you already know — or worse, to believe without question people who say or imply that *they* know.

This includes *me*, by the way. I've had a direct experience of True Nature that settled things for me, and allows me to speak and write with confidence about what was found, but do not take what I say to be true. The only thing my words, or anyone's words are good for, is to possibly inspire and help you in your own search. Unless and until you've had a *direct experience of Truth*, you've got nothing.

The seeker's task is to *unbelieve the world*. Where once you looked upon a world you "understood," now you admit you see only mystery. The spiritual path is not to accumulate more and more knowledge and understanding, but to back away from what you think you already know, and to live in a state of *unbelief*. In this state of innocence, of becoming as a little child, we quite naturally have questions.

In essence they are the same questions we had as a child, but that were satisfied then by pre-packaged explanations that killed our curiosity. Having arrived at this state of unbelief, we are back in

183

childhood again, but this time we want the Real Answers. The pursuit of the real answers is often referred to as *Self-Inquiry*, and is one of the most powerful practices seekers of Truth have at their disposal.

The basic process of Self-Inquiry is to obsessively ask questions that can only be answered with a *direct experience of Truth*. They cannot be answered in words or in any way that is "understandable" to the mind. You are asking the Divine questions that can only be answered by *the realization your true Self*.

The iconic Self-Inquiry question is "Who am I?" and it's a good one. It's even better phrased as "What am I?" because *who* implies a person, and thus strays into belief in individual personhood. Other good Self-Inquiry questions are:

What is witnessing this life?
What's really going on here?
What is my True Nature?
What is God?
What does it feel like to be God?

And many others you may think of that are even better for you. The important thing is that it's a question you have a burning desire to have answered, and that it can only be answered by direct experience, not satisfied by any intellectual or spiritual mumbo jumbo. It's also important that it be short and specific — a mantra, not a dissertation. Keep these questions in your mind and heart as you go about your life, and closely observe what the Universe displays for you in return. Within the nuances of your life, signs and opportunities will manifest that could trigger Self-Realization.

Meanwhile, as you wait for that fortunate accident, do all you can to find the answer yourself. Read enlightenment literature, consult the masters, living and dead, study metaphysics and the occult. Turn over every rock that might hold a clue. These efforts will not be what does the trick, but effort and intense curiosity are essential ingredients in becoming vulnerable to Grace. It is not until we have allowed the ego-mind to do everything it can think of to figure it out and "do it myself," that it will collapse in the exhaustion and utter defeat that opens the floodgates of Truth.

Self-inquiry is also a good practice on the level of the illusory ego-identity. We can call this "small-s self-inquiry." Here we are not asking who we *really* are, but investigating the characteristics and attributes of the *false self* we believe ourselves to be.

On the superficial level, this is something most everyone loves to do. We take magazine and online personality tests that ask, "Do you like cats or dogs?" "Are you a morning person or a night owl?" Whatever. Then the author of the article says your answers reveal that you should live in Bali and be an artist.

The value of even the most vapid of tests like this is that you actually have to take a look at yourself for a moment before answering. Thoughts run through your head. "Well, I don't know. I like getting up early, but I usually stay up late, so it never seems to happen."

A more sophisticated version of these quizzes is the Meyers-Briggs personality test, which after asking many questions, reduces you to a four-letter code for who you are. And we love it. We proudly tell others, "I'm an INFJ." The Enneagram is also in this category of investigation, and again, we proudly identify with the output: "I'm a 7." Whatever.

We like these because all we need to do is answer some generic questions, then receive a non-judgmental description of ourselves. We also love astrology and Human Design, where all we need provide is our birth date, time and location, and in return we are assigned identifiers we proudly display when asked: "I'm a Scorpio." "I'm a Manifestor." Whatever.

I do not mean to make light of these instruments. They target and satisfy our entry-level interest in self-inquiry, and provide a good source of information for further consideration and study. In fact I created a similar instrument myself, which I call the Identity Attributes Matrix (IAM).

In it you are asked to rate yourself on a scale of 1 to 100 on forty-five different character traits and life parameters. It's like taking personal inventory. These numbers can be put into a matrix and run through a program that will output some information, but to me that is not the value of it. The value is in the amount of *self-inquiry* one puts into deciding whether to assign one's self a 39 or a 40 in *audacity*, a 52 or 53 in *charisma*.

Another common form of self-inquiry is talk therapy with psychologists and psychiatrists. When I was holding weekly group meetings, I did much the same thing. When people asked questions or talked about their situation, I'd use what they said as an entry point to *guided self-inquiry*, by asking them questions about it that would require introspection on their part.

What I tried to do at the same time, was to shine a light on the very idea of *selfhood*. Does this entity with a name, and history, and memories, and characteristics, and problems actually exist in the way you think it does?

Guided self-inquiry can be very effective because the other person may see things about you that you are blinded to, and will take you in directions you may not be willing to take yourself. It's probably most beneficial with a good teacher, but is worth doing peer-to-peer with sincere friends, as well.

The process sometimes involves *confrontation* about characteristics and blind spots, which while often unpleasant, can open up valuable avenues of thought, and shed light on things we keep in shadow. Rose held separate *confrontation sessions* for this purpose alone, and encouraged his students to do it among themselves.

But more often confrontation occurs organically during guided self-inquiry, or in conversations among true friends. Most common friendships are based on the principle, "I won't call you on your shit, if you won't call me on mine." A spiritual friend, however, will tell you the truth about what he sees in you, and hope you'll return the favor.

Another benefit of working with others is that whatever you see in other people is also true of you, and vice versa. We all have the same human characteristics, just in different percentages and formulations. What I discover about myself I know is also present in you. And what I see in you, I know is also present in me. All our secrets are the same.

The capacity to have *empathy* with others is valuable in this regard. This is not sympathy or compassion for others, but empathy *with* them, meaning you can feel what they are feeling, and to a degree hear what they are thinking. This is a skill that can be developed, and which starts by simply learning to take your mind off yourself when with others, and tuning in to *them*.

This capacity has benefits in other situations as well, as in for instance being able to feel that someone intends to do you harm, or at the other end of the spectrum, has a crush on you. Empathy is closely aligned with *intuition*, which is an extremely valuable skill to nurture and apply on the spiritual path, and to life in general.

Most self-inquiry is done alone, though, and involves things like introspection, self-observation, recapitulation, and brutal self-honesty. The objective is to shine a light into all your dark corners, and to clearly see all aspects of the vehicle you inhabit—to not be a stranger to yourself.

It is important to note, however, that our objective with self-inquiry is merely to *see* these characteristics, not to *fix* them. That gets into self-help, which is not our purpose here. That's working on becoming a better robot, which may be useful in other aspects of life, but does not apply to the pursuit of Self-Realization. Seeing the truth about yourself is enough.

There's nothing wrong with self-help activities, except that they can become a seductive distraction from our real work as seekers. If during self-inquiry you see something about yourself that is a true block to Self-Realization, then yes, you need to address it. But you may also find that in your clear seeing of it, it shrinks in power and becomes less of an issue.

One of the things I've found useful for Self-Inquiry and self-inquiry is to keep a journal. Thoughts come and go quickly, and a potentially fertile insight can easily get lost if not written down. Plus, once on paper or on the screen, it can be contemplated, critiqued, edited and revisited.

I've been keeping a journal for decades and have found it interesting to go back and see the progression and evolution of my questions, investigations and insights. I also discovered recently that in the two years prior to my experience on Flight 99, my journal entries became more intense, focused, and surprisingly "not-wrong" about truths I did not yet "know."

My process had evolved by then to writing down my deepest questions, then capturing whatever occurred to me in "answer." I even compiled those entries into a book, *Self to No-Self: The Last Mile*, which I may someday publish.

Another kind of writing I fell into and think is worth mentioning is *haiku*. For me, writing haiku was a practice that combined both mindfulness and self-inquiry. I didn't know that when I started, I just enjoyed doing it. But I later realized that the reason I enjoyed writing haiku was that it quieted and focused the mind, and opened the door to insight.

Formal Japanese haiku has a rigid set of rules, but they need not be slavishly adhered to for our purposes. The rules say a haiku is exactly 17 syllables, arranged into three lines of five, seven, and five syllables. It also should have something that hints at the season, and something that hints at the mood or interior landscape of the author.

The aim is to produce a concise snapshot of the inner and outer experience of the author at a precise moment—now.

To do this you need to be very observant of the so called exterior world—wildlife, insects, the play of light on leaves—and very observant of what's going on in your inner experience as you write—sadness, elation, contentment, nostalgia, wonder... Most of my writing is done directly into the computer, but I like writing haiku with pen and paper. I sometimes think of it as *stalking thought.*

I just sit quietly watching the flow of thoughts and write down a few here and there. The more random and spontaneous the better. I don't judge the thought or image as to it's worthiness, just capture it. This is not journaling or essay writing. Neither is it an automatic writing exercise where you try to keep the words flowing no matter what. That's a focus on writing. This is a focus on the process of thought.

You may only jot down a few thoughts or images, none of which may be useful for haiku. Results are not the point, but like most other things, the more you do it the "better" you'll get at it. The process is the point. The idea is not to have a lot of thoughts, but to be aware of those that do come up, and to be aware of the process. Stalking thought is an opportunity to think about thinking. What's really going on, or seems to be going on?

There is the *source* of thought, which I may think is the brain, but how can I know that? Then there is the apparent *receiver* of the thought, which I presume to be the individual "mind"—but is it? Then there is the *observer* of the thinking process—but is that also just the mind? What's the difference between my brain and my mind? Does my mind live in my brain, or does my brain live in my mind? Are brain and mind themselves only thoughts?

Am I the generator of thoughts, or am I in receipt of them? Or both? Some thoughts seem to come out of nowhere. Others seem to logically follow a previous thought. When I intentionally think about something, where did that intention come from? When my intentional thoughts are interrupted by seemingly random, unrelated thoughts, where did those originate? Who's in charge here?

While all of this is going on, you'll find you have words appearing on the page. At some point you may want to arrange and edit them into a short poem or haiku, and if you do, wonderful. Either way, you've already gained the benefits of stalking thought, and inquiring into the workings of your mind in the present moment.

# THE CLOSE REALM

Our most basic desire is to exist—to know that I AM. "I am" can only be experienced, however, if there is "I am not." It can only even be conceived of in a world of Am and Am-not.

Sometimes I think and talk about Self-Inquiry and self-inquiry in the context of *realms*. In this paradigm I talk about each of us existing in, and *as*, three realms simultaneously: the outer realm, the inner realm, and the *close realm*. The inner realm is the mindbody complex we believe was born and will die—everything we consider *Me*. The outer realm is the perceived world we appear to be alive in—everything we consider *Not Me*.

The close realm is the point from which the inner and outer realms emanate—from which they both are created. It is located deep "inside" the inner realm, at the heart of the heart of *What Is*. It is ground zero of what we consider to be *Here*. It is where *God* abides. In the close realm there is no *I Am* or *I am not*.

These are the three realms we must investigate if we want to take seriously the Oracle of Delphi's admonition to *Know Thyself*.

The "divisions" between these realms are fluid. For instance, usually we perceive the body as Me, but in meditation or contemplation we might experience it as external to the "I-thought," and we often refer to it as "my" body, implying that we experience it as separate from "me." We may also sometimes have a beautiful experience of feeling "at one" with nature, or with another person. And sometimes we may feel the close realm leaking into the inner realm in the form of an ecstatic experience.

Self-Realization happens when the close realm floods the inner realm completely, and reveals with crystal clear self-evidence that these three realms are in fact One—the Close Realm. God. Until that happens, however, our experience and beliefs tell us we are not that which we perceive to be outside the body, and that we are not that which creates our world.

Virtually everyone who ever tried to follow the Oracle's advice has focused almost completely on the inner realm in their investigations, and for good reason. It is our firm belief that this is the entirety of our being. We certainly are not the external world of trees and mountains and "other" people, and even more certainly we are not the Creator of All That Is. Or so we believe.

When the outer realm gets dramatic, frightening, seductive, thrilling, our attention is riveted on it, and thoughts fade into the background. When we are consumed by feelings or "lost in thought" in the inner realm, we literally are not conscious of what's right before our eyes in the outer realm—bumping into things, missing exits on the highway, staring blankly without seeing, losing stuff, forgetting why we came into the room we find ourselves...

In the same way, when awareness drifts into the close realm, the inner realm of thought fades, and no-thought happens. The close realm is completely intimate and immediate. Here. Now. More intimate than "me." More immediate than "now." Closer than "here." Now and Here are the same. Neither describes what it is pointing at. Now is an aspect of *time*, which is not a real thing. Here points to a spot in *space*, which is not a real thing.

In a realm without time, when is Now? In a void without dimension, where is Here? Without time and space, here and now are meaningless. Follow either to it's essence and you fall through to the same no-place.

## MEMORY

Absolute Now cannot be experienced in the same way the "present" can be experienced. It is beyond the physiological capabilities of the mindbody robot to experience life in real time. The fastest synapse in the brain still has a lag time of some small duration, and the time it takes the mindbody to process those electrical impulses into conscious thoughts and perceptions is actually quite lengthy. I have heard of studies that say this takes 10 seconds or longer. So the "present" is really the most recent "past." Is this just picking at words or does it hint at something about the phenomena of *experience* that's worth looking into more deeply?

If we admit that what we experience as the *present* is actually the most recent *past*, does it follow that all of life is transpiring in memory? Am I living this life or remembering it? And if my life is only transpiring in memory, how do I know that my life experiences are ordered chronologically?

Yes, memories usually come with a time stamp, but that does not mean it is meaningful or accurate. It's just a part of the memory. A more accurate reporting of my actual experience in the moment is to say that memories appear spontaneously out of nothing right Now, and there is no way to validate they are what they claim to be.

My actual experience is that memories appear to be created in the moment on an as-needed basis. What we think are recurring
190

memories could just as easily be unique and spontaneously created memories that have a feeling of familiarity and recognition created right along with them.

My experience is that there is an apparent succession of now moments, some of which are retained in memories, most of which go unnoticed. But is this apparent succession of now moments an illusion caused by thought? It is also my experience that when thought is absent, time stands still, so where does that leave me?

If I am shown a photograph or video of someone who resembles the face I see in my mirror and told it was taken of me at a previous time, all of that is only taking place now. My actual experience is that the photographs and videos are materializing right now out of nothing. Explanations as to their supposed origin and meaning exist only as thoughts that have spontaneously appeared out of nothing right along with the "evidence."

All evidence of the concept of "past" can only be presented here and now. It is impossible for the past to actually exist. At best it can be spoken of as a mythical realm, like heaven or hell. That is my actual experience. No matter when I check and recheck, it is always Now. There can never be a time other than Now. If you invent a time machine and go to a place where they wear different clothes and the newspaper says it is 1874, all of that happens only Now.

And so, it can quite truthfully be said that all of the recollections of my past I've written down for this book never happened. I have memories of these incidents, but what exactly is memory, and should I trust it?

You think I'm a replicant, don't you?

In the movie *Blade Runner*, the Rachel character is a replicant, an android, who believes she is human because she has detailed memories of her past. But those "memories" are just part of her program, and she is in fact only a few days off the assembly line.

How is that different from your experience of memory? In the razor-edged moment of Now, what validates your memories or mine more than hers? Do our vague personal memories in the here and now prove the metaphysical existence of such a state as *past*?

To say that a story is true, or factual, really only says that the story teller is accurately reporting what is in memory. To say that memories are the result of actual events that took place in a physical universe in some past time, is only one of many possible explanations for their appearance in consciousness here and now.

As near as I can figure, my sense of who I am in the world is solely derived from memory notes I supposedly carry in my head on a variety of personal history topics and past behaviors. And who would I be without them?

In the movie, *Memento*, a man with no memory function whatever has learned to store scraps of memory *externally*—as Polaroid pictures, written notes, tattoos on his body. Because he has no internal memory, he needs to frequently review these external notes and pictures to re-construct his identity and purpose in life.

It soon becomes clear, however, that these notes are deeply flawed and bear little resemblance to the truth. And yet the man acts upon them as if they were completely true because he trusts them to be his guide, to tell him who he is and how to act. Then, as the movie progresses, on some level the man begins to realize that he can't necessarily trust these notes, but that in reality, it doesn't matter if these notes reflect the "truth" or not.

What matters is how the notes affect his future identity and actions. And so the man begins taking intentionally inaccurate notes in order to propel himself to a future identity and actions that serves the purpose of the present identity—the one jotting down the current memory notes. In this way, the man ends up tricking his future self into murder by having his present self write down false memory notes—knowing what his future self will be compelled to do when he reads them.

We do the exact same thing. It is the notes I've supposedly been taking in my head since childhood—the ones that are quickly accessed and reviewed whenever I arise from sleep—that tell me who I am and how I act in the world. The notes I store in my head may be more complex and richly textured than the terse tattoos on Memento man, but they are no less flawed and self-serving.

These mental notes I have been collecting and trusting as my only guide to living are so incomplete and selective, so distorted and tightly spun, they are all but useless for anything but maintaining consistent behavior in a robot.

192

What then is the truth about who I am and what I should do? If the notes in my head cannot be relied upon, where does that leave me? I seriously have no clue about anything. I only know what the Note Taker of the past wanted me to know — and he is apparently not to be trusted. He is often clearly seen in the present to be both ignorant and duplicitous, and to make matters worse, he's the only one available to debunk himself.

Memories are useful for some self-inquiry activities, like recapitulation, but they can also get in the way by rushing in to answer questions intellectually that are better left as open invitations to a deeper realization. Do not use memories as justification for current beliefs, habits, attitudes, or circumstance. Do not allow memories to define you or limit the infinite possibilities of the Moment.

Objectively study your memories, and observe how easily they can be altered and edited to "make a better story," or cover up unpleasantness. Notice that when you modify the telling of a story, that edited version becomes the "new" memory, and the "raw footage" of the original memory begins to become less accessible.

Memories are a useful tool, but they in no way describe you in the present, nor are they proof of a past. In short, they are not to be trusted. Memories provide provenance when the dream demands it, but otherwise serve only to obscure the present empty moment, which is all there ever is — whether or not it's actually happening.

If all this leaves you feeling like Wile E. Coyote after he's chased Road Runner over a cliff and finds himself in midair, good. You're beginning to get a sense of your existential situation.

Guy Pearce in *Memento*

# Prayer

*Pray without ceasing.*
—1 Thessalonians 5:17

If I could give only one suggestion to seekers of Truth it would be this: Ask for it in prayer, then live your life in a manner consistent with that prayer. Because, as Rose said, "When your whole life becomes a prayer, it will be answered instantly."

So what is prayer? How is it best done? To me prayer is basically just maintaining an open line of communication with a higher power, whatever you envision that to be. If you do not sense the presence of a higher power in your life, if you think that the mindbody character is solely in charge and is the cause of all that happens to it—or that what happens in life is totally random and there is no one in charge—then you have no reason to pray and nothing to pray to.

If, however, you sense at any level of your being that what happens to the character is governed by the "will" or "intention" of a power greater than the mindbody, then it's probably a good strategy to make contact with it and stay in touch. The word *God* is problematic for many people because of all the religious baggage, so don't try to force that word on yourself if it gets in the way. "It" has no name anyway.

The fact that this higher power is actually your True Self is beside the point until you have a direct, in-your-face, self-evident realization of that Truth. Until then, you need to relate to it as separate from and superior to you, because in the paradigm of the dream world you believe you inhabit, it is. Admit to it that you are powerless without it. Tell it what you want in no uncertain terms. Constantly ask for help, to be shown the way. Let it know that you know it is totally in charge and that you are nothing but its avatar in this dream world. Thank it, curse it, it doesn't care. It's just glad to hear from you.

Come into alignment with its will, its plan for you. Be an advocate for your innermost desires, but resist not destiny. Ultimately, if we are lucky, we arrive at the one prayer that unites us with the higher power: "Not my will, but Thy will." This is the surrender prayer, and if there comes a moment when we mean it with all our heart and all our mind and all our soul, Oneness will reign absolute.

Prayer puts us in our place. No matter how semi-sincere and awkward, any act of prayer is an admission of helplessness, which is our true state. Prayer has been practiced in one way or another, in one guise or another, by everyone who ever discovered Truth, so why not play the odds?

Proceed as if there is a higher power that governs every outcome, and that this higher power takes requests and can be reasoned with. What name we give it doesn't matter—God, Divine, Higher Self. Whether or not there even is such a thing doesn't matter. What matters is that prayer breaks down our resistance to the gift of Truth.

To "pray without ceasing" is not to mumble memorized religiosities all day, but to simply stay in contact with the Divine 24/7. Commiserate. Call upon the highest aspect of Self for help. Negotiations can be tumultuous at times, and being meek and obsequious is not always the best posture when things get dicey, but gratitude and surrender always trump everything.

Jesus says, "Ask and you shall receive," and that is the simple truth. What's not so simple is learning *how* to ask, and *how* to receive. Most often, the little guy asking for help is what's standing in the way of that help. Learn to get out of the way.

It is also important to discover your *baseline prayer*, which is so deeply imbedded you probably don't even realize it's there. Most people who say they want Self-Realization carry a baseline prayer that doesn't necessarily support that desire—something more like, "to live a long, happy, abundant life." I know I did. That's the pressure point. That's where the rubber meets the road. There is no more effective spiritual action than tweaking the programming of your baseline prayer. God is just waiting for us to ask. This is where the asking must come from. This is the frequency being monitored. Learning how to pray for Truth *at all costs* on the level of your baseline prayer is true spiritual action.

But if God is the Absolute, an infinite clear emptiness, what hears and answers prayers? Is there anything monitoring that station? This is where the notion of an intercessor linking God and man comes in. This is the Christ, the Holy Spirit of the Father/Son/Holy Spirit trinity. It is not the historical Jesus, or Buddha or whatever, but the impersonal helping force that is our lifeline, our way back when we've wandered too far. This is the hand

196

that flips the switch that turns off the mind. Let your prayer be that it reaches for you.

On Flight 99 I deeply felt the presence of this Great Intercessor. I experienced it as Love, as the Giver of All Gifts. It was in the presence of the Intercessor that I stood in awe and wept at my unworthiness. But the Intercessor is not God. God swallows the Intercessor like he's never been, leaving only the One. I am left with faint impressions of this — of being God, of being the One — and even those faint "memories" are unreliable, being created in a mind that was not present as it occurred.

The mind cannot enter the Absolute, and so to believe that what it says about it has validity is delusion. Bart and his mind vanished, and there was no one there to miss him. To rely on Bart to tell you what the "experience" was like is not a good strategy. Even with the greatest teachers this is a bad idea. To believe in another's words, whether they be Jesus or Buddha or whoever, and think that you have gained something is ludicrous. Unless the switch is thrown that reveals you as the infinite clear emptiness of God, you've got nothing.

Make your intention for enlightenment known in prayer and a way will be shown to you, a path through the intricacies of your fears and desires. The fewer fears and desires you have, and the less intensely they are felt, the more direct the route.

Your helper, your guide, your guardian angel, is like an internal GPS system. Tell it where you want to go and it will chart a route. Tell it only one destination and the route will be very direct. Program in a lot of destinations you want to visit along the way, along with others you want to avoid, and the route to your main destination becomes long and circuitous. So circuitous that your vehicle may run out of fuel before you get there.

Hidden within the circumstances of your life is a roadmap Home. Most people don't think to look for it because they have no notion they're lost. So a very basic step in all this is to suspect you're lost. Not just slightly off track, but totally lost. So much so that there is nothing — absolutely nothing — you know for sure.

We much prefer to feel that we have everything under control, that "I am the master of my fate, I am the captain of my soul." But is that just the ego beating its chest in bravado as it's tossed about on a tumultuous sea of uncertainty in vast uncharted waters? And is that the best posture to assume while seeking Truth?

Feeling lost is a good thing. The more lost you feel, the more motivated you are to find your way home, the more likely you are to check out anything that might hold a clue, no matter how crazy-sounding or preposterous, the more likely you are to ask for help.

> *Amazing Grace, how sweet the sound*
> *that saved a wretch like me.*
> *I once was lost, but now am found.*
> *Was blind but now I see.*

What beautiful phrasing: "I am found." It does not say I once was lost, but now I've found my way. Because the finding has nothing to do with you. You do the looking, then are found by a power that dwarfs the seeker into non-existence.

What shall we call a force with the power to reveal such a wonder? To expose the True Nature of All Existence? *Grace* is as good a word as any — the force by which something is given not as a reward for hard work, or because the recipient is somehow worthy of it, but as a pure gift bestowed in unimaginable Love.

> *Ask and it shall be given you.*
> *Seek and you shall find.*
> *Knock and it shall be opened to you.*
>
> *For everyone who asks receives,*
> *and he who seeks finds.*
> *and to him who knocks, it shall be opened.*
>
> *For the one who speaks is also the one who hears,*
> *and the one who sees is also the one who manifests,*
> *and the one who seeks is also the one who reveals.*
>
> *Let him who seeks continue seeking until he finds.*
> *When he finds, he will become troubled,*
> *and when he becomes troubled he will be astonished,*
> *and he will rule over the All.*

-- Jesus of Nazareth (from *Christ Sutras*)

# Meditation, Mindfulness, No-Thought

As you no doubt have noticed by now, topics I've treated separately in their own chapters—between-ness, self-inquiry, prayer—have a good deal of overlap, because they are all part of a single gestalt, a way of being, a way of life. This chapter adds a couple more topics to the mix, which also are a part of that singularity—*meditation* and *mindfulness*.

Even though all these practices are really the One Practice, it may help to draw some distinctions between them to aid in understanding how I use these words:

> Between-ness aims at *desire* in a state of *indifference*.
> Self-Inquiry aims at *introspection* in a state of *doubt*.
> Prayer aims at *communion* in a state of *surrender*.
> Meditation aims at *awareness* in a state of *no-thought*.

I say these practices "aim at" a certain state because those states are elusive and often not arrived at, but with continued practice we can edge ever closer. Another way of looking at it is:

> Self-Inquiry is asking the Higher Self for answers.
> Prayer is asking the Higher Self for help.
> Meditation is shutting up.

*Mindfulness* is similar to meditation, but has more to do with the way we hold our head as we move through waking life. Meditation is done while at rest, usually sitting, sometimes lying down, and aims at inner silence and no-thought. Mindfulness is a way of being while you're up and about. It aims at focusing on the task or person at hand. It is really just *paying attention*.

For most of our lives we do not. We do one thing while thinking of something else. We cook while talking on the phone. We listen to music while running. We eat while driving. We text one person while in conversation with another. We go through our daily routines by rote while our mind is elsewhere.

Mindfulness is to do one thing at a time, to give the thing you are actually *doing* your undivided attention. The spirit of it is encapsulated in the title of the iconic book by Ram Das, *Be Here Now*. It's a wonderful, and perhaps spiritually helpful, way to go through life, and certainly far superior to the clutter of "multi-tasking."

I have several ball caps embroidered **Be Here Now** that I ordered from the Ram Das website, and I wear them as a reminder to myself, and perhaps to those who see it, to be *here* now, not off somewhere else. Let your mind and body be doing the same thing.

*Meditation* is the one spiritual practice most everyone is familiar with, whether or not they are on an intentional spiritual path, and most everyone on an intentional spiritual path has practiced at least one kind of meditation. Many of us have tried several different practices.

But what is meditation? There are many definitions and varieties of practices, but do they all point at the same thing? Rose, for instance, said meditation was "productive thinking," but for me that more accurately describes *self-inquiry*.

For me, meditation has the aim of empty awareness in a state of *no-thought*. This is not easily arrived at, and so we sit, and sit, and sit, and hope for the best. For some, the act of sitting *is* meditation, and so sitting and meditation are synonymous for them.

For me, the act of sitting is *courting* meditation, not the thing itself—though sitting has its own benefits, like putting the body into a deep state of rest. Many sitting sessions do not arrive at meditation, but when they do, and *inner silence* reigns, the difference between sitting and meditation is unmistakable.

There are many meditation techniques taught and practiced, such as mantra, breath work, zazen, vipassana, and so forth. None of them are inherently better than any other. They can all be used to quiet the monkey mind so that inner silence might happen, and from there perhaps, no-thought.

In my own experience I have also found that meditation can happen without sitting in a formal practice. I did Transcendental Meditation (TM) off and on for a number of years, and practiced zazen to some degree. But my most consistent practice was what I call *spontaneous meditation*, which is really more of a non-practice.

Sitting with the intention to formally meditate was always difficult for me. Too much like work. But I could sit for hours on a porch or staring out a window. If meditation started to happen, I went with it. If not, I had a good time anyway. Some of my deepest meditations have come upon me while sitting on a screen porch staring into the middle distance, a glass of ice tea nearby.

I still sit to intentionally meditate sometimes, though I'm not entirely sure why. I'm no more disciplined about it than I ever was, but it seems like a good thing to do once in awhile. TM is still my go-to technique when I intentionally sit to meditate. If thoughts come, I replace them with the mantra—a supposedly meaningless sound, a

200

thought that leads to no other thoughts. More and more, though, I just pay attention to my breath. I'm beginning to think that the TM mantras, or any sound, really, are not entirely meaningless, and that on some level they, like all words, conjure subtle manifestations.

Regardless, meditation techniques are just temporary tools that will fall away after a few minutes, or even seconds, as you "descend" towards inner silence, and perhaps no-thought. No-thought cannot be experienced, but upon re-emerging from it you will be conscious of having been "gone." As you follow thought to ever more subtle levels in meditation, you may arrive at our most primal thought: *I Am*. This is the last thought to go before the trap door to no-mind opens under you.

What role does *external* silence play in the courting of inner silence? In theory, nothing. Even when meditating in a city apartment with the windows open, inner silence can happen. But practically, external silence is far more conducive to arriving at inner silence. I live alone on secluded rural property, and my days are spent in what might be considered "total" silence. But there's still birdsong, wind in the trees, rain, clothes in the dryer... All of which tend to produce thoughts.

The deepest external silence I've personally experienced is alone above the treeline in the Rocky mountains. In those situations of almost complete external silence, inner silence is but a breath away, and the distinction between internal and external disappears.

Some people choose to live in monasteries so they can dedicate their lives to meditation, prayer and silence. This is wonderful for those who are drawn to it. But spending your life in a monastery is not necessarily a better strategy for Self-Realization than periodic short isolations. Rose, in fact, recommended periodic isolation retreats of not more than a month. The theory here is that having limited time tends to focus our efforts to make the most of it.

It makes sense. The best home video of my kids I have is the first I ever shot, using a borrowed camera. Because I knew I only had it for a week, I used it to the max. Once I bought a camcorder of my own, the amount and quality of the footage dropped off dramatically, until I hardly ever used it. The same with travel vacations. We try to cram in as many experiences as possible into a short defined time.

In the larger picture, what effect does knowing we have only a limited lifespan have on how we use that time? For those on the bottom rung of the spiritual pyramid, who live totally in their animal nature, probably not much. For others, it is a spur to experience and accomplish as much as they can in the world in the time allowed.

For earnest spiritual seekers—and anyone who suspects that things are not what they seem—it's an invitation to pursue Truth as though a fire were raging in your hair.

# The Way of the Warrior

"A man goes to knowledge as he goes to war, wide awake, with fear, with respect, and with absolute assurance. Going to knowledge or going to war in any other manner is a mistake, and whoever makes it will live to regret his steps."        —Don Juan Matus

In the Toltec shamanic tradition of Don Juan, the goal of the practitioner is to become a *man of knowledge*. This is basically the same as what is referred to as *enlightenment* in eastern traditions, but also includes intimate knowledge of the natural world, and of what could be called magical realms—planes of existence not experienced in ordinary life.

Don Juan goes on to say: "In order to become a man of knowledge one must be a *warrior*. One must strive without giving up, without complaint, without flinching, until one *sees*."

In this chapter I'd like to build on the metaphor of approaching the spiritual path—and life in general—with the actions and mood of a warrior. I will also borrow the template of Buddha's Eightfold Path to propose eight *ways of being* that inform and define the way of the spiritual warrior.

The Eightfold Path of Buddha is:

Right view
Right intention
Right speech
Right action
Right livelihood
Right effort
Right mindfulness
Right concentration

Countless volumes have been written about Buddha's Four Noble Truths and Eightfold Path, so we won't go into them here, but you may notice they have quite naturally found their way into this book in one way or another—both up to now, and in what follows.

The eight ways of being I've chosen to highlight are more specific than those in the Eightfold Path, and I have phrased them as imperatives, which makes it sound like I'm telling you what to do, but that is not my purpose. They are merely suggestions based on observations I've made about how earnest seekers of Truth—how those aspiring to become men of knowledge—might strategize their efforts and lead their lives in such a way as to invite the accident of Self-Realization, to become vulnerable to Grace. It is in this spirit I offer *The Eightfold Way of the Spiritual Warrior*:

Befriend Death
Maintain Vitality
Be Self-Sufficient
Question Everything
Know the Terrain
Reconnect with Nature
Embody Integrity
Be a Friend

In the same way the items in Buddha's Eightfold Path might be summarized as "Right living," these eight ways might be summarized as "Right being." They are not "practices" to be made into a job, but rather, simply things to keep gentle on your mind as you go through life, until perhaps, they become your natural way.

## BEFRIEND DEATH

For a warrior, death is a constant possibility. This is also true of everyone else, but they do not live as if they know this. A warrior does. A warrior-sage enters into an intimate relationship with his death. This is described succinctly in a poem in *Verses Regarding True Nature*, so I'll save myself some writing by including it here:

*The multitudes fear death
and try not to think about it.
When it approaches, panic ensues.*

*The sage sees death as the companion of life.
He holds it in high regard,
and treats it like a childhood friend.*

*Death inhabits his thoughts.
Death informs his actions.
Death walks at his side.*

*When deciding what's worth doing,
he asks the advice of death.*

One of the main reasons it's important for seekers to be comfortable with death is that fear of death can abort a conclusive spiritual experience just as it's about to happen. The ego-identity senses its imminent unveiling as being non-existent and activates the fear of death as a last-minute defense. And it often works. I've had a number of people tell me they "almost" had a major spiritual experience, but got scared and turned away.

Why does the fear of death kick in just as we are about to enter the kingdom of God? Because our greatest fear is the *unknown*. Death is the Great Unknown and so we fear it. Enlightenment is also a great unknown, and so no matter how earnestly we might pursue it, we also fear it. The false identity sees enlightenment as death and treats it accordingly

What can be done? How does one overcome the fear of death, and thus, fear of Truth? There is no formula, but a good general principle would be to do the opposite of what most people do, which as it says in the poem, is to "try not to think about it." So think about it. Think about it a lot. Make friends with death and treat it as an ally, not a nemesis. Don Juan says that death is always just to our left. Turn to it. Give it a nod. Acknowledge its preeminence. Thank it for not touching you yet.

In Vietnam I became acclimated to death in certain ways—to being accustomed to seeing a lot of it, and to the knowledge that at any moment it could be lights out. But I had no sense of what death was, nor had I ever really thought about it in any meaningful way.

The closest I came to this was when digging up bodies the enemy had buried in retreat, looking for intelligence materials. As I was pulling one out of the dirt I became viscerally aware of its utter *lifelessness*, and the words "rubber dummy" came to mind. It was so completely obvious that whatever had animated this dummy, whatever had given it life, was gone. What left? Where did it go?

Later, as a seeker, I began to think about death more deeply, and gravitated to situations where I could be close to it. I was a hospice volunteer for five years, for instance, partly as an act of service, but mostly so I could be with people facing imminent death, and vicariously face my own death with them.

On the physical level, it also helped demystify the actual process of dying. The body does not give up easily, and death is often a slow, sometimes painful process. Seeing the different ways people live with the reality of their looming demise helped me learn that terrain, and led me into deep self-inquiry. Being fairly empathic,

I could at times feel what they were feeling at this most profound and uncertain time of life, and so get a taste of how it might be for me on my deathbed.

I also did various "thought experiments" around the theme of death, which would give me fertile ground for inquiry. In the famous short story, "An Occurrence at Owl Creek Bridge," by Ambrose Bierce, a southern civilian in 1862 stands with a noose around his neck, about to be hanged from a bridge by Union soldiers. His executioners tip the plank on which he stands, and the condemned man drops towards the river. When he reaches the end of the rope, however, the rope breaks, and he plunges into the water, where he makes his way to shore and escapes. The story then goes on to describe the long, happy life he lives with his family. Turns out, though, the entire story of his life we read about only transpired in his mind as he dropped towards the river. In actuality, when he hits the end of the rope, his neck breaks.

This story invites inquiry on multiple levels about the nature of existence. It also inspired for me a thought experiment, in which I did not survive the explosion in Phan Tiet, in which my prayer between shrapnel wounds, "Not head, not, head, please not my head," went unanswered, and my entire life has been lived — and is being lived — in the micro-second before a fatal head wound.

Most everyone has at least one time in their life where they dodged a bullet, so to speak, where death could have happened but didn't. But what if the actuality is that it *did*, that in fact you died? What if the experience you call your life is actually the experience of your death? What if you are "already" dead? What happens when this death experience ends?

This is only a thought experiment, and is not meant to point at any particular truth, but if you contemplate these kinds of things deeply enough, you'll find your mind on shaky ground, which is right where you want it as an earnest seeker of Truth.

It may also lessen your fear of death. I mean, if I'm already dead and loving it, what's there to be afraid of? If all of life transpires in thought only, is not death only a thought? What is the source of thought? What is the source of life? What is the Source of All? If death is just a thought, who's thinking it?

I look in the bathroom mirror. The infinite clear emptiness of the single eye is in receipt of a face. Lines from a poem by George MacDonald recite themselves in thought:

*Where did you come from, baby dear?*
*Out of the Everywhere, into the here.*

I ask the mirror of emptiness, "Is it to Everywhere I return?" The Everywhere replies, "You've never left."

## MAINTAIN VITALITY

Staying healthy is important no matter what you're up to in life. It's true what they say: "If you don't have your health, you don't have anything." Would you rather be healthy in a shack, or on chemo in a palace?

Good health is generally defined as being free of illness and disease. But one can be disease-free and still not feel good — lethargy, depression, worry… The list of life-sucking mental states is long. One also needs vitality. This is true for everyone, but for earnest seekers of Truth, even more so.

Rose once said about the experience of enlightenment, "You're going to walk through death, and that takes some vitality." I was in my mid-forties when I heard him say that, burdened by job and family, struggling with the ordinary, and I knew I had to stoke my fire if I ever wanted to discover the extraordinary.

Vitality includes strength, energy, enthusiasm, curiosity and drive. It's what makes the difference between being excited at the prospect of a trip to Bhutan, or thinking it sounds exhausting. As coach Vince Lombardi said, "Fatigue makes cowards of us all."

In the early days of Rose's work with students he told them, "If you haven't become enlightened by the age of 30, hang up your spurs. This is an undertaking for the young."

Part of his reasoning was that as we age, our heads harden. We get set in our ways and thinking, and become evermore impervious to ideas that challenge our beliefs. The other part is that as we age we lose the vitality it takes to pursue this Quixotic adventure called spiritual seeking, and to absorb the impact of enlightenment should it happen.

All of this is true, but it is not necessarily linked to chronological age. For most people aging does indeed harden the head and sap vitality. But for some it does not, especially if we fight against it. If we are conscious of these tendencies we can actively work to keep all our channels open, to expand our thinking in all directions, and to engage in actions and activities that maintain and increase vitality.

Being in good physical health is an important part of it, of course—even a common cold saps vitality. So doing things like eating nourishing food, exercising, and getting sufficient sleep are advisable for everyone. But turning the pursuit of health into a religion is not necessarily beneficial.

There is such a thing as too much exercise, for instance. I have a friend who was an extreme athlete when younger, competing in numerous Iron Man triathlons, and is now beset by all sorts of pains and physical maladies as a direct result of it—including heart surgery and other operations.

Too much emphasis on food misses the point, too. Being vegan or strict vegetarian is fine if you are naturally drawn to it, but pursuing it as a "spiritual" practice, or using it as a political statement against omnivores, is not helpful if your objective is Truth.

I think, too, that a fixation on being healthy often stems from an unhealthy fear of death, and thus can be counter-productive if taken to the extreme. My mother, for instance, was an early health food advocate as far back as the '50's, and even testified at U.S. Senate hearings on food topics. She also exercised regularly to a workout TV show hosted by Jack Lalanne, an early fitness and nutrition guru. (Who, when he got ill later in life, told his doctor, "Don't let me die. It would be bad for my reputation.")

All of which I'm sure did my mother good, and I no doubt benefitted from the healthy food she served us. But as she got older,

she increasingly saw nutrition as the way to fend off her death, swallowing large amounts of supplements and "superfoods" every day, and worrying about even the slightest indulgence or "break-over" she allowed herself in her diet. She died at age 83 with cancer. I sometimes think, though, that she worried herself to death worrying about death, and the cancer was just a physical manifestation of that anxiety. Her mother, who died healthy at age 96, never exercised a day in her life, subsisted on desserts, and never worried 'bout a thing.

Which brings up the subject of longevity. Why do some people live longer than others? Certainly DNA is a factor, but what else? Ask thirty people in their 90's or 100's what their secret to longevity is and you'll get thirty different answers. The actor Ernest Borgnine said, "Frequent masturbation."

One common theme being discovered is that many long-lived people have resisted trusting their health to doctors. Most people rush to the doctor at the slightest provocation, hoping for a pill or shot that will make things right, and accept whatever they are told by someone in a white lab coat as gospel. But is that wise?

Studies have shown that the *U.S. medical system* kills 225,000 people a year, making it the third-leading cause of death, behind heart disease and cancer—and those are just the numbers reported by a system that is extremely reluctant to admit mistakes or culpability. When asked his secret to longevity one centenarian said, "I lived where the doctors couldn't get at me."

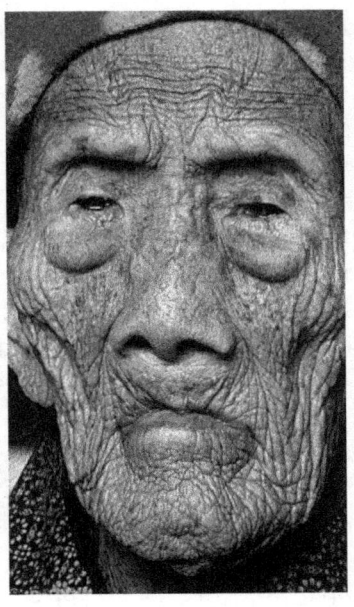

The oldest person on record was Li Ching Yuen, who was documented to be 256 years old when he died in 1933. He was a beloved member of his community, who reportedly married 23 times and fathered over 200 children. His advice for longevity was this: "Keep a quiet heart, sit like a tortoise, walk sprightly like a pigeon, and sleep like a dog."

Longevity has its place, but it's not the point of life, nor is it particularly desirable unless accompanied by health and vitality. Stay interested. Stay open. Stay curious. Stay strong. Stay enthused. Stay ready for anything in life— including death.

## BE SELF-SUFFICIENT

What does it mean to be self-sufficient, self-reliant? Why is it desirable? As a warrior it's important to be able to sustain yourself while on the move, and not be dependent on external resources that may or may not be available when you need them. You carry your food with you, or better yet, be able to live off the land as you go, hunting and gathering.

In Vietnam we went on month-long long-range operations into remote jungle, and carried about a week's worth of freeze-dried rations in our rucksacks, meaning every week we had to be resupplied. This was a problem if we were in areas of heavy enemy concentration—helicopters landing with food would be a dead-giveaway to our location. So we would be resupplied in conjunction with napalm bombing as cover. Live napalm bombs would light up one area of jungle, while nearby, blank napalm canisters with our food and ammunition would be dropped. An extreme but workable solution.

When I was backpacking the Appalachian Trail later in life, I carried a 40-pound pack with everything I needed to be totally self-sufficient on the trail. But again, a week or ten days of food would be all you could carry, so if you wanted to stay on the trail longer you needed to have a back-end support person who would send food packages to the post office of towns near the trail, which you could then hike to and pick up.

The point here, I guess, is that no matter how physically self-sufficient one might be in the short-term, we are only self-sufficient up to a point—unless and until we are able to survive and thrive in the world by our wits and skills alone. I'm not suggesting this is necessary, and I fall well short of this myself, but having a basic knowledge of what might be involved in surviving under extreme circumstances is not a bad idea in these times, and it informs your thinking about self-sufficiency at less daunting levels.

It also fosters self-inquiry about your physical and mental capacities in the face of great challenges. What if I lost everything? Would I drown in a puddle of self-pity or be able to rise to the occasion?

It's also not a bad idea to have your home base, your headquarters, be as self-sufficient as possible. This strategy is visibly adopted by "preppers," who keep several months food and water on hand as a hedge against natural or man-made disasters. The most self-sufficient preppers live on rural acreage with their own well, have gardens and orchards, and know how to hunt and fish.

This is how I live, mostly because it's my preferred lifestyle, but also because I'm uncomfortable being totally dependent on a supply chain that's vulnerable to interruption and even total breakdown—not to mention the potential for economic collapse, and the fragility of fiat currency. Five years ago Venezuela was one of the most prosperous countries in the world. Now people struggle to eat.

It's a good idea for everyone to be a prepper to at least some degree. Hope and work for the best, but prepare for the worst. It's not only a good practical strategy in disturbing and uncertain times, it also fosters an inner strength and confidence in yourself and your capacities that will serve you in other endeavors, like the pursuit of Truth—in which there is no support system whatever, in a landscape where you are utterly alone.

The bottom line truth is that the *Real You* is the One. You are the Totality of all that is. There is nothing that is not You. That's about as alone as it gets. More to the point for this chapter, perhaps, is that the *ego you* is also alone in the manifest world. No matter how many children, friends, lovers, allies and admirers one might claim, the hermit and the rock star die equally alone.

We all feel this at an existential level, and seek to counteract it by surrounding ourselves with "other people," and trying to convince ourselves that "we're all in this together." To a degree this is true, in the sense that we all face the same ultimate task—to discover our True Nature before death touches us. But it is folly to think that by linking arms and singing "Kumbaya" we all enter the kingdom of God as a pack. The journey is solitary, and unique to you. What you *are*, what you carry with you and inside you, is all you have to work with and to offer.

In keeping with the idea of physical self-sufficiency, it's also a good idea to cultivate psychological and emotional self-sufficiency. This in no way means being cold and distant with others, but simply to not be *needy* in your relationships with them. In fact, not being needy yourself allows you to be more generous and loving with others.

Many love relationships are founded on the basis of mutual need, of feeling "completed" by your partner. This is premised on the feeling that you are somehow incomplete or insufficient in yourself, which is neither true in the ultimate sense, nor a desirable position to adopt in life. The most beautiful relationships are between two people who are totally self-sufficient, who could live just fine without each other, but who choose to live and love together anyway, while allowing each other to pursue their own unique paths.

Another aspect of self-reliance is self-trust. One who is self-reliant does not give the ideas and opinions of others more weight than his own—no matter how many degrees and credentials they might have, no matter how firmly entrenched in history or spiritual lore they might be. One who is self-reliant does not accept the words of Jesus, Buddha or any great philosopher or religious figure, for instance, without testing them against his own experience and findings.

People who are always quoting authorities but never have anything original to say, who are merely spokesmen for conventional wisdom and institutional thinking, are not self-reliant. They have nothing of their own to rely on. After Self-Realization, one trusts himself or herself completely on matters of spiritual importance, not external authorities. One becomes self-affirmed, and speaks with deep conviction, borne of direct experience.

Being self-sufficient is easier when traveling light, which also allows for greater freedom in life. The more physical and psychological baggage we carry, the more restricted our movements. Traveling light lets us take advantage of unforeseen opportunities, and more quickly respond to changing circumstances, to the ever-shifting sands of the times.

The song, "Me and Bobby McGee," contains the line, "Freedom's just another word for nothing left to lose." It's a wonderful, memorable line that resonates with my inner vagabond. In the context of the song, it's a state of poverty and lack, but in the context of self-sufficiency, one might tweak it to say, "Freedom's just another word for living without need."

Freedom is not having nothing, but wanting nothing, and being prepared to do without whatever you might "have" — be it wealth, possessions, relationships, beliefs, or the good opinions of others. Don Juan says, "A man of knowledge has no honor, no dignity, no family, no name, no country, but only life to be lived." This is not a state many people would aspire to, and yet it is our true state. The belief that we have any of these things in the first place is a false one.

It is our common experience these days that life on planet Earth is speeding up at an incredible, almost unbelievable rate. Why this is happening, or why at least it *seems* that it's happening, is a topic for it's own book, but it is important to note here in the sense that being prepared for sudden change — for life to turn on a dime — is a sensible response and strategy, now more than ever. Self-sufficiency, flexibility, mobility, adaptability — these are more than vaguely desirable qualities in the abstract. They are a logical response to the truth of our existential situation.

212

An important component of being free and self-sufficient is simplicity—living a simple life. The less you need, the easier it is to be self-sufficient. We may look at the wealthy and think their money makes them self-sufficient. But are they? Is that guy posing on the tarmac with his Bentley and his private jet self-sufficient? Maybe, but only if his self-sufficiency is internal and not propped up by his wealth, only if he can leave it all behind at a moment's notice and do just fine.

Jesus said, "It is easier for a camel to pass through the eye of a needle than for a rich man to enter the kingdom of God." This was not meant as a condemnation of wealth, or of those who have it. It is merely an observation that wealth, possessions and attachments will not fit through the narrow gate of the Absolute.

It's also true, however, that one who has spent his life focused on earthly wealth is unlikely to be prepared for Truth. *Store up your treasure in heaven, for where your treasure is, there will your heart be also.*

Simplicity is a valuable practice in all aspects of life, and is extremely applicable to the spiritual search, and to all the complex questions and recommendations we encounter. *Occam's razor* states that, "The simplest explanation or solution is usually the right one," and I have found it an invaluable guiding principle and compass in life, and in my spiritual investigations.

When I was an art major in college I had a memorable example of this in a class on color theory. As part of our class materials we had to buy a pack of 300 clay-coated sheets, which were different colors in various subtle shades. We used these to cut up and create our projects.

At the beginning of the semester the instructor gave us an assignment that if we got it right, we'd get an "A" for the semester no matter what our other grades were. It was a complicated problem, he said, so we would be given the entire semester to solve it. He then handed out a list of 10 color qualities that would be present only when three of the colors in our packs were displayed together.

At the end of the semester we all pinned our solutions to the corkboard for his evaluation. The classroom was abuzz as students talked about how challenging this was to their thinking, and about how many hours and days they spent trying out different subtle shades together, testing the combinations against the 10 criteria. Every solution on the board was different, and every one wrong. Except mine.

The instructor unpinned it from the board and held it up for all to see. It was the primary colors — red, blue, yellow — the simplest, most obvious solution. It had been ignored and dismissed by everyone because they were told the problem was so complicated it would take a semester to figure it out.

For me, the solution came in the moment of the assignment as I sat there looking at my deck of 300 sheets, listening to him read the 10 color qualities that must be satisfied. I had not heard of Occam's razor at the time, but instinctively I sensed the solution could not possibly lie in testing the literally millions of combinations possible in the color deck. So what then? He said three colors, and there are three primary colors. I looked no further.

Applying the principle, *The simplest explanation or solution is usually the right one,* to the questions and problems we face in life cuts through false complexity, sharpens intuition, and invites insight.

In the medical profession there's a saying that also expresses this principle: "When you hear hoof beats, think horses not zebras." In other words, a patient with common symptoms likely has a common malady, not a rare disease.

When you are self-sufficient you are much better positioned to help others than if you are needy or in need yourself. But no matter how self-sufficient you are, you are not a fortress. No man is an island. We all need help sometimes, and should not be hesitant to accept it. This has always been somewhat difficult for me. It is in my nature to be self-sufficient, sometimes to a fault. A girlfriend once told me, "You pack a tight suitcase."

I've always been the strong one, the one who helped and advised others. I was self-sufficient and liked it that way. I freely gave help, but had a difficult time accepting it, feeling it was somehow an admission of weakness. This is not wise, either in life or in the spiritual search. One must be able to *receive* as well as to give.

In the summer of 2004 I was in conversation with my friend Kendra, who is quite intuitive, even psychic. I rambled on about my spiritual frustrations, at having worked so hard for 37 years on the path with nothing to show for it, about feeling like a defeated warrior. I was depressed, and uncharacteristically forthcoming about my fears and doubts about my capacity to ever discover Truth.

She listened patiently until I ran out of steam, then said simply, "You need someone to be kind to you." Her words softened me to the core.

Two months later I was in England with Douglas Harding for a workshop known as "The Gathering." Douglas was so kind to me it broke my heart wide open, and caused me to fall in love with everyone there, leaving me on the verge of tears for most of the weekend. When the Gathering ended, I boarded Flight 99 for Home.

## QUESTION EVERYTHING

From childhood on, we are programmed to believe without question what we are told by parents, teachers, governments, religionists, and self-proclaimed experts of every stripe. And the programming works. We are a nation — and a world — of sheep, who spend little or no time questioning what we are told by our television sets and authority figures.

This is not good for the soul. The soul yearns for truth, but the mindbody avoids it, preferring the comfort of herd mentality to the dangers of doubt, and mindless acceptance to the effort required for critical thinking and independent research.

Nothing new has ever been discovered by following the beaten path. Nothing great has ever been created by conformists. Nothing of value has ever been learned by accepting conventional thinking. No one has ever become enlightened by clinging to prescribed beliefs.

Rose used to say, "Doubt everything," and I could not agree more. I have modified this a bit to "Question everything," because of a slight nuance of connotation. To doubt something does not necessarily lead to action in the resolution of that doubt. Whereas, to question something implies a curiosity that leads to investigation in search of an answer. It's a minor linguistic difference to be sure, but hey, I was an English major.

A good place to start with our doubts and questions is with what our TV, governments and institutions tell us — and there is abundant material there, as we'll touch on in the next section. But this is essentially the low-hanging fruit. When we talk about questioning everything, we mean *Everything* — the very stage this soap opera is being played out upon.

In the movie, *The Truman Show*, Truman is a man who has been raised from birth on an incredibly elaborate and detailed movie set, and is the star of a highly-popular TV show he doesn't know he's in. The set is a complete world, with town, neighborhood, sea, and Truman is surrounded by family, friends and neighbors — all of whom are actors. They appear and disappear in his life according to a script, and the whim of an all-powerful director residing in the artificial moon that's part of the set. Truman is the only one who doesn't know it's all fake. He is being punked on the most elaborate, long-running "Candid Camera" show ever.

For those with a bent for self-inquiry this begs the question, "How do I know I'm not living in a similarly fake world, surrounded by phantoms playing a role in a movie I don't realize I'm in? If all of my life experience is an elaborate play being acted out on an exquisitely complex set, and it has been all I've ever experienced since birth, how would I know?"

In the movie, Truman slowly begins to question things, and to investigate his circumstances. Little by little things start to unravel and become revealed, until in the climactic scene Truman sets sail in a boat to find the truth. The director in the sky throws everything he can at him — thunder, lightning, raging winds — but Truman sails on, until finally he comes to the "other side" of the sea — a wall painted like the horizon of sea and sky.

His boat hits the wall with a thump. Truman climbs out, feels his way along the wall and finds a camouflaged door. He opens it and steps through to the backstage of the movie set. Workers, props, cameras, actors, script girls and gaffers... He staggers through the equipment, both bewildered and enlightened, then exits through a studio door into the sunlight of the real world.

To find the truth Truman had to have the courage and conviction to question *Everything* about his life and existence, and it's a wonderful allegory for the depth to which we need to question everything about our own world.

Our most basic assumption is that we are alive in an infinitely vast, infinitely old universe of solid separate objects, of which we are one. But where did we get that idea? Just like Truman, we got it from selected sources made available within the closed system of the paradigm that sells that idea. When looked at totally objectively, it is only one of many possible explanations for what we are experiencing as "my life."

As discussed in "The Single Eye" chapter, every culture has it's creation stories and myths. In the western world of today, there are two main competing creation stories. One is Genesis, in which a god creates the world and man out of nothing in six days. The other is Evolution, in which a mysterious Big Bang kicks things off and billions of years later man, and the world he lives in, somehow magically come to be.

As a thought exercise, let me elaborate a bit on one of the alternate explanations offered in that chapter, the one where the world is a computer program, a simulation, a multi-sensory holographic virtual extravaganza of monumental proportions, and the computer is the energy field and plasma that "fills" the Universe.

In this story the Earth "program" is upgraded by the "architects" from time to time. The last major version was 15,000 years ago, during which the current operating system, or *matrix* of the planet, was put in place. It was a beautiful thing, a Golden Age.

Then, 8,000 years ago, it was "upgraded" to a vastly more challenging environment for the purpose of accelerating the growth of human consciousness through stress and trauma. Essentially, everything was reversed. Evil was good, lies were truth, the few were entitled to enslave the many, war and strife were inevitable, struggle was necessary, and misery was the norm. It was, quite literally, the *inverted matrix,* and in galactic circles Earth became known as the "prison planet."

Today, in our time, the plug has been pulled on this inverted matrix. All support for it has been withdrawn and only the original, "organic" matrix is being supported. Change will not be immediate, but those who are supposedly in contact with the architects say the transition will be complete by 2030. The world and its systems will be drastically different, and vastly more delightful to live in than what we are now experiencing.

In the meantime, we are likely to be subject to the dangerous thrashings and death throes of the old paradigm, and to witness the fall of those who have been the manipulators and beneficiaries of this inverted madness. This is coming to be known as the "elite apocalypse." The rest of us are being given the opportunity to step into the next dimension of human/spiritual experience, which is being referred to as "The Great Awakening."

The architects of all this are said to be non-corporeal, inter-dimensional beings that interact and consult with us and other stellar species on the "soul" level. This story also includes highly advanced galactic civilizations, however, with technologies far beyond what even the most creative among us could fantasize.

A little over fifty years ago I was communicating with Morse code on a telegraph key in the jungle, and computers were housed in refrigerated rooms the size of a grocery store. Today most everyone in the world carries a feather-light mega-computer that far exceeds the power of a 1968 warehouse-sized computer system, and with which, among myriad other things, they can call anyone in the world in a matter of seconds. Fifty years. Imagine what a civilization a million years more advanced than ours—a mere blip in universe time—might be capable of.

When looking into this story, you will find these advanced species variously called pre-Adamites, ancient builder race, progenitor race, and annunaki, among other terms—and these terms do not necessarily refer to the same species or beings. It's all pretty vague still. Knowledge of these things is being released slowly, as we become more capable of taking it in. Too much too soon might blow our circuits.

In this story, man is not an organic accident of evolution, but a species created by one or more of these progenitor races through genetic engineering. Allegedly, we are a "hank of hair and a piece of bone" from a primitive ape-like species, combined with DNA from the progenitor race ("in His image"). The new humans quite naturally worshipped these advanced beings—their creators—as gods. And so perhaps parts of Genesis are not that far off, just a little light on details. Was Yahweh an annunaki?

Artifacts have been found indicating intelligent life on Earth as far back as two billion years ago, but that's a different story. In this story it is said the progenitor race first arrived on Earth from another star system about 450,000 years ago, and that about 200,000 years ago they created humans, initially to be used as slaves.

These advanced beings are believed to be the builders and inhabitants of Atlantis, as well as everywhere on earth pyramid architecture is found—which is everywhere. Their presence on Earth was almost completely wiped out in a massive cataclysm that is recorded in one way or another in the mythology of virtually all cultures now on Earth. Most famously for many of us, is the flood spoken of in the Bible. Those who did not escape in their craft, either perished or continued to live on and interbreed with surviving humans.

I do not present this story as true, or as one that should be believed, but merely as an example of the myriad stories that exist—or could be imagined—seeking to explain who we are and how we happened. Yet we are encouraged to believe that Genesis and Evolution are the only possible explanations.

Rose used to give a talk called, "The Lecture of Questions," which is included in the book, *Profound Writings, East and West*. It

218

consists entirely of questions intended to stimulate inquiry, and challenge conventional thinking and beliefs. Questions like:

> Do trees create wind by waving their branches?
> Is thought limited to the brain?
> Do we think, or imagine that we think?
> Are you a hero or a victim?
> Do you have possessions, or are you possessed by them?
> Does time pass, or is it only you who passes?
> What is the relation of memory to time?
> Does a given color cause the same reaction in all people?
> Is silence a sign of wisdom even when caused by cowardice?
> Does a man own a house or does the house own him?
> Does a man enjoy or is he consumed?
> Can you start thinking? Can you stop thinking?
> In what part of the body is the seat of life?
> If we can observe our thoughts, who is looking?
> Do you believe more than you know?
> What is equality? Is a baby equal to a dying man?
> Who or what are you?
> Is there a soul?
> Is space-time a stable matrix while we are transient visitors?
> What does a lifetime feel like?
> Do we see this world infallibly or obliquely?
> Is the hum of insects orchestral, or a bedlam of screaming?
> Is life a dream or an illusion?
> What is a state of mind?
> What is beauty? What is wisdom?
> What is intuition? How does one arrive at it?
> How would you react to an incontrovertible discovery of inescapable immortality?

Obviously, Rose was a man who questioned everything, and he relentlessly spurred those around him to inquiry, no matter whether they were on a spiritual path or not. In fact, his standard greeting—in much the same way as everyone else says, "How are you doing?"—was to ask, "What do you know for sure?" He said he only got one good answer in his lifetime, and that was from an old hillbilly who said, "The road goes two ways."

# KNOW THE TERRAIN

In war it is essential you know the terrain of the battlefield you are about to enter, or upon which you find yourself. On unfamiliar terrain you might advance in the direction of a closed canyon ambush, or retreat in the direction of an unknown cliff.

There was a TV show in the early '90's called *Quantum Leap,* in which Sam, a scientist, was trapped in a time-loop where he would spontaneously "leap" from one life to another, and while in "someone else's" life he would have to solve their problems or get them out of a jam. So for instance, he might be a radio DJ for an episode, then when his work is done, suddenly find himself in the body of a boxer getting punched in the face.

The first thing he needed to do when he landed in a new life was to learn about his situation. Where am I? Why am I here? What am I up against? What's the paradigm of this world and time?

It's like that for us, too, though less dramatic and sudden. Every morning we awaken into a world and time not of our choosing, with myriad laws, rules, restrictions, duties, expectations and imposed responsibilities that bind us tight, restrain our movements, and limit our options and activities. This is the terrain we must navigate and find our way within.

We are extorted by governments for our money under the threat of violence and ruin, and forced to obtain a license for every conceivable action we want to take in life. Our every movement is surveilled and tracked, and every detail of our life entered into a central database for scrutiny and approval by authorities.

We have financial credit scores that limit our buying power, and in China (coming soon to a country near you), *social* credit scores — based on how compliant and obedient you are — restrict your access to goods and services, and can be used to imprison you.

As I write this, the world is on lockdown, with everyone basically under house arrest, and you can't so much as buy food without being required to wear a mask that is bad for your health. Vaccinations with untested and potentially dangerous formulations that synthetically alter your RNA are being mandated for a "virus" that has not been isolated or proven to exist, which allegedly causes a "disease" with a 99.95% *survival* rate. Microchip implants that will give governments total control over your life and finances are starting to happen, and will soon no doubt be mandated along with vaccinations.

220

The "elites" behind all this seek a central world government with total control over an enslaved population of docile, obedient robots who do their bidding while of working age, then succumb to diseases the elites have nurtured, and give their money to a corrupt medical system the elites control, then die—which is really their ultimate agenda. They are even starting to introduce the idea of depopulation into the conversation, trying to numb us to it. Not birth control—*depopulation*. Genocide.

Some elites even admit allegiance to the mysterious "Georgia Guidestones," stone monoliths that prescribe a goal of reducing the total population of Earth to 500 *million*. If we estimate there are around eight *billion* of us now, that means 7,500,000,000 of us are on the chopping block.

In America we like to think and say, "It's a free country," but under what distorted definition of the word can we claim to be *free*? At best, we are tax slaves on a long leash, with targets on our backs.

This is the terrain of the world we awaken into each day. The vast majority of people accept it as "normal" and have no questions about it. They accept their fate and knuckle under to every increased infringement and aggression. They even berate, shame and rat out their fellow citizens who do not comply with the dictates of the elites.

This is not the way of the warrior. The spiritual warrior does not bend the knee to man, only to God. At times this may require openly fighting tyranny on one or another level, but the tyranny is so pervasive and dominant that often the savvy warrior must keep his head down as he moves through the battlefield, living to fight another day. He adopts the strategy of the *sly man,* as described by G.I. Gurdjieff, and makes his way through the madness of the world like a soldier behind enemy lines.

How did all this insanity happen? How did it get this far? Why do we accept it without question? Who or what is responsible? What if anything can be done? Are we destined to become trans-human automatons under the total control of Big Brother?

As mentioned in the previous section, much of this could be explained by the concept of the "inverted matrix," in which the Earth program supports all this tyranny. Our history books reflect this idea, telling us war, slavery, poverty, tyranny and misery have been the way of man for millennia. This may or may not be true, but either way it encourages us to think our slavery is inevitable and necessary, and prevents us from looking behind the curtain of our current paradigm of oppression.

To understand our current existential situation, it is more appropriate to investigate history on a shorter timeline. There are many ways to connect the dots we find when looking into this, and many, many details that can be expanded upon, but one short version goes something like this:

In 1913 the Federal Reserve, a private corporation of billionaire bankers and "illuminati" families, was created and given the keys to the financial kingdom of the United States. It was authorized to print all the money it wanted and lend it to the U.S. government at interest. Woodrow Wilson regretted signing it into law, later saying, "I am a most unhappy man. I have unwittingly ruined my country."

The IRS was created that same year, 1913, for the sole purpose of taxing citizens' income to pay the interest on these loans. Prior to 1913 there was no income tax. Central banks like the Federal Reserve have also been forced upon all but two or three other countries in the world, and the profits to these banking families with this ponzi scheme are incalculable.

But their greed and lust for power knows no bounds. They started World War I and sold weapons to both sides. They caused the stock market crash of 1929, then bought up depressed stocks and ruined businesses at pennies on the dollar. They financed Hitler and made untold billions on World War II. They wanted Hitler to win, but when that didn't happen they forced the U.S. to take in high-level Nazis and German scientists during "Operation Paperclip," and allow them access to all levels of government and industry.

The Third Reich was not defeated. It was moved to America and became the Fourth Reich—which is one of the names for the criminal cabal that now rules the world with a heartless hand. It has infiltrated and taken over government, finance, education, medicine, technology, entertainment, agriculture, and most everything else you can think of. And it does not have your best interests at heart.

"They" are deathly afraid you will discover the truth about who they are and what they are up to, and therefore pump out lies and misinformation 24/7 over virtually every channel, website and

222

publication generally available to the public. People trying to speak the truth in these times are censored, de-platformed and murdered.

If you lived in 1930's Germany and believed the Nazi information ministry was telling you the truth, you did not know the terrain. If you live in 2020's America and believe your TV and government is telling you the truth, you do not know the terrain.

Thirty years ago there were 1500 independently-owned TV stations, newspapers, magazines, radio stations and entertainment companies. Now, they have all be bought out and acquired by six mega-corporations, which in turn are all controlled by this consortium of central bankers and arch-villains, each of whom would make the worst James Bond nemesis look like a girl scout.

You only see and hear what they want you to — spun in a way that makes you think what they want you to think — and all of the war, strife, discord, unrest, protests, riots, fighting, division and "terrorist" attacks their news outlets "report," have been planned, financed and executed by these same villains. All of it. That's the world paradigm of 21st century planet Earth. That's the terrain.

Before you scoff at this as "conspiracy theory," I invite you to look into it a bit yourself — with critical thinking and an open mind. Do not rush to debunk it by parroting the propaganda you are fed by your TV. Take a little time. Dig a little.

And if you consider yourself a serious spiritual seeker, I also invite you to take a good look at the one who has been so easily taken in by all these lies. How did I miss this? If I'm so blinded to the relative truth of a manifest world right before my eyes, how much more must I be blinded to Ultimate Truth?

Do not be embarrassed by what you see in yourself. We've all been there. We've all been taken in by these masters of deceit. Also, resist pushing aside this kind of investigation as irrelevant to spiritual work because it is merely looking into the illusion, the dream. Work done ferreting out the relative truth of the dream paradigm builds inquiry muscle, and can pay dividends in the search for Truth. Plus, by knowing the truth about the way of the world, you no longer have to be these arch-villains' bitch — at least not as much — and that's worth something in itself.

Richard Rose saw little difference between investigating relative truth and seeking Ultimate Truth. "Truth is truth." He saw through the bullshit, and constantly railed against "the crooks that run this madhouse." He was a loose cannon, a thorn in the side of the establishment who fought City Hall at every opportunity. He recognized that every government—city, state, country, world—was corrupt to the core, and he refused to bend the knee.

In the movie *The Matrix*, Morpheus offers Neo the choice of taking the red pill or the blue pill. Take the blue pill and you'll stay asleep, believing the world paradigm is as we are told. Take the red pill and you will experience the truth of your situation. Neo takes the red pill and discovers the horrific truth.

Learning the terrain of the relative, worldly paradigm in these times is difficult, even dangerous, so proceed with courage tempered by caution. You will encounter things that shock you to the core, twist your stomach into knots, and invade your sleep. Those who pursue it—who have the courage to take the red pill—are to be highly commended, and the red-pilled leaders who try to reveal the truth to others, who have their heads above the parapet, are the true heroes of our time.

The decision whether to take the red pill or the blue pill is up to you, but for what it's worth, my personal observation these days is that those diving deep into the rabbit holes of relative truth display more capacity to receive the gift of Self-Realization, of Ultimate Truth—even though that is not their conscious purpose—than do blue-pilled seekers pursuing traditional spiritual paths who still believe what their TV tells them to.

Learning the terrain in the paradigm of *Absolute Truth* is even more challenging, and we need to go at it with all we've got. We need to be familiar with religions and spiritual traditions, physics and metaphysics, mystery schools and the occult, enlightenment literature and accounts of Realization—with anything that might provide clues and possibly trigger Realization. We need to, as Rose said, "turn over every rock."

224

The teachers who were most important to me in this regard are mentioned throughout this book, but there were many others. I have hundreds of spiritual books I've accumulated over the years. I particularly recommend the teachings of Nisargadatta Maharaj, especially the book *I Am That*. I also recommend becoming familiar with the ancient eastern texts anthologized in *The Perennial Way*, especially *Ashtavakra Gita*. These books will give you a good overview of the terrain of Absolute Truth. Other books and teachers that are suited to you and your path will appear as you proceed. Be on the lookout.

Read. Find teachers. Listen to podcasts, Watch videos. Let it all get in there and swirl around, bumping into itself. Try to figure it out. Try to understand it, knowing it's impossible. This is an elemental aspect of the path.

It's also worth noting, however, that as inspiring and compelling as good teachers can be for us, paradoxically, they can become our greatest obstacle. Being a disciple is easy, but a boy cannot become a man in his father's house. Rose recognized this when he told his students, "You'll need to leave me if you want to have any hope of having a spiritual experience." He was, like every Zen master worth his salt, saying, "I am a finger pointing at the moon. Do not mistake the finger for the moon."

And so, even as I recommend diving deep into the literature and teachings, I also recommend knowing when it's time to throw away the crutches. On a recent Skype call with a seeker who said he's read *I Am That* at least fifteen times in a row I immediately said, "Stop!" To someone who doesn't read, I say read. To someone who reads too much, I say stop. If you understand this for yourself, you are getting to know the terrain.

## RECONNECT WITH NATURE

Another aspect of the terrain we are born into is the natural world — mountains, oceans, plants, rivers, animals, fish, fowl, insects, dirt, clouds, snow, lightning... Most people are too distracted to notice these wonders, and if asked to sketch a tree would draw a green lollipop atop a brown pole.

A warrior notices everything about his surroundings, whether urban or wilderness, and looks upon them with great curiosity and interest, understanding that knowledge of his surroundings may mean the difference between life and death.

My experience is that urban surroundings are less helpful spiritually, but that may just be me. I find them too artificial, too reflective of greed and confusion and ill-placed priorities to offer much help in my pursuit of truth and authentic life.

In nature, especially wilderness, I find my natural inner stillness taking center stage, and the sense of oneness with all things easier to come by. I find myself more compelled by hawks and clouds than by traffic and neon billboards, by a herd of elk or glimpse wolf, than by a parade or shop window.

As children we are naturally fascinated by nature. Every flower, bird, insect, squirrel and pebble is magical. Somewhere along the way we "outgrow" that, and begin taking everything for granted. Instead of childlike wonder, we adopt a stance of aloof superiority to the things of the natural world. We no longer witness the miraculous, no  longer feel a part of it. The natural world becomes merely a playground and backdrop for our recreations.

For shamans like Don Juan, the natural world is a magical realm of infinite possibilities. Their relationship to it is one of reverent fellowship, and they are in turn granted intimate knowledge of its inner workings. They apologize aloud to the power plants they harvest, and thank them for the service they provide. They thank the animals they hunt for providing them nourishment. They engage with the seen and unseen forces of nature as conscious entities, and use them to perform stupendous feats.

In the earlier days of my spiritual seeking I aspired to be like Don Juan. I actively worked to see the natural world through the eyes of a shaman, and to act within it with reverent fellowship. I saw this as an integral part of becoming a *man of knowledge*.

What I found was that it also increased my joy of being alive tenfold. I was seeing the world as a child sees it, not hesitant to marvel at the first dandelion of spring, or the texture of a toad. In the Taoists also I found a tradition that reveres and flows with nature, and I nodded my head, yes, this is somehow important to finding the truth of what *I am*.

I saw this trait in Richard Rose, as well. As we walked in the woods that first weekend we met, he would stop to point out interesting plants, and the first sprouts of spring beginning to appear. He was a keen observer of animal behavior, both wild and domestic, and would describe what was going on for them internally as they exhibited certain behaviors. He also recommended his students be more observant of nature, and often used animals as examples of what he called *barnyard psychology* to elaborate on human behavior, saying, "We're no different."

Our feeling that we are separate from the natural world, and somehow more "evolved," is an obstacle to discovering Truth. It is in itself an untruth. We are not separate from anything, least of all from that which physically nourishes and supports us. Reconnecting with our childhood experience of the natural world is an easy and enjoyable way to begin feeling the dissolution of the sense of separateness that imprisons us in our mindbodies.

Feel the earth beneath your feet. Compliment the lizards and lichen on their beauty. Be a friend to wild things. Embrace the natural world and it will embrace you.

If this seems like a leap, start slow. If wilderness is a bit much, start by noticing the plants growing in the cracks of streets and sidewalks, and compliment them on their temerity. When your ball goes into the golf course rough, admire the mushroom growing there in the shade. Listen to the ebb and flow of insect harmonies as you sit on your deck at night. Thank the apple tree for its bounty. Compliment the mockingbird on its virtuosity. Talk back to the chattering squirrel.

Nothing is ordinary. Everything is a miracle, everything a gift. Experiencing the truth of this fully comes naturally to one in whom the illusion of separation has dissolved, in one who has become One. So why not dip your toe in the water now? Reclaiming your intimate connection to the natural world brings beauty into your life, and invites the revelation of your True Nature.

## EMBODY INTEGRITY

*Integrity* is a word with multiple definitions. Most commonly we use it as a measure of character, as to whether one possesses or lacks certain positive *character traits*, such as honesty, morality, reliability, and so on. It is also used to describe the *soundness* of a building or structure, how well it's constructed, how well-suited it is to withstand and survive earthquakes, for instance. A third definition is "the quality or state of being *undivided*, of being *complete*."

A warrior seeks to embody a unified integrity that encompasses all three definitions. On the level of character, a spiritual warrior lives according to a strict code of ethics and decency, and deals with his fellow men with honesty, fairness, kindness, and transparency. He does not cheat, or make sharp deals that take advantage of others. He does not lie to get his way or hide hidden agendas. He does not manipulate others, or use his power to restrict their freedom in any way. He stands tall and looks you in the eye without a trace of guile. He wants the best for everyone, not just himself. He is, in every way, an honorable man.

A warrior is also *sound*, inside and out. His body is strong and vital, and able to withstand and survive hardship. His mind is sharp and ready for any eventuality. His spirit is unwavering, and undaunted by overwhelming odds against his endeavors.

The third definition, of being undivided and complete, applies both to his True Nature as the One, and to his stance in the relative dreamworld. A warrior does not equivocate. Once a decision is made, a warrior goes all-in. He is not divided in his purpose. He cannot afford to be. Every choice, every action in life could result in his death. One cannot be conflicted in a swordfight.

The warrior approaches the search for Truth in this same way. With an unwavering single-ness of purpose, he navigates the seemingly endless, convoluted, circuitous Way that unfolds before him. He is certain of his purpose in a landscape of total uncertainty.

This takes courage. In small, sometimes seemingly insignificant ways, the courage of our convictions, the soundness of our integrity, is constantly tested. How much pressure does it take to

228

make us retreat to the comfort of conformance? How many obstacles to Truth are we willing to confront? At what point do we find an excuse to cave, and get back to "normal" life?

Are you all-in, enlightenment-or-bust, give-me-Truth-or-give-me-death? Or is Truth just a nice-to-have if it's not too disruptive? The opportunities to abandon your conviction will be numerous, and the more serious things get the higher the stakes are raised.

In 1943 this 17-year-old girl was part of an underground freedom movement. Her captors told her they would let her go if she told them who the other members were. She refused and was hanged. Integrity. Warrior.

We all aspire to be courageous, or better yet, we think, to be fearless. But fearlessness can get you in trouble. We over-reach, become reckless, show off. And besides, all of that is faux-fearlessness. True fearlessness is not possible in a human being that is functioning properly. Any primitive ancestors who may have had that trait, long ago eliminated themselves from the gene pool.

Fear alerts us to danger in our surroundings, makes us think twice about the consequences of our actions, and keeps us from all sorts of foolishness. It is a necessary component of life on earth. To experience fear is not only natural, but desirable.

What is not desirable, is to let it stop you from taking right action. The painter Georgia O'Keefe, who lived a life of visible courage, said, "I've been absolutely terrified every moment of my life, but I've never let it keep me from doing a single thing I wanted to do." Courage is taking right action in the presence of fear.

Spiritual seekers encounter fear in myriad guises. Some are afraid of the opinions of others if they are found out as looking into weird stuff. Some worry about losing their jobs for the same reason. Some fear disrupting family activities, or facing disapproving relatives, or going to hell, or getting an unfortunate reincarnation if they deviate from prescribed beliefs and scriptures — or any number of other social and cultural fears.

To have these fears is natural. Your ability to forge ahead anyway is a measure of your courage and integrity. It also has to do with the degree of *authenticity* with which you live your life. If you have an inauthentic face you show people whose opinions you fear, or whom you wish to delude, you are divided. You are not being authentic, you are not living with integrity. Almost everyone in the world lives their life like this. They put on masks, play roles, and self-censor their speech.

For much of my life I lived like this, too, though I like to think less so than most others. Still, I never felt completely at home in my life. No matter what I was doing or who I was with, it always felt like I was playing on someone else's turf. I joked to myself that if I ever wrote an autobiography I'd entitle it, "Away Games."

To fit in I accentuated some things and hid others. To protect the hidden aspects, I was disarming, cagey, inscrutable, always on guard. I had a team of subtly different personas available to trot out, depending on the situation and who I was with. I was a chameleon, so no matter how much I might be accepted or admired by those around me, I felt estranged, knowing that their opinions were based on an incomplete picture of me, a false face.

When I was driving to meet Rose that first weekend I had the recurrent thought, "If he likes me and accepts me he's not the real deal. He is capable of being fooled by an inauthentic face." It was a variation of the Woody Allen joke, "I don't want to be in any club that would have me as a member." Even though I was determined to be totally open and authentic with him, I knew my ability to "read the room" and play to it would be operating in the background.

What I felt in those first hours with him, though, drinking tea in his kitchen, was that he saw right through me, and — wonder of wonders — liked me anyway. What I saw in his eyes and felt in his presence even made me like myself more, and whatever mask I may have had on, fell away.

In the aftermath of Flight 99 my inner actor mostly naps in the wings now, but he still knows how to come on stage and play a role when the situation calls for it. Don Juan calls this *controlled folly*. All of our actions in life are folly, he says, but most everyone is blinded to this and takes their folly as serious business. The man of knowledge knows his actions are folly, but in order to interact with his fellow man, he must act anyway and join them in their folly. Controlled folly.

To be a man in full—a person of integrity, soundness, courage, completeness and authenticity at all times is perhaps impossible, but aspiring to it, and living one's life accordingly, is an essential aspect of the way of the spiritual warrior, and nurtures a way of being that may prove magnetic to Grace.

## BE A FRIEND

When I was holding meetings and retreats I'd often get questioned, and sometimes argued with, about my take on the role of compassion on the spiritual path. Compassion is a major teaching in mainstream Buddhism, of course, and for Buddhists and many others, spirituality and compassion are virtually synonomous. I think genuine compassion is a wonderful thing, and certainly should be encouraged, but I do not think the intentional *religious practice* of compassion is an effective path to discovering Truth.

There's a sort of inside joke among earnest seekers that "Buddhism sells enlightenment, but delivers compassion," and I think there's truth in that. Christianity has it's own version of this, with its emphasis on being a "good person."

There is absolutely nothing wrong with these teachings, and they are very appropriate for helping people take the first steps away from selfish ignorance—and Lord knows the world is full of people who need to hear and follow these principles.

My issue is more with teaching compassion and good works as a *means to an end*, as a way to accumulate merit and set yourself up for the "reward" of enlightenment, or heaven, or a fortunate rebirth. Do good and be good for its own sake, not because you expect to be repaid in this life or the next.

I also think these teachings can be a distraction if your purpose is to discover Truth, to have a direct experience of True Nature. The point of a spiritual path is not to become more compassionate, not to become a more kind and caring person. The point is to wake up. Only by waking up do you serve the world.

To be honest, I'm not a fan of the word *compassion*. The subtext is that I am superior to you and feel compassion for you because you are not as fortunate as I am. It implies and creates a separation. It also gets co-opted into institutional and political "compassion," and used to drum up support for charities and missions and government programs, and to guilt you into writing a check, or get you to accept extravagant use of your tax dollars for "humanitarian" projects that do little beyond line the pockets of corrupt officials. For these and other reasons I tend to leave the word *compassion* in the arena of religiosity, politics and armchair philanthropy. For genuine acts of one-on-one human kindness I prefer the word *friendship*.

It's all well and good to have so-called compassionate political opinions and support worthy causes at a distance, but the rubber meets the road in every *personal contact* you have with people. Is that person better off for having encountered you that day?

Friendship can be as simple as complimenting the fingernail polish of a depressed cashier, or comforting a flustered young waiter when he spills your drink, then leaving him a big tip. Life is hard for everybody. Get your eyes off yourself and ease the burden of others a bit. Be of service however and whenever you can, but don't make yourself out to be some grand beneficent bestower of compassion, or pat yourself on the back for being evermore worthy of heaven.

Jim Burns said, "Unconditional love is to give someone exactly what they need in the Now moment." This is true friendship. It does not require that you feel compassion — although you might — only that your actions are that of someone who truly wants the best for a fellow traveler.

This picture breaks my heart. The man's simple gesture of friendship, bowing to give a barefoot stranger his sandals, is part of it, but mostly it is the woman's reaction. In the angle of her head, in the hand to her down-turned face, we see her life, a life of hunger and hardship and lack, a life where no one ever treated her with kindness, nor did she ever expect it. She is overwhelmed that such a simple kindness as this even exists, let alone be offered to the likes of her. She can't even bring herself to look.

In my grandmother's house was a framed needlepoint she'd stitched that read, "Build your house by the side of the road and be a friend to man." Richard Rose lived this way his entire life. Everyone

232

in town knew that if a person in need showed up, they could send them to Rose and they would be taken care of. He'd house the homeless as best he could in old trailers and sheds on his farm, and despite having little money, find a way to help feed them. But I never once heard him even use the word *compassion*, let alone preach it.

Rose often said, "There is no religion greater than human friendship." His life was a living example of this, but to him friendship was not a "practice," nothing to make a job out of. His compassion, if we want to call it that, came to him as naturally as breathing, and was expressed without any thought of reward or obedience to scripture.

Even when "teaching" it to others he treated it offhandedly. Once he took a student with him when visiting a dying man in need of emotional and spiritual help. The student, unused to situations like this, asked Rose how he should act while they were there. Rose said, "Just be a friend."

In the "Energy, Rapport and Transmission" chapter Mike mentions the feeling of deep friendship we shared as I sat with him during his experience. This is friendship between souls free of the false idea of separation. It is on the one hand special and rare, but on the other, not qualitatively different from any connection of true friendship, of literal *kinship*, with the legion of fellow travelers — of fellow warriors — navigating the mysterious uncharted terrain of their lives.

Everyone is fighting battles and facing obstacles we can't imagine. How can we not wish them well? Even if they temporarily play the role of "enemy," I have no less kinship with them. Every war is a civil war. To the spiritual warrior there are no enemies, only worthy opponents who push him to ever greater versions of himself.

Boxers can spend 15 rounds trying to destroy each other in a championship fight, then, if they're both still standing, embrace when it's over. Which imperative is more innate? The desire to destroy, or the desire to embrace?

See everything as Self and all becomes clear.

*Friendship*, by Richard Rose

*I passed through a deep crevice at twilight,*
*And I saw a narrow vista of trees,*
*Magical in the mists —*
*Vocal to the hush of meaning —*
*Whispering to the wisdom of shades —*
*Of degrees —*
*Before the backdrop of eternity...*

*And I had a friend,*
*Whose dust with mine was not the bond,*
*Whose love with mine was not the bond,*
*Whose teaching with me was not the bond.*
*Both of us had been to this same place,*
*To the twilight in the narrow crevice,*
*And because of this place, we are eternal.*

# A Long Obedience in the Same Direction

So, we're well over 200 pages now. That's a lot of words about how to become what you already are—an undertaking I sometimes refer to as, "The long hard journey from here to Here."

So, how to end this tome? What final words will sum things up, place proper emphasis, inspire and encourage, focus effort and make the way straight? I'm gonna go with *commitment* and *persistence*.

Rose was big on commitment as an essential ingredient to success on the spiritual path. In his farmhouse he had a framed Goethe quote on the wall:

"Until one is committed, there is hesitancy, the chance to draw back. Concerning all acts of initiative (and creation), there is one elementary truth, the ignorance of which kills countless ideas and splendid plans: that the moment one definitely commits oneself, then Providence moves too. All sorts of things occur to help one that would never otherwise have occurred. A whole stream of events issues from the decision, raising in one's favor all manner of unforeseen incidents and meetings and material assistance, which no man could have dreamed would have come his way."

He advised students to practice commitment in small things as a way of building that muscle for spiritual work. "Make a decision and carry it out," he said. "Make a commitment to walk around the block every day for a month, then *do it*. You'll be amazed at the power that small act will give you to perform ever greater deeds."

Most of us have a long history of starting things we never finish, resolutions we fail to keep, commitments we don't follow through on, and as seekers we generally keep that streak going. We resolve to meditate twice a day, attend weekly meetings, read two pages of *I Am That* in bed before sleep... And for awhile we do. Then we don't. Then we do again. In the parable of the tortoise and the hare, we are the hare. We lack what the tortoise exemplifies: Persistence.

Persistence is not only a quality necessary to follow through on commitments, it is also an essential element of prayer. Jesus talked about the power of continual asking, saying:

"If you knock upon a friend's door at midnight and say, 'Friend, lend me three loaves, for a guest has arrived and I have nothing to set before him.' And your friend answers from within, saying, 'Do not trouble me. My door is shut, and my children are with me in bed. I cannot rise and give to you.' I say to you, that even though he will not rise and give to you because he is your friend, if you persist, he will rise and give you as many loaves as you need because of your persistence."

Growing up my parents often criticized me for being *stubborn*, which is a sort of negative spin on persistence. For better or worse it is in my nature to, as Churchill says, "Never, never, never give up!" When my mother was being more generous in her description of this trait in me, she'd say things like, "If you ever put that determination to work in the right direction, something good might happen."

One of my favorite movies is *Cool Hand Luke*, with Paul Newman, and my favorite scene is the fight between Luke and the George Kennedy character, who is a head taller and outweighs Luke by 100 pounds. Luke fights with all he's got, but every time Kennedy hits him Luke goes down. Luke gets back up swinging, then gets knocked down. Again, and again, and again... Kennedy starts feeling bad for him. "Stay down," he says. Luke staggers back up and swings, and gets knocked down. "Stay down!" He gets up and swings. "Stay down!" Luke gets back  up and swings. He never, never, never gives up—until he's out cold.

If I tell you that writing about that scene just now brought tears to my eyes, you will know a lot about me. It may also offer insight into why, after 37 years as a wayward, outmatched seeker, Realization finally happened for me. My path was not elegant, or skilled, or romantic. Tenacity was all I had. I had no special talents or gifts or qualities, no nothing. But I guess, as Luke says after winning a poker pot on a bluff, "Sometimes nothing can be a real cool hand."

Recently I came across a Nietzsche quote that resonates for me, which I have edited slightly, and with which I will conclude:

"The essential thing in heaven and on earth—for everything of the nature of freedom, elegance, boldness and mastery, everything to do with virtue, art, music, reason and spirituality, everything that is transfiguring, everything that makes life worth living—is premised on one thing: *A long obedience in the same direction.*"

All that exists is you reading this.

Also published by
# REALFACE PRESS
www.realfacepress.com

**Christ Sutras**: *The Complete Sayings of Jesus
from All Sources Arranged into Sermons,*
compiled and composed by Bart Marshall

**The Perennial Way**: *Expanded Edition,*
translations by Bart Marshall

**Bhagavad Gita**: *The Definitive Translation,*
translated by Bart Marshall

**The Triune Self**: *Confessions of a Ruthless Seer,* by Mike Snider

**Letters of Transmission**: *The Enlightenment Method of
Zen Master Alfred Pulyan,* edited by Bart Marshall

**After the Absolute**, by David Gold with Bart Marshall

**Magic, White and Black**, by Franz Hartmann, M.D.,
edited by Bart Marshall

**Verses Regarding True Nature**, by Bart Marshall

**Ashtavakra Gita**, translated by Bart Marshall

**The Torah**: *The Five Books of Moses,*
*King James Reader's Version,* translated by Bart Marshall

**Poetry and Wisdom of the Old Testament**,
*King James Reader's Version,* translated by Bart Marshall

**The Conquest of Illusion**, by J.J. van der Leeuw,
90th Anniversary Edition, edited by Bart Marshall

**Pearl of the Orient**, a screenplay by Bart Marshall

**Book of Psalms**: *A Psalter for Seekers in Extraordinary Times,*
translated by Bart Marshall

**The Emerald Tablets of Thoth the Atlantean**,
edited by Bart Marshall

**The Four Gospels and the Gospel of Thomas**,
*King James Reader's Version,* translated by Bart Marshall

CPSIA information can be obtained
at www.ICGtesting.com
Printed in the USA
FSHW020956260521
81847FS

9 780999 258330